CANDIDATES '80

Timely Reports to Keep
Journalists, Scholars and the Public
Abreast of Developing Issues, Events and Trends

January 1980

Congressional Quarterly Inc.
1414 22nd Street, N.W., Washington, D.C. 20037

Congressional Quarterly Inc.

Congressional Quarterly Inc., an editorial research service and publishing company, serves clients in the fields of news, education, business and government. It combines specific coverage of Congress, government and politics by Congressional Quarterly with the more general subject range of an affiliated service, Editorial Research Reports.

Congressional Quarterly was founded in 1945 by Henrietta and Nelson Poynter. Its basic periodical publication was and still is the CQ *Weekly Report,* mailed to clients every Saturday. A cumulative index is published quarterly.

The CQ *Almanac,* a compendium of legislation for one session of Congress, is published every spring. *Congress and the Nation* is published every four years as a record of government for one presidential term.

Congressional Quarterly also publishes paperback books on public affairs. These include the twice-yearly *Guide to Current American Government* and such recent titles as *The Washington Lobby, Third Edition* and *The Supreme Court and Individual Rights.*

CQ Direct Research is a consulting service that performs contract research and maintains a reference library and query desk for the convenience of clients.

Editorial Research Reports covers subjects beyond the specialized scope of Congressional Quarterly. It publishes reference material on foreign affairs, business, education, cultural affairs, national security, science and other topics of news interest. Service to clients includes a 6,000-word report four times a month bound and indexed semiannually. Editorial Research Reports publishes paperback books in its fields of coverage. Founded in 1923, the service merged with Congressional Quarterly in 1956.

Editor: Charles W. Hucker.
Contributors: Christopher Buchanan, Rhodes Cook, Larry Light, Warden Moxley, Robert E. Healy, Edna Frazier-Cromwell.
Index: Diane Huffman.
Cover Design: Richard A. Pottern, drawing by George L. Rebh.
Production Manager: I. D. Fuller. **Assistant Production Manager:** Maceo Mayo.
Book Department Editor: Patricia Ann O'Connor.

Copyright 1980 by Congressional Quarterly Inc.
1414 22nd Street, N.W., Washington, D.C. 20037

Library of Congress Cataloging in Publication Data

Congressional Quarterly, inc.
   Candidates '80.

   Bibliography: p.
   Includes index.
     1. Presidents — United States — Election — 1980.
I. Title.
E875.C66   1980   324.973.0926   79-26925
ISBN 0-87187-190-4

Table of Contents

Introduction v
    1980 Presidential Primary Dates vi

Candidate Profiles
    Jimmy Carter 1
    Jerry Brown 9
    Edward M. Kennedy 15
    John B. Anderson 23
    Howard H. Baker 28
    George Bush 34
    John Connally 40
    Philip Crane 46
    Robert Dole 51
    Ronald Reagan 57
    Other Candidates 65
    Explanation of Voting Studies 67

Appendix
    Candidates' Races for Governor,
        House and Senate 71
    1976 Presidential Primaries 73
    Key Votes 1977 79
    Key Votes 1978 89
    Key Votes 1979 99

Selected Bibliography 109

Index 111

Introduction

The United States entered the 1980 presidential election year under some of the most extraordinary conditions in its history.

An incumbent Democratic president faced the possibility of losing the nomination of his own party for a second term. That had not happened since 1856. His main challenger was the last surviving brother of a previous Democratic president. And the president also was under attack from the Democratic governor of the nation's largest state, California.

On the Republican side, the early favorite was a former actor and ex-governor of California who would become the oldest president ever inaugurated if he won. But as could be expected in the "out" party, numerous candidates had entered the Republican field and were trying to dethrone the front-runner.

All this activity was being played out against a background of continuing rapid change in the way the American political game is played.

The explosion in the number of presidential primaries continued. In 1980, primaries were to be held in 35 states, plus Puerto Rico and the District of Columbia, compared to a total of 30 in 1976, 23 in 1972 and only 17 in 1968.

Moreover, the Democrats had instituted delegate selection rules that mandated a transformation in who would attend their national convention and how they would be chosen. Delegates were to be allocated among presidential candidates in proportion to their showing in the caucuses and primaries. Half the delegates were to be women. To a lesser extent, Republicans also had changed their rules to provide for some proportional representation and for voluntary efforts to gather more minority and women delegates.

The electorate also had undergone massive changes in the previous decade. More and more voters were casting split ballots — choosing the candidate of one party for president and another for congressional or state office.

The number of voters calling themselves independents climbed to about one-third of the electorate. That left the Republicans, who have the allegiance of less than a quarter of the voters in most polls, in third place behind independents and Democrats.

Presidential candidates also have to deal with a complicated and restrictive set of campaign finance laws and regulations. In response to campaign abuses related to the Watergate scandal, Congress rewrote the rules of financing federal elections.

Departing from traditional American political campaign financial practices, Congress enacted laws providing for public financing of presidential elections and national conventions through federal tax dollars, limits on private campaign contributions to federal candidates, complete disclosure of contribution sources and establishment of the Federal Election Commission to oversee and enforce the new laws.

In addition, there was a huge untapped reservoir of non-voters potentially available to the blandishments of the candidates. Relatively few of the large bloc of "baby boom" Americans born in the years following World War II, had been drawn into the political process. Pollster Robert Teeter reported in late 1979 that of the 75 million Americans who had reached voting age since 1960, fully 50 million had never even registered to vote. Not since the 1930s, he pointed out, had there been such a large bloc of voters up for grabs.

The 1980 Cast

The cast of characters attempting to deal with these realities spanned the political spectrum from left to right.

The "out" party, the Republicans, had come forth with several candidates by December 1979. Far and away the front-runner was Ronald Reagan, the 69-year-old former actor and two-term governor of California (1967-75), making his third try for the Republican presidential nomination.

Reagan's candidacy was a good test of the recent trend for early front-runners to collapse as the primary season develops. Memories of Michigan Gov. George Romney's precipitate fall from his leading position for the 1968 Republican presidential nomination and Democratic Sen. Edmund S. Muskie's similar demise in his run for the 1972 Democratic presidential nomination would haunt the dreams of any front-runner.

And only one man in history has lost his party's nomination twice and then gone on to win both the nomination and the presidency — James Buchanan of Pennsylvania, who won the presidency on his third try in 1856. Buchanan also was the oldest man ever to be inaugurated president for a first term.

1980 Presidential Primary Dates

By the beginning of 1980, 37 presidential primaries had been scheduled — in 35 states plus the District of Columbia and Puerto Rico.

If a primary or filing deadline applies only to one party, it is noted in parentheses. The filing deadlines listed below are the last dates which a candidate can gain access to the states' primary ballots.

	Filing Deadline	Primary Date
Alabama	Jan. 14 (R) Jan. 15 (D)	March 11
Arkansas	April 1	May 27 (D)
California	March 21	June 3
Connecticut	Feb. 8	March 25
District of Columbia	March 7	May 6
Florida	Jan. 22	March 11
Georgia	Feb. 10	March 11
Idaho	April 28	May 27
Illinois	Dec. 31	March 18
Indiana	March 7	May 6
Kansas	Feb. 12	April 1
Kentucky	April 2	May 27
Louisiana	Feb. 29	April 5
Maryland	March 21	May 13
Massachusetts	Jan. 4	March 4
Michigan	March 21	May 20
Mississippi	April 4	June 3 (R)
Montana	March 15	June 3
Nebraska	March 14	May 13
Nevada	April 25	May 27
New Hampshire	Dec. 28	Feb. 26
New Jersey	April 24	June 3
New Mexico	April 3	June 3
New York	Feb. 7	March 25
North Carolina	Feb. 5	May 6
Ohio	March 20	June 3
Oregon	March 11	May 20
Pennsylvania	Feb. 12	April 22
Puerto Rico	Jan. 14	Feb. 17 (R) March 16 (D)
Rhode Island	Feb. 28*	June 3
South Carolina	Jan. 8	March 8 (R)
South Dakota	April 1	June 3
Tennessee	March 4	May 6
Texas	Feb. 4	May 3 (R)**
Vermont	Feb. 12	March 4
West Virginia	March 29	June 3
Wisconsin	March 4	April 1

* *Rhode Island was not in compliance with Democratic Party rules that require filing deadlines to be no more than 90 days before the primary. State legislative action to change the filing deadline was considered possible early in 1980.*
** *Texas Democrats were considering holding a non-binding primary on May 3. A final decision was not expected until March.*

As the 1980 campaign began, the task for Reagan was to break those recent precedents and maintain his front-runner status through the national convention in Detroit in July. His dedicated band of supporters, his continued strong showing in the polls throughout 1979 and the strategy of keeping his distance from his competitors by beginning his campaign late and refusing to join in debates all were taken as signs by his backers that Reagan was in a position to stay in front of the rest of the pack.

The other Republican candidates adopted a variety of strategies to try to dethrone Reagan. Former Texas Gov. John B. Connally, who converted to Republicanism from the Democratic Party in 1973, gathered a massive campaign war chest to use in competing with Reagan on a nationwide scale. But his plans for running large numbers of TV spots were scotched by the refusal of the networks to sell him the desired time before January 1980. So instead he decided to forego federal matching funds, which would free him from observing state-by-state campaign spending limits. He then could use his ample funding for an all-out effort in the early primary states.

Another major Republican candidate, Sen. Howard H. Baker Jr. of Tennessee, the Senate minority leader, planned to use his Senate position to gain public exposure and enhance his image as a thoughtful, moderate leader. He was especially counting on a dramatic debate on ratification of the SALT Treaty with the Soviet Union to shove him forward into a key role. But with the postponement of consideration of SALT, Baker was forced to change his strategy and begin personal campaigning in the early primary and caucus states.

George Bush, former head of the Central Intelligence Agency and onetime Republican National Chairman, adopted a third strategy, similar to the one forged by Democrat Jimmy Carter in 1976. Although he remained continuously low in the polls, Bush quietly constructed a thorough organization designed to identify all his supporters and get them to the caucuses and polls. His aim was to score early in the year and considerably better than the media and political professionals expected. He then could garner the publicity and support that he lacked throughout 1979.

The six remaining Republican candidates at the end of 1979 all were scrambling to break out of their lagging status, hoping for a breakthrough that would catapult them to the forefront sometime early in the campaign.

Rep. Philip M. Crane of Illinois was counting on a hard core of conservative activists for support. Rep. John B. Anderson of Illinois was presenting a moderate campaign, appealing to the party's moderate-to-liberal wing that has been in the minority since the early 1960s.

Sen. Robert Dole of Kansas was following a recent tradition of defeated vice presidential nominees later seeking the presidency. Others who have followed that tradition over the past 20 years have been Henry Cabot Lodge Jr., Edmund S. Muskie and Sargent Shriver.

Benjamin Fernandez, a Los Angeles businessman, and the old political warrior Harold Stassen of Minnesota, starting his seventh campaign, were seen as the longest shots for the nomination.

Democratic Battle

The Democratic contest pitted the power of an incumbent president against the charisma of the last of the Kennedy brothers, Sen. Edward M. Kennedy of Massachusetts. Squeezed out at the edges, at least in the early days of the campaign, was Gov. Edmund G. Brown Jr. of California, who had defeated Carter in three direct confrontations during the 1976 primary season.

Kennedy's and Brown's challenge to Carter also was a challenge to the power of an incumbent president. Even a president perceived as weak and ineffective can still mobilize a number of resources to stave off an attack. And Carter began to do this shortly after it became clear that Kennedy would challenge him.

Chief among an incumbent president's powers are patronage, access to the public and policy initiatives. All these can be used to keep challengers off balance. Carter gave evidence in the fall of 1979 of using all of these weapons. His appointments often went to supporters, potential supporters or their friends, and he was careful to recruit blacks, Hispanics and women in conspicuous numbers.

The Iranian crisis also allowed Carter to dominate the news and practically froze the campaign in place for awhile. From Nov. 4, when Iranian militants seized the American embassy in Tehran, through the end of the year, Carter's actions to deal with the crisis enhanced his popularity and prestige. However, after the Soviet invasion of Afghanistan in late December 1979 some of the other presidential candidates began to criticize the president's handling of the situation.

In the summer of 1979, Kennedy had a two-to-one lead in the Gallup Poll over Carter. But by December, Carter had turned that around to an eight point lead for himself. The question remained of how ephemeral that lead would be, but it was a vivid demonstration of how an incumbent can make sudden gains by his shaping of or reacting to events.

Shifts of that sort may indicate that the identity of the Democratic nominee will not be known until close to the time of the party's convention in New York in August.

Inside Candidates '80

This book profiles the players in the 1980 presidential drama. Included are Congressional Quarterly voting studies and group ratings for those candidates who are members of Congress, a review of the candidates' backgrounds and positions on outstanding issues, a rundown on the candidates' staffs and an overview of the candidates' early campaign strategies.

Only one of those strategies ultimately will be successful. Whichever one triumphs will be not only the product of skill, foresight and industry but a good deal of luck and chance thrown in.

—*Warden Moxley*
January 1980

Jimmy Carter

Running With the Leadership Issue

Leadership — and Jimmy Carter's capacity for it — have emerged as leading issues of the 1980 presidential contest.

Carter began his presidency as an honest Washington outsider in a political atmosphere still crackling from the excesses of Vietnam and Watergate. But it was not long before disillusionment set in and the president's ratings in the polls began to drop. His highly publicized difficulties with Congress and his failure to gain quick enactment of his energy program contributed to his image as a political novice unable to deal with the demands of his office.

As the Democratic presidential campaign got underway in the late fall of 1979 Carter's position looked bleak indeed.

According to a Gallup poll released in August 1979, only 20 percent of those contacted said Carter had done a good or excellent job and just 27 percent thought he displayed "strong leadership qualities."

Other polls taken about the same time showed Carter trailing Massachusetts Sen. Edward M. Kennedy by more than two to one as the choice of Democrats for the party presidential nominee. Measured against potential Republican opponents, Carter was in a dead heat with Ronald Reagan and trailed Gerald R. Ford (who had removed himself as an active candidate) by nearly 10 points. Kennedy, on the other hand, had substantial leads over both Republicans.

But all that was before Iranian students seized 50 hostages at the American Embassy in Teheran on Nov. 4, 1979, triggering a foreign policy crisis and focusing national attention on Carter and his leadership abilities.

Carter's handling of the early stages of the crisis won overwhelming public approval. A Gallup survey released Dec. 11, 1979, showed a dramatic reversal of his political fortunes. Carter surged past Kennedy to become the first choice of 48 percent of Democrats; Kennedy was selected by 40 percent. The same poll showed that 61 percent of those surveyed expressed approval of the way Carter was handling his presidential duties.

He also improved his position against Reagan, with 60 percent of voters favoring Carter to 36 percent for the former California governor.

But the president's new-found popularity could prove temporary. Traditionally the public supports a president in time of crisis. John F. Kennedy registered his highest approval ratings after the Bay of Pigs invasion and the Mayaguez incident boosted Gerald R. Ford's ratings, even though American lives were lost.

Because of the situation in Iran, Carter's Dec. 4, 1979, formal announcement of his candidacy was very low key. Campaign duties for the duration were turned over to Vice President Walter F. Mondale and various members of the president's family.

Carter's position, while improved by his actions during the Iranian crisis, was still not totally secure. He inevitably would have to face the problems of the economy and the growing energy shortage that would return to center stage upon resolution of the problems in Iran. He also could expect renewed attacks on his leadership abilities.

Political Obstacles

Carter's past political woes, and those he was likely to face, were not entirely his fault, students of presidential politics contend. They appeared to be the outgrowth of two things — the institutional constraints on the presidency and the personal attributes of Carter himself.

Institutional Constraints

High Expectations. Rightly or wrongly, such an aura of omnipotence surrounds the modern presidency that the office's occupant gets the blame when things go bad.

The inability of Carter to solve the inflation and energy problems have hurt him with the public, despite White House protests that it is doing all in its power and that quick solutions are unrealistic.

Disappointments Inevitable. A built-in political disadvantage to being president is that someone will be displeased by your actions. Carter's budget austerity and his go-slow attitude toward a potentially expensive national health insurance program have disappointed a number of important liberal, black and union figures, who are mainstays of the Democratic Party.

Some of them call Carter "the most conservative Democratic president since Grover Cleveland."

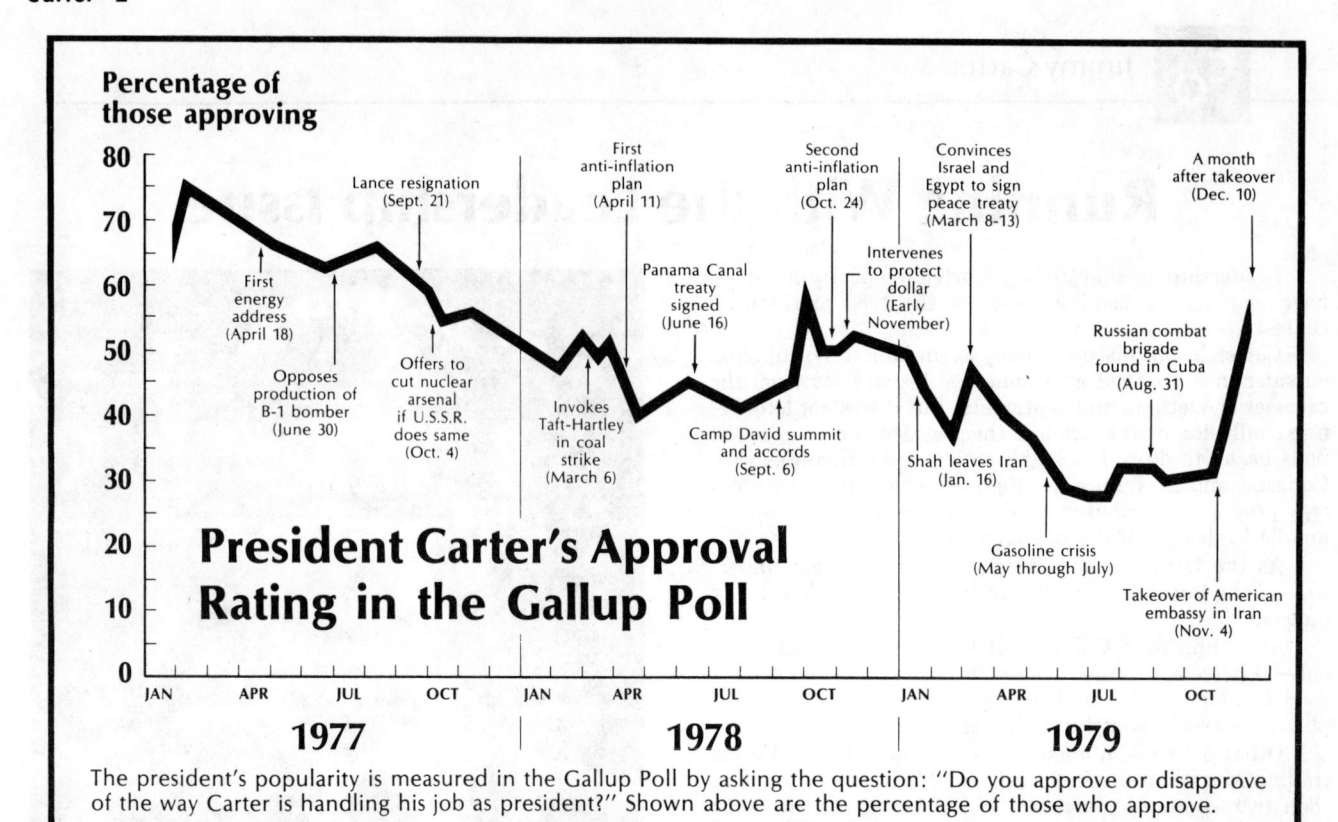

President Carter's Approval Rating in the Gallup Poll

Percentage of those approving

Annotations on chart:
- First energy address (April 18)
- Opposes production of B-1 bomber (June 30)
- Lance resignation (Sept. 21)
- Offers to cut nuclear arsenal if U.S.S.R. does same (Oct. 4)
- Invokes Taft-Hartley in coal strike (March 6)
- First anti-inflation plan (April 11)
- Panama Canal treaty signed (June 16)
- Camp David summit and accords (Sept. 6)
- Second anti-inflation plan (Oct. 24)
- Intervenes to protect dollar (Early November)
- Shah leaves Iran (Jan. 16)
- Convinces Israel and Egypt to sign peace treaty (March 8-13)
- Gasoline crisis (May through July)
- Russian combat brigade found in Cuba (Aug. 31)
- Takeover of American embassy in Iran (Nov. 4)
- A month after takeover (Dec. 10)

The president's popularity is measured in the Gallup Poll by asking the question: "Do you approve or disapprove of the way Carter is handling his job as president?" Shown above are the percentage of those who approve.

Administration pressure on Israel to soften its line on the Palestine Liberation Organization (PLO), which the White House believes is necessary to maintain American influence in the Arab world, is one more example. U.S. Jewish groups are angry at Carter as a result.

Feisty Congress. Added to this is the changed nature of Congress in the 1970s. With the decentralization of authority into subcommittees, it is much harder than before for a president to push through legislation.

As a reaction to the so-called "imperial presidency" of the Johnson and Nixon administrations, lawmakers are more willing these days to challenge presidential initiatives, even when the White House is controlled by their own party.

"Ford had the same problems [with Congress] as Carter, so did Nixon," said Stephen J. Wayne, a George Washington University political scientist. "But you didn't notice since Congress was controlled by the Democrats."

Another factor is the increasing value of incumbency in winning re-election to Congress, which may be diminishing the value of presidential coattails. An overwhelming majority of House Democrats ran ahead of Carter in the 1976 balloting and thus owe him nothing for their victories.

Lower Esteem of Office. Further, the esteem previously accorded the presidency has dropped — along with that of politicians generally — in the wake of Vietnam and Watergate. During his initial months in office, Carter enjoyed great popularity stemming from his professing to be a non-political type. As president, however, Carter had to move in a political world, making the tarnishing of his non-political image virtually inevitable.

Significantly, the erosion of the president's poll standing began with the September 1977 forced resignation of his first budget director and close friend, Bert Lance, due to alleged financial irregularities. Carter hurt himself by sticking with Lance to the end, drawing widespread criticism for valuing cronyism. In the public eye, that made him the same as other politicians.

Personal Liabilities

No Strongman Image. While polls show people look upon the president as likable and honest, he also is viewed by many as lacking the personal qualities of leadership — a forceful speaking manner, a commanding presence, an ability to persuade. These things are more highly valued in the political community nowadays than they were in the immediate post-Watergate environment of 1976.

If the presidency is, in Theodore Roosevelt's phrase, "a bully pulpit," lay preacher Carter finds it hard to stir his congregation. Even White House loyalists admit Carter's soft voice and singsong speaking delivery make for dull listening.

Only in his televised address in July 1979 following the "domestic summit" at Camp David did Carter finally display real vocal vigor. It remained to be seen whether he could maintain that style.

Beyond any oratorical defects, Carter suffers from the widespread perception that he is weak-willed — that he cannot knock Congress into line and is unable to discipline close associates who fail.

In national security and foreign affairs, conservatives lambaste him for canceling the B-1 bomber and for not being more forceful about the Russian combat brigade in Cuba.

In an interview before the Iranian crisis, former California Gov. Ronald Reagan said the Carter foreign policy reminded him of "the sorry tapping of Neville Chamberlain's umbrella on the cobblestones of Munich," an allusion to the British appeasement of Hitler

While Carter's actions regarding Iran had won high praise from many by the end of 1979, not everyone agreed with his policy. However, criticism was restrained by a concern for the safety of the hostages and a general feeling of the necessity of presenting a united front in time of crisis. But in early January 1980 both California Gov. Jerry Brown and Senator Kennedy attacked Carter on his handling of the crisis.

The situation in the Middle East deteriorated further with a Soviet invasion of Afghanistan in late December 1979. In response to the Russian actions Carter, among other things, imposed an embargo on grain shipments to the U.S.S.R., a move that angered many American farmers who were dependent on foreign grain sales and drew harsh criticism from Kennedy.

Object of Ridicule. Editorial cartoons tend to depict Carter as a bumbling, clown-like gnome — short in stature, with comically big lips and teeth, wearing a bewildered expression as he gets his foot stuck in a bucket or is trussed up with a rope by Teddy Kennedy. When the news got out that Carter reportedly was attacked by a swimming rabbit while fishing in Georgia, cartoonists and comedians had a field day.

White House aides feel Carter is the subject of so many jokes due to his unconventional — by Washington establishment standards — background. He is a Southerner and devout Christian, his sister is a faith healer, and his brother has a history of drunken escapades and outrageous remarks.

No Inspirational Goals. Carter, critics say, is hurt by his inability to convey a grand vision of national goals and to rally the public to attain them.

Calling the Carter administration "the passionless presidency," James Fallows, once chief speech writer for Carter, assessed the deficiency this way in a May 1979 *Atlantic Monthly* article: "Carter thinks in lists, not arguments; as long as the items are there, their order does not matter, nor does the hierarchy."

This purported absence of an overarching inspirational philosophy usually is blamed on Carter's training as an engineer. He is portrayed as absorbed in details and indifferent as to how they fit into a larger framework.

In his 1979 State of the Union message, Carter unveiled a slogan for his administration, the "New Foundation," which apparently was meant to evoke other Democratic presidents' catch phrases, such as Franklin D. Roosevelt's New Deal and John F. Kennedy's New Frontier. But the New Foundation, representing stability rather than bold venturing, was quickly dropped after it met with ridicule.

Carter is blind to political nuance and historical lessons, wrote Fallows.

He commented that the president "wanted to analyze the 'correct' answer, not to understand the intangible, irrational forces that had skewed all previous answers.... When he said that, this time, tax reform was going to happen, it was not because he had carefully studied the tales of past failures and learned how to surmount them, but because he had ignored them so totally as to think that his approach had never been tried."

Dislike of Horsetrading. The performance of Carter in office has been affected by his disdain for wheeling and dealing — a staple of the Washington world — according to detractors.

Carter's Background

Profession: Farmer and businessman.
Born: Oct. 1, 1924; Plains, Ga.
Home: Plains.
Religion: Baptist.
Education: Georgia Southwestern College, 1941-42; Georgia Institute of Technology, 1942-43; U.S. Naval Academy, B.S., 1946; Union College, Schenectady, N.Y., 1952.
Offices: Chairman, Sumter County (Ga.) Board of Education, 1955-62; Georgia state senator, 1963-67; governor, 1971-75; president, 1977- .
Military: Navy, 1946-53; discharged as lieutenant.
Family: Wife, Rosalynn; four children.

At the outset of the administration, this sentiment manifested itself in Carter's reluctance to grant patronage and favors to foster goodwill among other Democrats. More administration bills would have passed in Congress if the president had been generous with government largess from the start, the reasoning runs.

While the White House has loosened up on this a great deal as the 1980 election nears, Carter reportedly still feels uncomfortable with another aspect of the Washington political game, arm twisting.

"Carter still thinks he can persuade by reasoning with these guys," said one Capitol Hill aide, referring to members of Congress. "You've gotta show them you mean business."

In an attempt to secure a good legislative record, Carter has started to meet regularly with and entertain members of Congress. Nevertheless, his approach remains softsell — a vast departure from the last Democratic president, Lyndon B. Johnson, whose personal confrontational style, a blend of flattery and bullying known as "The Treatment," changed many a mind.

Lack of Washington Roots. Unlike his immediate predecessors, Carter has no roots in Washington. Even the oft-maligned Richard M. Nixon had a core group of steadfast supporters who years before had served with him in Congress or received his help campaigning.

Yet Carter's government experience was entirely on the state level — four years as a Georgia state senator and another four years as Georgia governor. He can assemble no die-hard cadre of loyalists on Capitol Hill to stand by him.

Aside from an absence of longstanding allies, Carter's performance was hobbled by a lack of federal government experience on the part of the president and many of his aides.

The administration gradually has been improving its internal functioning, but it continues to retain its reputation for amateurism. Instances of crossed signals abound — such as inflation-fighter Alfred Kahn saying one thing about economic policy and other officials saying the opposite. One of the professed goals of the mid-1979 Cabinet shake-up was to bring about tighter management.

Georgian Inner Circle. White House insularity, called "the Fortress Georgia Syndrome" in Congress, has contributed much to Carter's problems, especially on the Hill. Or so say the non-admirers of chief of staff Hamilton Jordan, press secretary Jody Powell, lobbyist Frank Moore and other insiders.

Indeed, the president does depend a great deal on his close aides, mostly young Georgians who have spent their public careers almost entirely in Carter's service.

Carter defenders protest that the so-called "Georgia Mafia" is hardly as arrogant and cloistered as they are painted. Regardless, the July shake-up — in which Jordan was elevated to the head staff job and Washington establishment types such as Joseph A. Califano Jr., secretary of health, education and welfare, were fired — produced a wave of vilification for the White House insiders.

"They're cutting down the biggest trees and keeping the monkeys," said Rep. Charles Wilson, D-Texas.

The stories about Jordan's social misadventures have soiled his reputation and have not helped that of Carter, whose judgment in choosing advisers has been called into question.

Carter Assets

"[Carter] is not on the canvas and down for the count," said Senate Majority Leader Robert C. Byrd, D-W.Va. "An incumbent has the power to quickly change poll standings. Public opinion polls don't elect a president. He's a good campaigner and people view him as being a good man."

The truth of Byrd's statement was graphically demonstrated by Carter's jump in the polls in December 1979. But the White House is aware that poll match-ups are misleading, and standings can drop as quickly as they rise. They understand that, when it comes down to pulling the voting lever for one of two declared candidates, both of whose records have been publicly aired, anything can happen. Therefore Carter is taking advantage of the assets available to a president that can enhance his position.

Power of Incumbency. When Pope John Paul II visited Washington in late 1979, scores of Catholic Democrats were invited to the White House reception for the pontiff. Democratic members of Congress who have endorsed Kennedy have found their invitations to the White House, and the resultant favorable publicity, severely restricted. Pro-Carter Democrats in Congress reportedly will have a say in distributing 1980 census jobs. These are examples of the power to grant and deny favors that an incumbent enjoys.

Although Carter rebuked President Ford for using patronage to bolster political support four years ago, he has resorted to the same practice himself.

Recently, he made a pitch for the Spanish-speaking vote by naming Hispanics as Navy secretary and chief of protocol. His wife, Rosalynn, emphasizes in speeches to civil rights organizations the number of blacks and other minorities her husband has appointed to high positions.

Moreover, Carter has been targeting federal favors at early primary and caucus states.

In New Hampshire, which has a primary Feb. 26, he has pledged sufficient home-heating oil for this coming winter. A new plywood factory in Claremont, N.H., got its government loan guarantees boosted thanks to the president. At an estimated cost of $3 million, residents of the six New England states (four of which have early primaries) this fall are receiving free pamphlets offering energy-saving tips and free plastic devices for shower heads to conserve hot water.

When Florida and Alabama, which have primaries March 11, were hit by Hurricane Frederic, Carter hurriedly flew in and vowed to speed disaster aid. For Iowa, where delegate selection caucuses were scheduled for Jan. 21, he promised there would be adequate diesel fuel to run farm machines.

An incumbent president always takes advantage of the news media spotlight constantly trained on him. An evening seldom passes when he does not make the network television news. In 1976 Ford, seeking to demonstrate that he was in charge of the nation while others were merely playing politics, scheduled a series of bill signings to command media attention — a strategy dubbed "running from the Rose Garden."

Beyond these tangible benefits, incumbency invests a person with a certain magic that turns out crowds. In August 1979 when Carter traveled down the Mississippi River on vacation, throngs of well-wishers appeared on the banks to greet him, even in the middle of the night.

As a consequence of all this, no 20th century president who has fought for renomination has been denied it.

Carter Record. As the business magazine, *Forbes*, commented, if Carter is to be blamed for so many problems, "shouldn't we also credit him with fat dividend checks, record high employment, cheaper airline fares and a general level of economic well-being without parallel in the history of the world?"

Calling Carter's reputation for ineptitude "a bum rap," Stuart E. Eizenstat, his chief domestic policy adviser, says that administration accomplishments are "vastly underrated."

Inflation is one area where public preoccupation with the negative has obscured forward strides, Eizenstat told Congressional Quarterly.

"The inflation rate for the industrial sector of 7.5 percent is not bad. It's the [overseas] oil costs that have hurt. But nobody could forecast them. Meanwhile, we've reduced federal expenditures from 23 percent to 21 percent of our gross national product and are moving toward a balanced budget."

Among the achievements the Carter camp lists: A 50 percent reduction in the budget deficit from the Ford administration, the international trade bill, civil service reform, airline deregulation, 1977 economic stimulus measures that helped generate eight million new jobs, ending the Turkish arms embargo, creation of separate departments for energy and education, refinancing of the Social Security system and extension of the ratification period for the Equal Rights Amendment to the Constitution.

Carter supporters point to two feats previous presidents had failed to bring off — the Middle East peace agreement and the Panama Canal treaties — as evidence of their candidate's prowess. Further, they say, his human rights campaign and his siding with black majority rule in Zimbabwe-Rhodesia have won America new influence in the Third World, and his recognition of the People's Republic of China was a deft geopolitical move.

Another major theme in the Carter re-election effort is, in Rosalynn Carter's words, "the restoration of honesty and integrity." Carter supporters play up his reputation for decency and describe him as the best president for current times, when the public is suspicious of government.

Although Carter's judgment of people has been questioned because of the Lance investigation, his own probity has not. The Jordan and Lance inquiries concern allegations of personal misconduct. Neither is related to government; abuse of power and graft are not involved.

Personal Attributes. An August 1979 Gallup survey disclosed that, despite a drop among those who thought the president had done a good or excellent job, about 80 percent regard him as "a man of high moral principles" and as "a religious person."

Plus, more than half looked upon him as "bright and intelligent," as "a likable person" and as a man "who says what he believes even if it happens to be unpopular."

It is significant that, even when there were great public doubts about his competence, Carter continued to be a well-liked president. In addition, by the end of 1979 his approval rating began to rise again.

Carter also receives general praise for his diligence and his insight. Brock Adams, although ousted by Carter as transportation secretary, nonetheless gives high marks to the president on these scores. "He has an ability to analyze problems and I think he works at it very hard," Adams said.

"He is probably smarter, in the College Board sense, than any other president in this century," wrote former speech writer Fallows.

Supporters of the president lament that, if only he could meet everyone in a small group, the nation would be smitten by him. In person, Carter blends folksy charm and a fine intellect that often wins over his listeners, according to those who have met him.

These qualities reportedly enabled him to bring off the Middle East peace agreement at Camp David, where he dealt personally with Israel's Menachem Begin and Egypt's Anwar Sadat.

Politically, the two most important traits of Carter may be his self-confidence and stubborn perseverance. They enabled an out-of-office governor of negligible renown from a predominantly rural state to trounce seasoned political veterans, capture the majority party nomination and defeat an incumbent president. Carter in 1976 was an indefatigable campaigner, willing to go days at a time with little sleep.

Philosophy and Issues

Carter parts company from past Democratic orthodoxy by not calling for a raft of new federal programs. In this, he is tacking to the political winds that are blowing against big government and high taxes — a course that many of his fellow Democrats are following.

"It is not enough to have created a lot of government programs," he said in his 1979 State of the Union address. "Now we must make the good programs more effective and improve or weed out those which are wasteful or unnecessary."

According to White House domestic adviser Eizenstat, "Carter has been a moderate and cautious president who has refused to . . . give glib answers that would appeal for a time, but would not have a lasting impact, and indeed might be proven incorrect by later events."

While a deepening recession may change his mind, Carter continues to give more attention to combating inflation than to fighting unemployment.

These priorities do not slight the unfortunate, Carter insists. "Inflation is a burden for all Americans, but it is a disaster for the poor, the sick and the old," Carter has said.

For now, the president is committed to attaining a balanced budget as soon as fiscal 1981, which begins in the fall of 1980.

Perhaps as an outgrowth of his religiosity, the Carter philosophy of government contains a spiritual component.

In the June 15 television talk following his Camp David sojourn, Carter decried what he called "a crisis of the American spirit" marked by pessimism about the future and selfishness. He urged citizens to marshal their inner strengths to "rebuild the unity and confidence of America." This speech was reminiscent of the 1976 Carter campaign in which he advocated "a government as good as the American people."

On national security matters, Carter favors a rise in the defense budget of 4.5 percent over inflation in an attempt to keep stride with the Soviet arms buildup. Nonetheless, he does not concede that America is falling behind the Soviet Union militarily. In his 1980 state of the union address Center advocated reinstitution of registration for the draft.

Under mounting conservative criticism for not asserting American might around the world, the president says he is hardly being soft, only realistic. In the modern world, he believes, neither America nor the Soviet Union can work its will on others. When asked at a Feb. 27, 1979, news conference about who lost Iran, he replied, "Iran was not ours to lose in the first place."

Certainly his view of the Soviet Union is laced with much more suspicion than prevailed in the early days of detente when amity between the two superpowers was a hallmark of American foreign policy.

The president contended that SALT was fair to the United States and in the national interest because it would cap the costly arms race. However, in the wake of the crisis in Iran and the Soviet invasion of Afghanistan, he withdrew the treaty from consideration and strongly condemned the Soviet intervention.

When Carter, to conservative dismay, scrapped the B-1 bomber and the fifth nuclear aircraft carrier, he argued that they were too expensive and not needed.

The distrust that such moves spawned among defense-minded senators imperiled the SALT treaty even before it was withdrawn and Carter has tried to counterbalance charges of U.S. strategic inferiority by deciding to develop the M-X missile system and cruise missiles.

Here are the Carter positions on other issues:

● **Energy.** He ordered the phase-out of price controls on domestically produced oil but advocated a windfall profits tax on the oil companies. The poor would receive aid to help them meet higher energy prices. In a bid to end dependence on OPEC oil, Carter also has proposed a massive federally underwritten program to produce synthetic fuels and a plan, known as "fast track," to cut red tape for energy projects. And he advocated standby gasoline rationing.

On atomic power — a potential political factor in 1980 because of the growing anti-nuclear movement — he favors its cautious development with tighter safeguards.

● **Health.** Carter wants a national health insurance bill to help Americans meet the soaring price of medical care. His plan features an arrangement where consumers and the government share the costs. The expenses of the poor would be met entirely with public funds. The plan is based on private insurance carriers and would be put into practice in steps.

Kennedy also has a health insurance bill. But his would take effect immediately and would cover more types of treatment than Carter's. It is more costly as well.

Another Carter initiative would impose controls on hospital costs and is considered a vital prerequisite to national health insurance.

● **Social Policy.** Carter's welfare reform proposal would set national minimum benefits, grant aid to two-parent families and give fiscal relief to states. Carter recently won approval for a separate Department of Education, keeping a 1976 campaign pledge to the National Education Association, the largest teachers' union.

- **Government Reform.** Apart from new departments for education and energy, Carter's reorganization of government did not appear to be as wholesale as he indicated in 1976. Earlier in 1979, he gave up on plans to consolidate natural resource agencies into a beefed-up Interior Department and economic development units into an expanded Department of Housing and Urban Development.

But, Carter established procedures to reduce the regulatory burden to American consumers and businesses. He supported "sunset" legislation for federal agencies and deregulating the trucking industry. Deregulation of airlines, which he advocated, led to a boom in air travel and a reduction in fares.

- **Taxes.** Carter did not repeat his efforts to overhaul the tax system, which went nowhere in the 95th Congress. He has resisted pressures for a stimulative tax cut, fearing its inflationary impact. Nevertheless, he left the door open to one in 1980, if the expected economic downturn is more serious than expected.

- **Environment.** For the most part, Carter was applauded by environmentalists for his conservationist management of federal lands and his skepticism about water projects. The environmental movement's major victory of 1979, passage of a law preserving vast wilderness areas of Alaska, benefited greatly from administration backing.

Their ardor for Carter cooled, though, with his synthetic fuel and fast track plans. They were bitterly disappointed as well when he signed a bill exempting the Tellico Dam in Tennessee from the Endangered Species Act, thus jeopardizing the snail darter, a rare fish.

Background

Carter, who came from political nowhere to attain the highest office in the land, has a history of taking on tough challenges and winning.

He showed determination early. A farmer's son from landlocked southwest Georgia, his greatest wish as a youngster was to go to the U.S. Naval Academy — a desire he had "before the first grade," he recounted in his autobiography, *Why Not the Best?*

Inadequately prepared in math at the local high school, which would have proved a detriment at engineering-oriented Annapolis, he boned up on the subject at Georgia colleges as he waited for his appointment to come through. Graduating from the academy in 1946, he finished 59th in a class of 820.

As a young commissioned officer immediately after World War II, Carter was chosen to work in the fledgling atomic submarine program under Admiral Hyman G. Rickover, whose personal motto Carter used for the title of his autobiography. He served aboard a nuclear sub, the *U.S.S. Sea Wolf*, and did graduate work in nuclear physics at Union College but did not complete a degree.

A promising military career was cut short in 1953 when Carter resigned from the Navy because his father, a state representative, had died and the family peanut business was ailing. Through the years, he doggedly built it into a thriving enterprise.

Home in Plains, Carter became active in civic affairs as school board chairman. In 1962 he won a state Senate seat only after a tough legal battle to get a recount in the Democratic primary, which the initial results said he lost. The new tally showed him the winner, and he moved on to the legislature, where he acquired the reputation as a moderate.

Georgia Governor

In 1966, Carter passed up a good chance to win a U.S. House seat to run for the Democratic gubernatorial nomination. He and his family tirelessly stumped the state, establishing a campaign pattern that would be repeated later. Carter came in third. Lester G. Maddox, a militant segregationist, went on to win the governor's office.

Utterly depressed by his defeat, Carter went walking in the woods with one of his two sisters, Ruth Carter Stapleton, a born-again Christian activist. Carter, a longtime Baptist churchgoer, claims he had a religious experience there, which he says has shaped his outlook on life since. This religious aspect about Carter helped make him a novelty in 1976.

Carter spent the next four years running for governor. With Maddox unable to succeed himself, Carter in 1970 soundly beat Sanders for the nomination by positioning himself to the right of his opponent.

He attacked busing, called himself a "redneck" and spoke approvingly of the former governor in neighboring Alabama, Democrat George C. Wallace (1963-67; 1971-79), who was a hero to the Maddox followers Carter wanted.

At his inauguration as governor, Carter did an about-face and made national news with this avowal: "I say to you quite frankly, the time for racial discrimination is over." He later hung the portrait of Martin Luther King Jr. in the statehouse and appointed blacks to high positions in Georgia government.

Thus began Carter's political alliance with blacks, who proved decisive in his 1976 victory. King's father, Martin Sr., and an Atlanta Democratic House member, Andrew Young, became key supporters. These black admirers proclaimed that Carter understood minorities and cited his refusal in the 1950s to join the segregationist White Citizens Council, a decision that supposedly harmed his business for a time.

King came to Carter's rescue in 1976, rehabilitating the candidate with blacks after he had advocated "ethnic purity" in neighborhoods.

Carter became interested in running for president after national politicians visited the "New South" governor. Upon meeting them, he figured he was easily their equal and started to look beyond the Georgia border.

To broaden himself in foreign affairs, he secured membership on the Trilateral Commission, a study group of the internationally prominent. To carve out a niche in nationwide party matters, he was active in the movement to deny Sen. George McGovern, D-S.D., the 1972 presidential nomination.

More important, he was named the Democrats' national campaign coordinator for the 1974 election, giving him the opportunity to travel the country meeting party leaders.

Running for President

After his one term as governor was over in early 1975, Carter and his devoted young aides roamed the country to gather followers. The campaign was based on a memo by Jordan that said the voters, sickened by Vietnam and Watergate, would want a fresh face, a non-Washington candidate who represented decency.

With his remarkable self-confidence, his broad grin and his startling appeal that "I will never lie to you," Carter built up a network of adherents in key states.

This and his exhaustive campaigning paid off in the January 1976 Iowa caucuses, where Carter beat better-known Democratic rivals. Although the undecided slate came in first, the fact that Carter topped all other candidates guaranteed him news media attention.

His victory in the vital New Hampshire primary catapulted Carter to fame. Then in Florida, he bested the previously formidable Wallace, whose chances were hindered by his confinement to a wheelchair.

A crowded field on his left cancelled each other out. With Wallace vanquished, the only competition for the blue-collar vote, Sen. Henry M. Jackson, D-Wash., could not get his labor constituency mobilized because of the possibility that Sen. Hubert H. Humphrey, D-Minn. (1949-64; 1971-78), might enter the race. Carter ran everywhere and was lucky, which enabled him to keep his psychological momentum going by always winning something on multi-primary days.

By the time Carter beat Jackson in the Pennsylvania primary, the nomination was his. The late-starting candidacies of California Gov. Edmund G. Brown Jr. and Sen. Frank Church, D-Idaho, who took several primaries from Carter, were to no avail.

In the 1976 general election, Carter started out ahead in the polls over President Ford. The Republican incumbent had been hobbled by the worst economic slump since the 1930s and by his pardon of Richard M. Nixon.

But Ford crept up on Carter in the polls, assailing the Democrat for being "fuzzy on the issues" — a reference to the Carter penchant for trying to please both sides on volatile questions, such as abortion.

The vote electing Carter was narrow: 50.1 percent for the Democrat, 48.0 for Ford, with the rest going to others. Electoral votes broke down 297 for Carter, 240 for Ford. Carter was predominant in his native South and the traditionally Democratic East. The regional character of the election also was demonstrated by Ford's strength in the Midwest and West.

The White House

The 39th president of the United States started out with high approval ratings. After the inaugural he walked, instead of driving, down Pennsylvania Avenue, a common touch that won wide acclaim. Despite his subsequent drop in the polls, Carter maintained his customary calm and grinning demeanor in public.

Any venting of spleen — such as his comment, "If Kennedy runs, I'll whip his ass" — took place in private groups. Carter is known to be thin-skinned, which was more readily seen in 1976 when he was constantly under press scrutiny and subject to daily campaign pressures.

His circle of assistants was broadened to include former Time Inc. editor-in-chief Hedley Donovan and Washington lawyer Lloyd Cutler, so that gray-headed wisdom could supplement the counsel of the young Georgia insiders. Another adviser has been Vice President Walter F. Mondale, whose Washington expertise and personal rapport with Carter have brought him great influence.

Yet the closest Carter confidant is his wife of 33 years. Called a combination of "sugar and steel," the former Rosalynn Smith is a staunch defender of her husband.

The first lady, also from Plains, has been a key participant in Carter's every undertaking — beginning with their struggle to save the family business, when she functioned as company accountant, and continuing to her present-day speaking tour to trumpet the administration record. The Carters have three grown sons and a daughter, Amy, who turned 12 on Oct. 19, 1979.

Carter Campaign Staff

Campaign Director: Robert Strauss, previously Middle East peace negotiator and special trade representative and one-time chairman of the Democratic National Committee.

National campaign manager: Tim Kraft, 38, former assistant to the president for political liaison; 1976 director of Carter campaign field operations and ex-executive director of the New Mexico Democratic Party.

Deputy national campaign chairman: Malcolm Dade, former executive assistant to Detroit mayor Coleman Young.

National finance chairman: Evan S. Dobelle, 34, former U.S. chief of protocol, ex-Democratic National Committee treasurer, former Massachusetts commissioner for environmental management and former GOP mayor of Pittsfield, Mass.

Deputy campaign chairman (labor and White House liaison): Diana Rock, 31, former associate director of White House personnel office and ex-legislative liaison for the American Federation of State, County and Municipal Employees.

Deputy campaign chairman (Northeast primaries): Chris Brown, 30, Carter 1976 campaign worker and former chief of staff for New Mexico Gov. Jerry Apodaca.

Fund-raising director: Tim Finchem, 32, former White House deputy adviser for intergovernmental relations under presidential inflation fighter Alfred Kahn and former vice-chairman Virginia Democratic party.

Treasurer: S. Lee Kling, formerly Democratic Party national finance chairman and former White House assistant special counsel for inflation and deputy to Robert Strauss.

Delegate selection coordinator: Tom Donilon, 24, previously on the staff of the White House lobbying office.

Legal counsel: Timothy G. Smith, 31, formerly deputy appointments secretary to the president, ex-staff director of the National Commission for the Review of Antitrust Law and Procedures, former special assistant to the assistant attorney general for the Antitrust Division, Carter 1976 campaign worker and lawyer with Washington firm of Rogers and Wells.

Press secretary: Linda Peek, 29, former special assistant to White House press secretary Jody Powell and 1976 Carter campaign worker.

By all accounts, Carter is an extremely hard-working president, rising before dawn and retiring at night with briefing papers. This self-discipline, publicly manifested when he is running for office, is found in Carter's recreational pursuits as well. He drinks very little, goes through several books weekly and jogs long distances.

Financial Holdings

The peanut business has made Carter a millionaire. He reports the worth of his assets at more than $1.2 million, which includes $228,750 in savings, a house in Plains valued at $89,400 and a "blind" trust for his holdings in the family enterprises of $785,345. Carter lists liabilities of slightly more than $200,000.

The trust actually is not so blind because details about it have periodically been made public. It is administered by a longtime friend of Carter, Atlanta attorney Charles H. Kirbo.

There are two Carter companies, both handling peanuts — a farm and a warehouse. Carter Farms Inc., consisting of a total 2,038 acres in two locations, is 91 percent owned by the president's trust. The trust holds 62 percent of Carter's Warehouse, with the remainder owned by his brother, Billy, and his mother, Lillian.

Billy Carter has borrowed some $250,000 from the farm to use as working capital for the warehouse, which has encountered financial difficulties.

The warehouse's complex financing was investigated by a special prosecutor, Paul J. Curran, a former U.S. attorney for the southern district of New York. He was charged with determining whether, among other things, warehouse money was illegally channeled to the 1976 Carter campaign. Curran's report, issued in October 1979, found no evidence of wrong doing.

Strategy

Early in the campaign the Carter strategy had three main elements — using the advantage of incumbency, stressing the president's accomplishments and running everywhere.

The third, an echo of Carter's 1976 effort, is an attempt to capitalize on the proportional representation feature of Democratic primaries and caucuses. Around the Carter camp, the phrase is "run to the last delegate," meaning the president will stay in the race despite possible early setbacks. If Carter loses a primary, the thinking goes, he at least gains some delegates in proportion to his showing. Beaten 60 percent to 40 percent, he would be entitled to 40 percent of the state's delegates.

In such a scenario, the race for the Democratic nomination might resemble the 1976 Republican battle between President Ford and former Gov. Ronald Reagan — a seesawing contest that culminates in a scramble to line up uncommitted delegates just prior to the convention.

An extra possible plus from running everywhere is psychological. Carter, just as he did in 1976, stands a better chance of compensating for a loss in one state with a victory in another the same day.

Of course, Carter also could be so thoroughly devastated in the early states that he might change his mind and withdraw. (However, that is not considered likely by most of Carter's close associates.)

The ability of the unexpected to alter the political landscape cannot be ignored either. On the fringe are the Lance trial and a probe of allegations that fugitive financier Robert L. Vesco sought to get the administration to drop extradition proceedings against him. Developments from these cases conceivably could wound Carter.

Carter says he will run with Mondale again, which might help him patch up relations with the vice president's old friends among liberals, labor and minorities.

The Carter-Mondale Presidential Committee, as it is called, has veteran political operative and former Democratic National Committee chairman Robert Strauss as national campaign manager.

In running against Kennedy, Carter plans to question the senator's record and whether he could do any better as president. In spite of Kennedy's nearly 17 years in Congress, Carter told a town meeting in Queens, N.Y., he has failed to attain his foremost legislative goal, national health insurance.

In addition, Carter might coyly use the "character" issue against Kennedy. "I don't think I panicked in a crisis," the president said at the Queens event, which some saw as an implicit reference to Kennedy's actions at Chappaquiddick. Carter afterward said he did not mean that.

How Carter would deal with California Gov. Jerry Brown is unclear. A number of observers believe Carter is overly cocky in believing that Brown poses little threat to him.

Jerry Brown

Striving for a New Political Coalition

California Gov. Edmund G. Brown Jr. has piqued more curiosity and caused more consternation than almost any other political personality in recent years.

Like his native California, Brown is a mixture of the traditional and the unorthodox, the practical and the idealistic, and the contemplative and the restless. And also like California, that sometimes makes him hard for the rest of the nation to understand.

Brown burst on the national political stage in 1974 when he was elected governor of the nation's largest state. Two years later, he made a sporadic though highly appealing run for the Democratic presidential nomination, winning three primaries and backing two winning uncommitted delegate slates. But his entry into the contest was too late to stop the momentum Jimmy Carter had built up in earlier primaries.

Re-elected by a landslide margin to a second term as governor in 1978, Brown saw his name immediately enter speculation for the 1980 presidential race. His espousal in his inaugural address of a national constitutional convention to propose a federal balanced budget amendment captured national attention and has formed a major theme of his prospective presidential campaign.

Brown's questioning of traditional American politics is what distinguishes him from other presidential aspirants and most other politicians in general. His often bold, sometimes startling, ideas have brought Brown both praise and scorn.

Detractors claim he flits from one new idea to another, some of them contradictory, shifting his concerns to fit the current political climate. Critics also charge that he challenges institutions for the sake of the challenge and is sometimes arrogant and insensitive in the process.

But supporters argue that Brown is zeroing in on some of the basic problems facing America in the 1980s, warning Americans of what must be done to ensure the country's security and stability. In the practical sphere he has a solid record of accomplishment as governor of California, Brown's backers say.

Brown's stream of statements and ideas over the past five years has led to confusion as to just what he believes. And yet, there are certain basic themes on which Brown has focused.

His concerns center around such issues as the powers, limits, and priorities of government; the need for a revitalized sense of community; the integration of women and minorities into the mainstream of American life, and the economic decline of the United States.

Political Synthesis

Often Brown's approach to the issues that concern him involves seeking a synthesis of seemingly conflicting ideas.

For example, when Brown first took office as governor in January 1975, he gained attention by probing with skepticism many of the methods and programs which had become sacrosanct in state government.

He delighted people by wondering aloud why educational administrators were paid more than teachers because teachers were carrying out the basic task of education. And when he asked to see the federal and state welfare regulations so he could study them, he was astonished that it took 28 binders to contain them.

He also attacked federal regulations and bureaucratic language as utter gibberish.

Brown concluded that an era of limits had been reached — including limits on what government was capable of doing effectively. He symbolized his belief in a less grandiose style of government by such actions as refusing to move into the newly-built governor's mansion, favoring instead a small bachelor apartment and riding in an inexpensive car rather than a limousine.

But Brown's emphasis on limits and criticism of bureaucracy did not mean he was reverting to some brand of traditional conservative Republicanism. His strong belief in the creation of productive jobs as the basis of a strong society and economy grew as he continued to hold office. He also backed union desires for an expansion of collective bargaining and labor rights.

His legislative proposals included collective bargaining bills for teachers and farm workers and a measure to bar employment of professional strikebreakers in the state, all of which were enacted. In the 1976 campaign, Brown endorsed the concept of the Humphrey-Hawkins bill, a measure designed to ensure employment for everyone able and willing to work.

More recently, Brown has called for a new emphasis on investment, especially in the areas of energy, mass transit and new technology.

Brown summed up his goal to Robert Shrum in an interview for *Politics Today* in mid-1979: "What I would want to do is put the priority on the rebuilding of domestic independence through conservation, energy development, technological leadership, space, electronics, and other places where America excels."

Another example of Brown's efforts to synthesize what have often been thought of as political opposites is in the social field.

He often has expressed his concern over the decline of a sense of community and many traditional values. He argues that one of the main reasons for the expansion of government is the decline of community institutions — the family, neighborhood, schools, for example — which provide physical and psychic support for the individual. At the same time, unlike many conservatives who stress the old-fashioned community values, Brown puts equal stress on bringing minorities and women closer to the center of national life.

Brown deplores the self-gratification ethic and harks back to the older concepts of duty and responsibility. In June 1976, he told *The New York Times*, "The whole self-fulfillment ethic is antithetical to the service of God. Pop psychology lets people expect they can be high 24 hours a day. The idea of duty is that there are certain rules you are supposed to follow and you just follow them. That is all falling apart in many cases."

Brown, then, appears to see a struggle in American life between a philosophy of "doing your duty" against one of "doing your thing" — an objective vs. subjective philosophy of life.

The first is an integrating mechanism, uniting society in a common sense of what is proper and desirable. The second is a fragmenting tendency, separating individuals into their own worlds and leading to the creation of demanding single-interest groups. Brown clearly feels there must be a new emphasis on a traditional sense of duty.

Criminal Issues

Brown also takes a largely conservative stance on crime. When Robert Scheer asked him in a *Playboy* interview in the spring of 1976 whether social problems were not well established as the basic cause of crime, the governor replied that he still believed in individual responsibility.

"I believe the individuals should assume that their actions are the product of their own free will and be treated accordingly," Brown stated.

While not abandoning attempts at rehabilitation, Brown has said more emphasis should be given to the penitent aspect of incarceration.

There is one area of criminal legislation where Brown has stood steadfastly on the liberal side, however. He has strongly opposed the death penalty. He fought the enactment of capital punishment in California throughout his first term, when opinion polls showed it to have a large majority of support among the state's voters. Finally, in 1977, the legislature enacted a measure over Brown's veto, although some liberals complained that Brown did not fight hard enough to have his veto sustained.

While emphasizing the need for revitalization of traditional community values, Brown has given a distinct liberal twist to this effort by attempting to expand the political community to include those previously left on the sidelines.

Brown Campaign Staff

Campaign chairman: Thomas Quinn, former chairman of the California air resources board and manager of Brown's 1974 gubernatorial campaign.

Campaign co-chairman: Richard Silberman, former executive secretary to Gov. Brown and former director of finance for the state of California.

Campaign co-chairman: Richard Maullin, former chairman of the California energy commission, former deputy secretary of state, associate manager of Brown's 1974 gubernatorial campaign.

Deputy campaign manager for field organization: Mike Fernandez, a lawyer with experience on George McGovern's 1972 presidential campaign.

Finance chairman: Anthony Dougherty, former legislative secretary to Gov. Brown.

Press coordinator: Larry Pryor, formerly with the *Los Angeles Times*.

Headquarters: Brown for President, 849 S. Broadway, Los Angeles.

His main instrument has been the appointment of large numbers of women and minority group members to judgeships, boards, commissions and other offices under his jurisdiction. These groups had previously been ignored, but Brown's efforts to bring them into the mainstream have been one of the highlights of his administration.

With appeals to both traditional and innovative ideas, Brown has sought to lift the political world out of what he sees as its current stagnation and "shake up" the Democratic Party.

Political writer Richard Reeves may have caught the psychological basis for this aspect of Brown's behavior when he wrote in *The New York Times Magazine* in August 1975, "Intellectually, Governor Brown may be farther left than anyone else holding high executive office in the United States.... Emotionally, he is extremely conservative."

One practical consequence of Brown's thinking is his belief in an amendment to the U.S. Constitution requiring a balanced federal budget — the linchpin of his political program. Such an amendment, Brown argues, would force the country to confront its profligate spending habits and make hard decisions about priorities. This process implies a reimposition of discipline as well, Brown contends, with individuals and interest groups discovering that they cannot get everything they want.

Brown told *The Boston Globe* in August 1979, that "we need a crystallization of the political will that the balanced budget amendment makes possible.... We need a change in the political chemistry that the amendment would encourage."

A mandatory balanced budget would impose a fiscal discipline replacing the constant deficits of recent years, Brown argues. The deficits have largely gone to fuel the consumptionist demands which must be reversed, says Brown. Brown's current favorite saying which summarizes what he sees as the detrimental effects of today's budget policy is, "America right now is not building for the future. It is stealing from it."

Brown also contends that traditional New Deal Democratic programs are simply distributing a declining wealth base. Unless the party learns to say no to some of its interest groups and instead takes steps to strengthen the economy, it will lose the confidence of the people.

Whether the balanced budget amendment would work out as beneficially as Brown supposes is another question. There have been strong criticisms of the concept of the amendment. Critics argue that devices could fairly easily be found to circumvent the amendment, thus creating more confusion and budgetary legerdemain.

Coalition Building

Brown's combination of skepticism toward government spending and large administrative bureaucracies with a belief that government has a legitimate role in shaping the American economy has placed him in a position of defying traditional political categories.

In trying to create a new consensus, combining traditional conservative and liberal values, Brown is attempting to transcend the current political divisions and gather a new coalition for the 1980s.

The question remains whether he can indeed build his new coalition — the prerequisite for translating abstract ideas into policy.

When he became governor of California, he pleased conservatives with a tight budget policy and liberals with such actions as appointment of minorities to state positions, conservation measures and some pro-labor policies. The stretch across the political spectrum represented by those actions was manageable with Brown drawing positive approval ratings across-the-board.

However, Brown may now be in danger of stretching the spectrum to the breaking point. The distance between endorsement of a balanced budget constitutional amendment and his closeness to left-wing activists Tom Hayden and Jane Fonda, whom Brown recently has cultivated, may be too great. How long he can satisfy his disparate allies depends on whether old political reactions can be overcome. If they cannot, each end of the spectrum may be alienated by Brown's actions towards the other.

Several other Brown stances may test his ability to span the breadth of traditional political positions.

For example, Brown Oct. 15, 1979, said he would establish diplomatic relations with Cuba if he were elected president. That is a position that some of his conservative supporters may find irritating.

He also has taken a bold approach to U.S. energy policy. He has expressed support for establishing a federal corporation that would explore for and develop energy resources on federal lands instead of private oil companies.

Brown has suggested federal legislation that would allow the president to appoint public members to the boards of oil companies. He also would set up a national oil import authority to purchase foreign oil instead of the oil companies.

Background

Brown did not get to the governor's office primarily by the force of new ideas or actions. His main asset at the beginning of his political career was that he was the son of Edmund G. Brown Sr., one of the best-known names in California politics. The senior Brown was California governor for eight years until he was defeated by Republican Ronald Reagan in 1966.

The elder Brown was an old-fashioned glad-handing politician in the stereotypical Irish Catholic mold. He was a New Deal liberal. While governor, the elder Brown initiated numerous projects such as a massive water development program to bring more of the precious resource into parched Southern California and more social benefits for the jobless and disabled.

Father and son seem to share little except a love of politics. Their personalities, policies and methods are about as divergent as two politicians of the same party could be. While the father is proud of his son's accomplishments, he has not played a major role in his administration. Some observers note a coolness on the part of the young governor toward his father.

Brown attended Catholic schools as a youngster, graduating from Saint Ignatius Preparatory School in 1955 and then entering the University of Santa Clara. However, he soon made a decision to prepare for the priesthood and in 1956 entered the Jesuits' Sacred Heart Novitiate. The discipline there was severe with novitiates allowed to speak at only brief periods each day. While he decided against becoming a priest, the training and contemplation he experienced at the novitiate helped shape his political outlook.

It also may have influenced his attitudes about personal finances because he has not acquired great personal wealth. A financial statement filed with the Federal Election Commission in July 1979, showed his income was derived from his salary as governor of California and interest amounting to less than $1,000 on a savings account. In addition, he owned approximately 160 acres in Nevada County, California, purchased in May 1978 for between $100,000 and $250,000. He also has a mortgage liability of between $100,000 and $250,000.

After leaving the novitiate in early 1960, Brown entered the Berkeley campus of the University of California, majoring in classical languages and obtaining his degree in 1961. He went on to Yale Law School, where he received a J.D. degree in 1964.

Political Life

At first clerking for a California Supreme Court justice and then joining a prominent Los Angeles law firm, Brown slowly became swept up in the turbulent politics of the latter half of the 1960s. He had spent a brief time in Mississippi in 1962 aiding the civil rights effort but did not become immersed in issues of national moment until he joined the anti-Vietnam War movement in 1967.

In 1968 Brown was the Southern California vice chairman and treasurer for Sen. Eugene J. McCarthy's presidential primary campaign in the state. The following year he made his first bid for elective office, winning a seat on the board of trustees of the Los Angeles community colleges.

By 1970, Brown was ready to move into big-time politics and entered the race for the post of California secretary of state.

Brown won the secretary of state's office by 308,000 votes in November 1970, when Republican Ronald Reagan was elected to his second term as governor. He was the first Democrat to win that office since 1886, although an appointed Democrat served from 1940 to 1942.

The weakness of California's political parties facilitated Brown's victory and future successes. His maverick style met less resistance in California than it might have elsewhere. And his image as an independent, disdaining politics-as-usual, became the base of his unusual appeal.

The new secretary soon started to shake up his office. Brown began enforcing stringently the state's campaign

Brown's Background

Profession: Attorney.
Born: April 7, 1938, San Francisco, Calif.
Home: Sacramento, Calif.
Religion: Roman Catholic.
Education: University of California at Berkeley, B.A., 1961; Yale University, J.D., 1964.
Offices: Member, board of trustees, Los Angeles community colleges, 1969-71; secretary of state, state of California, 1971-75; governor of California, 1975-
Military: None.
Family: Single.

contribution law, suing both individual candidates and companies for allegedly receiving and making illegal contributions.

Brown's popularity soared. His stewardship of the secretary of state's office coincided with the last years of the Nixon administration when Americans were particularly sensitive about government corruption and wrongdoing.

The culmination of Brown's four years as secretary of state was his support of Proposition 9, known as the political reform initiative. Placed on the June 5, 1974, primary ballot, the initiative provided for strict regulations on campaign contributions and expenditures and restrictions on the activities of lobbyists.

The lobbying regulations incurred the wrath not only of business but labor as well. The state AFL-CIO withdrew its endorsement of Brown in the gubernatorial primary because of his backing for the measure. Nevertheless, Brown had judged the public mood well. Not only did he win the gubernatorial nomination, but the proposition passed by a two-to-one margin.

Governor's Contest

Brown had announced his candidacy for governor in January 1974. He faced stiff competition for his party's nomination from four other major candidates: Mayor Joseph Alioto of San Francisco; Robert Moretti, Speaker of the California Assembly; William M. Roth, former U.S. trade negotiator, and U.S. Rep. Jerome R. Waldie. While Brown beat his closest competitor, Alioto, by 531,000 votes, he received only 37.8 percent of the vote in a crowded field of eighteen Democratic candidates.

Polls gave Brown a strong early lead against Republican nominee Houston I. Flournoy, the state controller, and Brown tended to coast during the fall campaign. With Flournoy a lackluster campaigner, it appeared that Brown would be an easy victor. But late in the campaign Flournoy started to close in on Brown. Some of Brown's advisers urged him to increase the intensity of his campaign, but he continued in the same rather stiff style, attacking the Reagan administration and criticizing President Gerald R. Ford for his pardon of former President Richard M. Nixon.

Brown won, but by a relatively small margin, 50.1 percent to 47.3 percent, with the remainder going to minor candidates. *(Election results, see p. 71.)*

Once in office, Brown repeated his pattern as secretary of state, surprising political leaders with his proposals, statements and behavior. In addition to probing the complexities of the state's bureaucracy, Brown had several solid legislative successes during his first two years as governor.

By far the most heralded was the passage of farm labor legislation. For years farm laborers, concentrated in California's Central Valley, had been fighting for the right to organize unions. In 1975, Brown became personally involved in negotiations among the growers, the United Farm Workers led by Cesar Chavez and the Teamsters Union to secure enactment of legislation designed to end violence in the farm areas. The result was that farm laborers won the right to secret-ballot elections to choose whether they wanted to be represented by a union.

Despite his aloof personality, Brown seemed to work well with the Democratic legislature in his first years as governor. Besides the farm labor legislation, he concentrated on the passage of environmental legislation including a comprehensive coastal protection bill and a nuclear safeguard bill — which was a forerunner of his opposition to nuclear-generated power.

Presidential Ambitions

Speculation about a Brown presidential candidacy began shortly after Brown's election as governor. Although he was only 36 years old, he was the governor of the nation's largest state and had demonstrated acute political talents in getting there. The speculation increased throughout 1975, but Brown hesitated to commit himself to a presidential bid.

On March 12, 1976, he announced that he would enter California's presidential primary as a favorite son. His campaign expanded from there as Brown entered other primaries. He made a good showing, upsetting Jimmy Carter in the Maryland preference primary in May and winning in his native California and neighboring Nevada. Uncommitted slates of delegates backed by Brown won in Rhode Island and New Jersey. And he came in a strong third as a write-in candidate in Oregon.

But it was too late to stop Carter. The Georgian had won impressive victories in early primaries and was able to win enough late primaries to keep ahead of the rest of the pack.

Brown was determined to win a big victory in his 1978 re-election drive as a launching pad for another try at the White House in 1980. In his three years as governor he had managed to retain his liberal following while picking up conservative support with his tight budget policy. He received some criticism in 1977 for the alleged red tape and complicated regulations involved in businesses getting permission to set up new facilities in the state.

But Brown moved quickly to counter the impression that the state was anti-business, adopting a "California Means Business" campaign geared to bringing business into the state and making the bureaucratic and tax situations more favorable.

Proposition 13

In his re-election campaign, Brown faced his most difficult political issue, Proposition 13. Placed on the June 1978 primary ballot through the efforts of anti-tax crusader Howard Jarvis, the initiative provided for a sharp rollback in property taxes. Brown at first opposed the proposition, but as primary day approached in June, he realized he was in the midst of a political hurricane of support for the proposition.

He dropped his campaign against it and began planning to cope with the consequences of passage. Estimates of revenue losses to local governments and schools ran up to $7 billion, and there were predictions of chaos.

Brown's handling of the issue was a political masterstroke. After its passage he in effect took over the issue as his own and began speaking of the opportunities the proposition provided for better government. He pointed out that he had begun his administration as an advocate of a tight budgetary policy and the message he received from the voters on Proposition 13 was that the voters wanted more of it.

In his address to an emergency session of the legislature two days after passage of the proposition, Brown urged use of the state's entire $5 billion surplus to help schools, cities and counties offset their losses. He also made some cuts in his original budget for the year and imposed a state employee hiring freeze.

In response, the legislature passed a series of grants and loans designed to ensure the continuation of basic services throughout the state. Furthermore, the state took over the counties' share of welfare and Medicaid payments. Brown's handling of the issue was so adroit that by mid-July, a *Los Angeles Times* poll found 41 percent of the respondents thought Brown had supported Proposition 13 all along. Republicans quipped they were now forced to run against "Jerry Jarvis." Brown's Republican opponent in 1978 was the state's attorney general, Evelle Younger.

Younger was a capable but colorless politician who had effectively run the Los Angeles County district attorney's office before moving on to two terms as attorney general. During the spring, polls indicated Brown was losing popularity with the voters, but with his handling of the aftermath of the Proposition 13 vote he rebounded quickly. The governor completely outclassed his opponent in political maneuvering, and by October the *Los Angeles Times* poll found that voters thought Brown, rather than Younger, would be better able to cut government waste, keep taxes down and make Proposition 13 work.

The election wound up as a landslide for Brown, with the governor winning 56 percent of the vote compared to 36.5 percent for Younger. Brown's popular vote margin of 1,352,000 was the largest in the history of the state in a contest where both major parties had nominees.

Nevertheless, Brown was unable to carry in his running mate for lieutenant governor, incumbent Mervin Dymally. He was beaten by Mike Curb, a 34-year-old music and record company executive. Curb has managed to complicate Brown's political life by taking advantage of a provision of the state constitution which says the lieutenant governor becomes acting governor whenever the governor leaves the state.

Curb has insisted on interpreting that as meaning he can make appointments and even veto bills whenever Brown is out of the state. With Brown needing to spend much of his time campaigning outside California, Curb could cause him major headaches. Brown has initiated court action to try to prevent Curb from continuing his activities.

Political Opposition

Brown's success in handling Proposition 13 was a two-edged sword. On the one hand, it enabled him to score a tremendous political success in California. But it also opened him up to sharp criticism in the national press and from political opponents that he was wishy-washy, inconsistent and an opportunist who shifted direction with every political wind that comes along.

Defending himself against those charges, Brown has argued that a person in public life has an obligation to respond to the will of the people and if he finds something is not working, then he should try something else. Also, he has pointed out that he has been consistent on a long series of issues, some of which have not been popular with the general public.

He also has encountered political opposition over his support for a national constitutional convention to propose a federal balanced budget amendment.

In his 1979 inaugural address, Brown couched his endorsement in near-apocalyptic terms:

"Today we see the ethos of our moment dominated by 'getting and spending' rather than innovation and risk. The depressing spirit of the age ungratefully feeds off the boldness of the past. Where there should be saving for the future, I see frantic borrowing. Where there should be investment in productive capacity, I see frenetic consumption.... It is time to get off the treadmill, to challenge the assumption that more government spending automatically leads to better living. The facts prove otherwise. More and more inflationary spending leads to decline abroad and decadence at home. Ultimately it will unwind the social compact that forms the basis of our society.... A constitutional convention to propose an amendment to balance the budget is unprecedented, but so is the political paralysis that makes effective decisions impossible."

Despite the governor's eloquence, the Democratic-controlled legislature was not impressed, refusing to join the call for a constitutional convention. Moreover, the fight over that issue seemed to bring to a head legislators' negative feelings about the governor and what they saw as his arrogance and self-righteousness.

During a raucous spring session, the legislature overrode three Brown vetoes in three weeks. That equaled the number of overridden vetoes in the last 33 years. Prior to 1979, Brown's only overridden veto was on restoring the death penalty. Finally, the state Senate rejected Brown's appointment of actress Fonda to the state Arts Council.

Democratic Assembly Whip Art Agnos remarked that "Jerry Brown is reaping the harvest of his five years of contempt for the legislature."

However, after a summer recess, the legislators seemed in a better mood and cooperated with the governor in passing a series of measures he supported, including a new job training program, a tax credit for businesses that hire welfare recipients and a bill to create an investment fund for renewal of natural resources. Earlier in the year, the legislature also passed another relief measure designed to continue to help local communities make up for the revenue lost by the passage of Proposition 13.

Strategy

From the time of his 1978 re-election, there was little doubt that Brown would run for the presidency in 1980. His strong showing in the 1976 primaries plus his attention to national problems made it clear that he was interested.

Moreover, President Carter's early weakness in the polls only made it more certain that Brown would enter the fray against him, even though no elected president has been denied renomination by his own party if he wanted it and fought for it since Franklin Pierce in 1856.

Brown's strategy against Carter was to be to hit him from both sides of the political spectrum. Hoping for support from conservatives based on his budgetary austerity and from the left based on his anti-nuclear stance and other administrative actions that pleased liberals, Brown had planned to construct a coalition that would squeeze Carter into second place in a two-man contest.

But the entry of Massachusetts Sen. Edward M. Kennedy into the Democratic presidential race confronted Brown with the most formidable challenge of his political life. At the outset of the campaign Kennedy was far ahead of both Brown and Carter in national opinion polls.

Even in his own state Brown might fare poorly in such a race. A November 1979 poll by Mervin Field showed Kennedy getting 49 percent of the vote among potential California Democratic primary voters compared to 15 percent for Brown and 23 percent for Carter. The same poll showed Kennedy beating Brown in a two-man race 67 percent to 23 percent.

However, Brown insists he remains undaunted by Kennedy's candidacy. His basic strategy is to run second in the early primaries, putting Carter in third place and eventually eliminating him. Then, as the only alternative to Kennedy, Brown might run strongly in the Midwest and West and pick up anti-Kennedy support in the South.

Edward M. Kennedy

The Long Delayed Quest Begins

Just as I went into politics because Joe died, if anything happened to me tomorrow, Bobby would run for my seat in the Senate. And if Bobby died, our young brother Ted would take over for him.

—John F. Kennedy, in 1959

During late 1967 Sen. Robert F. Kennedy agonized over whether he should challenge President Lyndon B. Johnson in the following year's presidential election. Most of his aides said yes. His younger brother, Sen. Edward M. Kennedy, said no.

The younger Kennedy feared personality and talk of a Kennedy dynasty would overshadow Robert's efforts to change Johnson's Vietnam War policy. "The opportunity for bringing about new kinds of directions, new departures, appeared to be elsewhere," Ted Kennedy told a biographer years later.

But 12 years after he counseled his brother against running for the presidency, Edward Kennedy found himself in the same position — challenging an incumbent president from his own party.

After removing himself from presidential politics three times, Kennedy, like his brother in 1968, could find no persuasive reason not to run in 1980. The previous obstacles have lessened. The emotional agony of Robert's assassination in 1968 that forced him to reject all draft efforts that year has waned. The memory of the 1969 automobile accident at Chappaquiddick, in which a woman campaign worker was killed and which removed Kennedy from the 1972 race, also has faded with time. And his troubled family situation, which blocked a try in 1976, has been smoothed over.

With the formal announcement of his candidacy on Nov. 7, 1979, Edward Kennedy finally picked up the fallen presidential standard of his brothers, Robert, who sought it briefly in 1968, and John F. Kennedy, who was assassinated in 1963.

But Ted's campaign won't necessarily be like Robert's. The 1968 Kennedy candidacy started late and was a very intense and emotional affair. Aside from his overall objections, Ted Kennedy was bothered by the fact that Robert waited until after the first primary to enter. His own campaign is starting much earlier and, at least in the early stages, at a much lower emotional pitch.

Kennedy's November announcement came as no surprise. During most of 1979 he had moved closer and closer to an open, declared candidacy. A giant step came Sept. 6 when Kennedy revealed that his wife and mother would support whatever decision he made about a presidential bid.

That was the first in a series of signals that Kennedy was about to move away from his long-held public pronouncement that "I expect the president to be renominated, I expect him to be re-elected and I intend to support him."

Within days more draft-Kennedy groups sprouted around the country. And, in the view of some political observers, the senior senator from Massachusetts began a rhetorical drift to the ideological center, away from his long-held liberal beliefs.

At a speech in New York Sept. 27, Kennedy said, "We do not ask to bring back the New Deal or restore the New Frontier to life." He added, "We reject the idea that government knows best across-the-board, that public planning is inherently superior and more effective than the private sector."

These statements and others raised questions of exactly where Kennedy stood, whether his positions were undergoing a swift revamping to be in line with the fiscally conservative trend in the country and how much he differed with President Carter on various issues.

The Liberal Image

During his nearly 20 years in public office, Kennedy frequently has employed the concepts of fairness and equal opportunity for the underprivileged in his public statements.

Often, Kennedy feels, government involvement is required to bring the "have nots" up to the level of the "haves." As a consequence Kennedy has acquired the tag of a "liberal, big-spender." The label comes as the inevitable result of a philosophy that urges the government to help those who can't help themselves.

He bases his long-time push for national health insurance on the desire to "make health care a basic right for all, not just an expensive privilege for the few." In opposing President Carter's plan to decontrol domestic oil prices

Congressional Quarterly Vote Study Scores...

	1963	1964	1965	1966	1967	1968	1969	1970
Presidential[1]								
Support	75	31	75	66	68	39	44	33
Opposition	4	5	11	16	18	5	44	40
Conservative Coalition[1]								
Support	5	2	11	1	0	4	3	3
Opposition	86	41	80	86	89	34	85	74
Party[1]								
Unity	84	37	81	67	69	26	78	73
Opposition	3	6	10	9	15	4	5	4
Voting Participation[1]	83	49	86	83	86	39	83	70

[1] *Explanation, see p. 67.*   NOTE: Failure to vote lowers scores so that total in each category will not be 100% in every year.

Kennedy termed it "the worst form of rationing, because it is rationing by price." He asked, "Is it fair to ask poor elderly citizens . . . to shift to cat food so they can afford to pay their heating bills?"

In the late 1960s, Kennedy fought for a change in the military draft law to "make it fair, just and predictable." He was one of a few liberals who opposed the all-volunteer army during a war in favor of the lottery, again on grounds that a lottery would be more fair.

But Kennedy's interest in fairness and equal opportunity also has been used to explain his effort to remove government involvement and regulation in other areas, such as the airline and trucking industries. Kennedy's advocacy of airline deregulation, which began in 1974, was seen by the senator, according to a top aide, as a "populist crusade." Kennedy said he wanted to get the government out of "naturally competitive" industries, such as airlines, to make fares lower "so more people could afford to fly, so people who did fly would not have to spend so much."

In 1978, with support from the Carter administration, an airline deregulation bill was passed. However, Kennedy's efforts to deregulate the trucking industry have moved much more slowly.

If there is a consistency to Kennedy's overall philosophy, the emphasis in his recent speeches has in fact changed. As a candidate for the presidency of a country whose people appear to be calling for less government, Kennedy prefers to mention his efforts to reduce the size of the federal government than talk about the need for more funds for environmental protection or food stamp programs. "There is a growing consensus, which I share, that government intervention in the economy should come only as a last resort," Kennedy said in late 1979.

Kennedy aides have been pointing out that his efforts on behalf of deregulation and for federal criminal code revision are not completely in the mold of a liberal.

But there has been no indication that he would back away from all of the government programs he has supported in the past — programs that are geared toward improving the lot of the underprivileged, the constituency he inherited from his two slain brothers.

Differences with Carter

In most instances, the issue differences between Kennedy and President Carter revolve around taking slightly different approaches to solve the same problems.

Most often these conflicts are resolved before they reach the Senate floor for a vote. Consequently, judged only on his voting record, Kennedy is in harmony with the administration's position most of the time.

In the first session of the 96th Congress, according to Congressional Quarterly's tabulation of recorded votes Kennedy supported Carter 73 percent of the time.

Kennedy and Carter generally agree on the major thrust of foreign policy. Kennedy backed the Panama Canal treaties all the way. He supports the administration's human rights initiatives, often urging Carter not to compromise his position in countries such as Argentina and Chile.

Although he opposed the sale of sophisticated jet fighters to Israel, Egypt and Saudi Arabia, Kennedy has praised Carter's Middle East peace efforts. He also took a leadership position in winning approval early in 1979 for the administration's legislation which implemented full diplomatic recognition of the People's Republic of China. That was one of the few areas in recent years where Kennedy has been out front on a foreign policy matter.

Kennedy was one of the first politicians to publicly criticize the way Carter was handling the Iranian situation. Many observers felt Kennedy's remarks were poorly timed and cost him some support. However, after the Soviet invasion of Afghanistan in late December 1979 others joined Kennedy in criticizing the president.

On national defense, Kennedy usually can be expected to join a group of approximately 35 liberal senators who oppose modest increases in new defense hardware, but rarely does he take the lead on any defense-related issues. One potential area of conflict between Kennedy and Carter is over the development of the M-X missile system, which Carter supports. Kennedy, critical of advancing more nuclear weaponry, is advocating a go-slow approach with continued research and development of the system.

...Covering Kennedy's Career in the Senate

	1971	1972	1973	1974	1975	1976	1977	1978	1979
Presidential[1]									
Support	30	22	30	31[2]/38[3]	43	21	76	80	73
Opposition	50	52	58	61[2]/49[3]	45	60	17	12	7
Conservative Coalition[1]									
Support	13	4	4	4	4	5	2	5	2
Opposition	76	82	85	80	84	84	88	88	88
Party[1]									
Unity	78	80	80	78	80	84	86	88	72
Opposition	10	8	5	8	4	4	5	5	5
Voting Participation[1]	83	80	86	84	84	82	89	89	74

[1] *Explanation, see p. 67.* [2] *During President Nixon's tenure in 1974.* [3] *During President Ford's tenure in 1974.*

Kennedy's major policy differences with Carter are in the domestic sphere. During 1979 Kennedy differed with Carter over budget priorities, national health insurance and the administration's energy program.

Although Kennedy supported Carter's effort to reduce the federal budget deficit to below $30 billion, he quarreled over where the president had imposed cuts. "The administration's budget asks the poor, the black, the sick, the young, the cities and the unemployed to bear a disproportionate share of the billions of dollars of reductions," Kennedy said of Carter's budget in January 1979.

Subsequent efforts by Kennedy to restore some of the cuts, particularly in the health field, were unsuccessful.

Recently Carter assessed his differences with Kennedy by saying: "Sen. Kennedy is much more inclined toward the old philosophy of pouring out new programs and new money to meet a social need. I'm much more inclined to try to make existing programs work efficiently and start up new programs only when it's absolutely necessary."

But Kennedy and Carter both support the idea of national health insurance. However, they take substantially different views on what it should cover and how to finance and administer the program. Carter wants Congress to enact just the first phase of his "lean" program, while Kennedy wants to enact the entire program immediately with benefits phased in over time. The Kennedy program is more comprehensive than Carter's and would be administered by private insurance companies rather than by the federal government, which was part of Kennedy's original proposal.

Kennedy's program is more costly in the short run to the federal government, as well as businesses and workers who would be required to pay increased premiums. But Kennedy argues over a number of years his program would cost less.

On energy issues Kennedy and Carter are on different wavelengths. Along with his opposition to decontrolling domestic oil prices, Kennedy has opposed Carter's natural gas deregulation moves and is skeptical about the administration's new push for development of synthetic fuels. Although not totally opposed to nuclear power, Kennedy supports the two-year moratorium on construction permits for new nuclear plants.

In July 1979, Kennedy offered his own energy program which stressed conservation and incentives to private industry for increased efficiency. The federal cost of Kennedy's program, he claims, would be $34 billion but would save the American economy $230 billion over the next 10 years in reduced oil imports.

In another domestic policy difference, Kennedy supported substantially more funds than recommended by Carter for the Law Enforcement Assistance Administration (LEAA), which channels federal funds to state and local agencies. However, Kennedy and Carter agreed on a general outline for revamping the embattled LEAA.

Leadership

The state of the economy, overriding all the other domestic policy questions, is the central issue on which Kennedy claims he would challenge Carter. But that is an area where the Massachusetts senator has not yet fully formulated clear alternatives to Carter's anti-inflation program.

In general, he supports Carter's voluntary wage and price controls but charges there has been an unfair burden placed on wages without clamping down on prices. He fears that interest rates have almost reached a point that will trigger a major recession. Kennedy agrees with Carter that a stimulative tax cut may be needed in 1980 but thinks the decision should be put off until then. Both Kennedy and Carter favored a similar tax cut in 1977 but have opposed "indexing" taxes to inflation.

Rather than focusing on economic policy differences, Kennedy has suggested that the intangible quality of "leadership" will be at the center of his challenge to Carter. The source of the country's current economic problems, Kennedy has charged, are the consequence of a lack of strong leadership. In his November announcement Kennedy said: "Only the president can provide the sense of direction needed by the nation.... The most important task of presidential leadership is to release the native energy of the people."

Kennedy's Background

Profession: Lawyer.
Born: Feb. 22, 1932, Boston, Mass.
Home: Boston, Mass.
Religion: Catholic.
Education: Harvard University, A.B., 1956; International Law School, The Hague, The Netherlands, 1958; University of Virginia Law School, LL.B., 1959.
Offices: Assistant district attorney, Suffolk County, Massachusetts, 1961-62; U.S. Senate 1963-
Military: U.S. Army, 1951-53.
Family: Married, Nov. 29, 1958 to Virginia Joan Bennett; three children.
Committees: Judiciary — chairman of full committee; member of Subcommittees on Antitrust, Monopoly and Business Rights; Criminal Justice; Improvements in Judicial Machinery.
Labor and Public Welfare — chairman of Subcommittee on Health and Scientific Research; member of Subcommittees on Aging; Education, Arts, and Humanities.
Joint Economic Committee — chairman of Subcommittee on Energy; member of Subcommittee on Priorities and Economy in Government.

Making leadership an issue may be a good tactical move for Kennedy as polls show that it is an area where the voters have given Carter bad marks in the past. The president's approval rating rose dramatically during the trouble in Iran, but historically Americans have supported their leaders in times of crisis. The ratings could drop again when the problem was resolved. Further, leadership is a quality that the public has associated with the Kennedy family during the last two decades. While Ted Kennedy may try to shy away from the policies of his brother's New Frontier, it is unlikely he will abandon its style.

Kennedy hopes to draw a stark contrast between the Carter's sometimes lackluster image and the vigor, activism and hard-driving approach that has characterized all three Kennedy brothers.

Background

The Kennedy style, the emphasis on strength and the devotion to public service can all be traced back to the patriarch of the Kennedy clan — Joseph P. Kennedy.

The elder Kennedy made millions in investments in movies, real estate, stocks and bonds. Each child was given a one-million-dollar trust fund.

Ted Kennedy used that nest egg to amass a personal wealth of several million dollars, much of which he keeps in a blind trust. (Of his disclosed wealth, about half is in real estate as he owns homes in Hyannis Port and Boston, Mass., Palm Beach, Fla., and McLean, Va. The other half comes primarily from stock ownership. His major investments are in American Telephone & Telegraph Co. and International Business Machines. He also has between $40,000 and $135,000 in gas and oil company stock.)

At the time of his announcement for the presidential nomination Kennedy released a report showing that he had an income of $702,697 for 1978 and paid taxes amounting to $315,508.

The youngest of nine children, Edward grew up in an intensely political family. "My babies were rocked to political lullabies," his mother, Rose, once remarked. Ted was still in prep school when his brother John, 14 years older, was elected to the House.

While the successful careers of his brothers John and Robert were already under way, Ted ran into the first of several troubles that would follow him through life. During his freshman year at Harvard, Kennedy arranged for another student to take his Spanish exam. When it was discovered, Kennedy was asked by university officials to leave school for a year.

Kennedy spent the next two years as a private in the Army, serving in Germany and France during the time of the Korean War. With his honor somewhat redeemed, Kennedy re-entered Harvard and graduated in 1956 with a bachelors degree in history and government and memories of starring on the Harvard football team.

During the next four years, Kennedy served a short stint as a reporter in North Africa for the International News Service, earned a law degree from the University of Virginia and managed John's senatorial re-election campaign in 1958. That was his first active political involvement. There was little doubt that John Kennedy would win easily. But the exercise proved a valuable training ground for young Edward, who had decided by then he wanted to make his career in "public service" like his brothers.

In 1960 his assignment was to round up delegate votes for John Kennedy's presidential campaign in the Western states. It was a second-string post as few expected Kennedy to do well in the West. But Ted worked hard and won praise from the candidate for being the best politician of the family.

When John Kennedy was elected president and Robert Kennedy decided he'd rather be attorney general than appointed to fill the vacant Massachusetts Senate seat, the Kennedy dynasty looked to Ted. He was only 28 years old, two years shy of the constitutionally-mandated minimum age. So the president-elect talked the governor into appointing a Kennedy family friend, Benjamin A. Smith II, to the Senate. Smith's job was to keep the seat warm until Kennedy was old enough to run. Under Massachusetts law a special election to fill the seat was required when the next general election was held in November 1962.

While waiting, Kennedy traveled around the world to become conversant with foreign affairs and worked at $1 a year as an assistant district attorney of Suffolk County (Boston). Three weeks after his thirtieth birthday, Kennedy announced his candidacy; Smith, as expected, said he wouldn't run. But Edward J. McCormack, the nephew of House Speaker John W. McCormack, was not so obliging.

The young McCormack challenged Kennedy for the endorsement in the state convention. Kennedy prevailed, employing the same sophisticated techniques his brother used at the national convention two years earlier. Lacking the party endorsement, McCormack continued his bitter campaign into the primary. During debates between the two, McCormack savagely attacked Kennedy's qualifications for the job. "If [your name] was Edward Moore, your candidacy would be a joke," McCormack taunted. McCormack's repeated efforts to get Kennedy to lose his temper failed and resulted in a backlash. Though Kennedy said his candidacy went beyond the fact he was the president's brother, his slogan — "He can do more for Massachusetts" — kept that fact high in voters' minds.

Kennedy easily won the primary, getting 559,000 votes to McCormack's 247,000. He coasted to an even larger win in November against Republican George Cabot Lodge, the great-grandson of Sen. Henry Cabot Lodge (1893-1924). It was the second time the Kennedy brothers had revenged their grandfather's loss in a 1916 Senate race to Lodge. In 1952 John Kennedy had defeated Lodge's grandson, Sen. Henry Cabot Lodge Jr. (1937-44; 1947-53).

In The Shadows

From the time he entered the Senate in 1962 until 1969, Kennedy was the youngest member of the body. As the youngest child in a large family, Ted had grown comfortable with his elders, which proved helpful during these years in the Senate. Many of his colleagues were twice his age. It was a time when Kennedy was in the shadow of his brothers, beginning a slow apprenticeship, learning how to work in the Senate.

His first day in the Senate, Kennedy asked veteran Georgia Sen. Richard Russell for advice. All Russell told Kennedy was, "You go further if you go slow." Kennedy followed that advice and the other unwritten rules about how to win acceptance in the Senate. He deferred to the senior members, kept quiet, did his homework on issues and went slowly.

After filling out the two remaining years of his brother's term, Kennedy ran for a full six-year term in 1964. On June 19, 1964, flying to the Massachusetts state party convention, Kennedy's small private plane crashed in an apple orchard near Westfield, Mass. The pilot and Kennedy's administrative assistant were killed. Indiana Sen. Birch Bayh, who was with Kennedy, pulled the severely injured senator from the wreckage.

For the next four months Kennedy was hospitalized, strapped between two canvas slings with three fractured vertabrae. Kennedy's wife, Joan, took over the campaign duties, which amounted to little more than informing voters her husband was getting better. If being the brother of a slain president was not already enough to carry Kennedy to victory, the sympathy from his accident eliminated any doubt. Against a little-known Republican, Howard Whitmore, Kennedy won by the largest plurality ever given a Senate candidate in the state.

During his convalescence, Kennedy embarked on a personal campaign to become what some have termed "a national senator." The first step was to hold a series of one-man seminars about national issues. He called upon the Kennedy brain trust and others at Harvard and M.I.T. to brief him on major national issues and help him develop liberal positions on each one.

Returning to the Senate in 1965, Ted Kennedy found himself still in the shadows. His older brother, Robert, had just been elected senator from New York. With the Kennedys, the family's seniority rule prevailed over the Senate's. It was Robert Kennedy, not Edward, who spoke out forcefully against the continuing escalation of the Vietnam War even though both opposed it.

Ted Kennedy's forum for the war came with his first subcommittee chairmanship in 1965 on the Judiciary Committee's Subcommittee on Refugees and Escapees. Ever since then Kennedy has championed the refugee cause. The first bill he managed on the Senate floor was the Johnson administration's Immigration and Nationality Act in 1965, which ended the national origins quota system.

In 1979 Kennedy won Senate passage of a bill, supported by the Carter administration, that revamped procedures for admitting refugees and increased their numbers. In between there have been countless hearings on refugee problems and human rights violations in Indochina, Bangladesh, Romania, Argentina, Cyprus and South Africa, among others.

Kennedy's Interest Group Ratings

Americans for Democratic Action (ADA) — The percentage of the time Kennedy voted with or entered a live pair in accordance with the ADA position.

AFL-CIO Committee on Political Education (COPE) — The percentage of the time Kennedy voted in accordance with or was paired in favor of the COPE position.

National Farmers Union (NFU) — The percentage of the time Kennedy voted in accordance with, was paired for or announced for the NFU position.

Americans for Constitutional Action (ACA) — The percentage of the time Kennedy voted in accordance with the ACA position.

Following are Kennedy's ratings since he became a member of the Senate in 1962:

	ADA[1]	COPE[2]	NFU[2]	ACA
1963[3]	94	100[4]	65[4]	0
1964	89	—	—	0
1965	94	100[5]	100	0
1966	100	—	86	8
1967	92	100	90	0
1968	71	100	88	0
1969	100	100	94	9
1970	84	100	100	5
1971	100	83	100	5
1972	90	89	90	5
1973	90	91	100	4
1974	81	70	100	0
1975	89	89	100	0
1976	95	90	92	0
1977	95	89	80	4
1978	95	95	40	4

[1] *Failure to vote lowers score.*
[2] *Percentages compiled by CQ from information provided by groups.*
[3] *Kennedy took office Nov. 7, 1962 after the adjournment of the 87th Congress. He did not cast his first Senate vote until 1963.*
[4] *Rating is for the entire 88th Congress.*
[5] *Rating is for the entire 89th Congress.*

The Darkest Years

Ted Kennedy was forced out of the shadows with the assassination of his only remaining brother, Robert, on June 6, 1968. It marked a significant turning point in Kennedy's life as an individual, a senator and a national figure. As Joseph Kennedy's sole surviving son, he became the surrogate father of his brothers' 13 children. In the Senate, he was at last on his own, at a time when he had enough seniority to have some senatorial power. And on the national scene, there were intense pressures for him to follow the path laid down by his brothers. For a 36-year-old, these were tremendous emotional pressures.

After a long brooding summer, mostly spent sailing off the Maine coast, Kennedy re-entered the public arena in August 1968 with his strongest denunciation to date of Johnson's war policy. At the conclusion of the speech, given at Holy Cross College in Worcester, Mass., Kennedy said, "Like my three brothers before me [the oldest, Joseph P. Kennedy Jr., had died in World War II], I pick up a fallen standard. Sustained by the memory of our priceless years together, I shall try to carry forward that special commitment to justice, to excellence, to courage that distinguished their lives."

For the time being, Kennedy had decided to make his mark in the Senate rather than seeking the presidency. It was widely accepted that Kennedy already was much more dedicated to his Senate responsibilities and more adept at them than either of his two brothers had been during their Senate careers.

Six months after Robert's death, Ted Kennedy decided to take his Senate career one step further by challenging Sen. Russell B. Long for his job as majority whip. The short campaign rekindled his enthusiasm for the Senate that had left temporarily with Robert's death. He was elected by a secret ballot, 31-26.

Kennedy looked on his new role as one that would enhance his reputation as a "national senator" — involving him in all subjects, giving him an activist role in a Democratic Senate developing alternative policies to those of a newly-elected Republican administration.

He was disappointed. He had to spend a lot of time on tedious, housekeeping details. The long hours on the Senate floor kept him from accepting national speaking dates. And working under Majority Leader Mike Mansfield, Kennedy's involvement in forming Democratic policy was quite limited.

Kennedy did not win high marks as a whip. Along with his growing disinterest in it, there were several external events which prevented Kennedy from undertaking the job with the attention it required.

In the winter of 1969-70 his father died, and Kennedy came down with a severe case of pneumonia. In the summer and fall of 1970, Kennedy spent a lot of time campaigning in Massachusetts. He needed to make sure that the repercussions of another personal mishap would not have an adverse affect on his electability.

That event, whose consequences have gone far beyond the whip's job, happened late in the evening of July 18, 1969. Driving home after a party on Chappaquiddick Island, Mass., Kennedy's automobile plunged off a bridge. Mary Jo Kopechne, a former campaign worker for Robert Kennedy who was in the car, died.

Kennedy escaped but did not report the accident to police until the next day. A week later he pleaded guilty to charges of leaving the scene of an accident. In a nationwide television address, Kennedy called his actions "indefensible" and asked for guidance from Massachusetts' voters about whether he should remain in public life. On July 30 Kennedy announced that the response from the public — though not necessarily the press — had been so overwhelmingly supportive that he would remain in office and serve a full term if re-elected the next year. That was his roundabout way of ruling out a 1972 presidential campaign.

Questions about the events at Chappaquiddick and Kennedy's judgment have continued for the last decade. It is almost inevitable that it will become a campaign issue in 1980.

After winning re-election in 1970 over Republican Josiah A. Spaulding with 63 percent, Kennedy sought to retain the whip's job. Many of Kennedy's colleagues already had decided he did not deserve another term as whip. West Virginia's Robert C. Byrd, who as secretary of the Senate Democratic Conference was the third-ranking Democrat, had taken over many of Kennedy's housekeeping chores. In doing so he accumulated enough votes to oust Kennedy from his leadership job by a 31-24 vote.

The National Senator

Although angry over losing — something Kennedys are unaccustomed to — the Massachusetts senator was free to pursue his own agenda in national legislative issues.

Two years earlier Kennedy had become chairman of the Judiciary Committee's Administrative Practice and Procedure Subcommittee, a panel whose jurisdiction was as broad as Kennedy's interests.

In the eight years Kennedy held that position, he conducted hearings on subjects ranging from the Freedom of Information Act to oversight of the Food and Drug Administration. The original Civil Aeronautics Board oversight hearings, which culminated in airline deregulation, began in that subcommittee. Oversight hearings on the Food and Drug Administration, begun in 1975, led to Senate passage of a consumer-oriented redrafting of the federal drug laws in September 1979.

Kennedy has been criticized in some circles for spreading his legislative cloak over too much area.

In a dispute over whether Kennedy's Judiciary Committee or the Commerce Committee should handle the trucking deregulation bill, Sen. Ernest F. Hollings, D-S.C., railed against what he termed "the Kennedy hegemony" in an unusual personal attack on the Senate floor.

Hollings charged that Kennedy's committee was "running all over the lot, trying to grab work to do." The Senate, in what amounted to a test of personal strength, lined up against Kennedy, who conceded the bill to the Commerce Committee, headed by the influential Howard W. Cannon, D-Nev.

Critics charge that Kennedy's legislative style leans heavily on grabbing headlines with little follow-up. Others view his approach to most legislation as being marked by a willingness to compromise and accommodate the interests of his colleagues to get his bills through.

Although one moment Kennedy may be speaking against lifting sanctions on Zimbabwe-Rhodesia and the next supporting the extension of the ratification period for the Equal Rights Amendment, the majority of his time is spent on the subjects that involve his current committee and subcommittee chairmanships — Judiciary and Health. Kennedy's Energy Subcommittee in the Joint Economic Committee has no legislative powers.

In the health field Kennedy has promoted a series of bills that for the most part expand the role of government regulation but at the same time provide more money for improved patient services and research programs. His current national health plan, which is substantially different from previous versions he has introduced, is in line with this overall assessment. It would require massive regulation of the private insurance industry but provide extensive health care to virtually all citizens.

Although a Catholic, Kennedy has supported providing government funds for indigent women seeking abortions. He became identified with that stance in 1975, when he successfully blocked an attempt to attach an anti-abortion amendment to a health services bill he was managing on the Senate floor.

Judiciary Committee Career

Serving on the Judiciary Committee since 1963, Kennedy has championed a number of liberal causes. He joined Indiana's Bayh in pushing through the constitutional amendment to lower the voting age to 18 in 1970. In 1978 he helped pass the first major legislation to control wiretapping in the United States for national security purposes. And he has been a strong advocate of gun control laws.

Perhaps the best example of Kennedy's willingness to compromise and barter to win approval of major bills is seen in his Judiciary Committee work.

For the last 10 years there has been an effort to recodify federal criminal laws. Liberal organizations generally supportive of Kennedy, such as the American Civil Liberties Union, criticized the effort. They felt many provisions dealing with sentencing and parole would inhibit personal liberties. In 1978 Kennedy abandoned his liberal friends and, with limited changes, supported the bill pushed by Sen. John L. McClellan, D-Ark., and Judiciary Committee Chairman James Eastland, D-Miss., both conservatives. It passed the Senate but not the House.

In 1979, as chairman, Kennedy attempted to mollify the ACLU by removing some of the sections it opposed. But the overall tone of the bill still had a fairly strong law and order ring to it, which Kennedy could use in a campaign to turn back any argument he is "soft on crime." In the latest version federal jurisdiction has been curtailed somewhat in response to criticism that rewriting the criminal code was really a back-door effort to increase the role of the federal government in law enforcement.

When Kennedy assumed the chairmanship of the Judiciary Committee in January 1979 he came in with the same kind of enthusiasm which marked his start as majority whip. A forceful, centralized committee, charging ahead in many areas was predicted. But by the end of the year Kennedy's accomplishments in the Judiciary Committee were limited. The committee also spent a substantial amount of time scrutinizing nominees to fill the 152 new judgeships that were created in 1978. Kennedy has been evenhanded in the hearings, allowing all dissenting views to be aired before voting on the nominations. Although Kennedy personally is committed to getting more minorities and women on the federal bench, he has not interjected himself in the Carter administration's selection process.

Two major Kennedy initiatives in the Judiciary Committee encountered serious opposition during the first session of the 96th Congress. One — designed to permit consumers to sue price-fixers for damages (the *"Illinois Brick"* bill)— cleared the Judiciary Committee on a slim 9-8 vote in May 1979. And Kennedy achieved that narrow victory only after making major concessions.

Kennedy also ran into strong resistance from big business to legislation that would bar mergers between large corporations.

The trouble Kennedy had with these bills may be useful to political opponents, when the question of leadership is discussed in the presidential campaign.

A Careful Strategy

Since winning a third full term in 1976 by trouncing Republican Michael Robertson with 70 percent, Kennedy has maintained a careful political independence from the Carter administration. And beginning with a speech at the Democratic midterm convention in Memphis in December 1978, Kennedy has sought to define his differences with Carter and offer the leftwing of the Democratic Party an alternative.

Virtually whenever the president would make a move, Kennedy would have a ready response. Although he stood by his litany of intending to support the president, Kennedy led many to believe he already had changed his mind.

His undeclared candidacy was nurtured in the spring and summer of 1979 by a draft movement that developed in several states. It was given added impetus in May when four Democratic House members endorsed the non-candidate. Throughout the year, public opinion polls showed Kennedy to be a stronger candidate against any of the potential GOP contenders than President Carter. A number of Democratic senators up for re-election in 1980 were reported to have quietly urged Kennedy to run.

Along with the obstacles of Chappaquiddick and renewed talk of resurrecting a Kennedy dynasty, Kennedy was faced with a family situation that would prove ticklish in a presidential campaign. In early 1978 Kennedy's wife, Joan, moved out of their home in McLean, Va., and rented an apartment of her own in Boston.

She wanted to build a new life, free from her admitted problem with alcohol, and centered more on her own interests in music and less on politics. She admits she is "not wild about politics," and her role as the wife of the only surviving Kennedy brother constantly has shoved her into an unwelcomed spotlight.

During the August 1979 recess, Kennedy pondered his political situation. If he was going to make a presidential bid, he could not wait until after the first primary, like his brother, because too many filing deadlines would have passed. Unlike 1968, when only about 40 percent of the delegates were elected in primaries, the 1980 party nominee will be forced to compete in nearly all the primary contests to have a shot at the nomination. About three-quarters of the delegates will be chosen in primaries in 1980.

One of Kennedy's chief concerns was that his candidacy would lead to comments by major Democratic leaders that he was splitting the party. But with California Gov. Jerry Brown already an obvious candidate, he was able to

---

Kennedy Campaign Staff

Campaign manager: Stephen Smith of New York City, husband of Kennedy's sister, Jean. Smith manages the Kennedy family business and financial affairs and was Robert F. Kennedy's presidential campaign manager in 1968.

Deputy campaign managers: Ron Brown, Joanne Howes, Gov. Pat Lucey (D-Wis., 1971-1977), Phil Bakes, James O'Hara.

National political director: Paul G. Kirk, Boston and Washington lawyer, Kennedy's personal political aide from 1969 until 1977.

Press secretary: Thomas P. Southwick, 30, formerly a reporter for Congressional Quarterly and later press secretary in Kennedy's Senate office.

Treasurer: Carolyn Reed, formerly assistant counsel for the House Administration Committee.

Legal counsel: Bill Oldaker, formerly general counsel with the Federal Election Commission.

Director of field operations: Carl Wagner, 34, former political operative for the American Federation of State, County and Municipal Employees.

Campaign headquarters: 1250 22nd St., N.W., Washington, D.C. 20037.

convince himself that such attacks against him would be muted.

The personal questions about handling the Chappaquiddick incident, possible threats against his life and the reluctance by his wife and mother also were worked out during a month of sailing and touch football games at the family compound at Hyannis Port, Mass.

Some have speculated that the objections from the family served as a convenient smoke screen to cover up the presidential maneuvering that began many months ago.

Whether or not that was the case, Kennedy's announcement that his family would support whatever decision he made provided a clear signal to draft-Kennedy operatives in New England, Florida and other places to continue their efforts.

During September, following his encouragement of the draft movement, Kennedy moved himself closer to becoming an actual candidate. Technically he became a candidate on Oct. 25, 1979, when nearly 100 supporters pledged more than $150,000 to his campaign at the home of Patricia Lawford, Kennedy's sister. Once an individual accepts money he is legally a candidate unless the money is returned, according to the Federal Election Campaign Act. On Oct. 29 a Kennedy For President Committee registered with the Federal Election Commission, preparing the way for the Nov. 7 announcement.

The National Arena

As a full-fledged presidential candidate, Kennedy at last began operating completely in the national arena. Although he has been a more effective senator than either of his brothers, Kennedy, like them, always has been more influential with the general public than in the Senate. There he has been subjected to the same roadblocks imposed by the competition of interests that hinder all senators.

Kennedy says the only way to pass national health insurance and the other elusive goals he has been working for in the Senate is to have a strong president who will forcefully advocate them. The incumbent, Ted Kennedy thinks, is not such a man. This conviction, it appears, has thrust Kennedy into the contest.

John B. Anderson

A Long Shot Running on the GOP Left

When John Connally promised tax cuts at a recent Republican gathering in Indianapolis, the audience clapped and cheered. When Benjamin Fernandez lauded big business, they applauded lustily. But when Rep. John B. Anderson of Illinois voiced the need for increased aid to Southeast Asian refugees, there was virtually no response at all.

Both the speech and the audience response were fairly typical for Anderson's long shot presidential campaign.

Widely regarded as one of the most able and articulate members of the U.S. House of Representatives, Anderson has made little effort to alter his unorthodox brand of independent Republicanism for more traditional party audiences. He has taken to the campaign trail intent on appealing to the conscience of the party as well as its pocketbook.

Over the course of his 10-term House career, Anderson gradually has gravitated from the right to the center of the country's political spectrum. But viewed inside the rightward-moving GOP, he is seen as a champion of the Republican left.

That is not an especially good place from which to mount a presidential campaign. Better known and better financed Republican liberals have gone nowhere in recent years in their bids for the GOP presidential nomination. And Anderson must guard his liberal base from overtures by Sen. Howard H. Baker Jr. of Tennessee and ex-Rep. George Bush of Texas.

But Anderson believes that he can, claiming that he is the lone candidate to support the liberal Republican position on controversial issues such as ratification of the SALT II treaty. His dark horse candidacy can succeed, he says, because he can construct a base, albeit a narrow one, solely for himself.

While other contenders are slicing up the conservative vote in the important early primaries, Anderson hopes to run surprisingly well by garnering nearly all the liberal votes. Once established as a serious contender for the nomination, he would hope to broaden his base by convincing other Republicans that he is the party's most viable general election candidate.

Political Odyssey

In the words of his campaign manager, William G. Bradford, "Anderson is a Republican who dares to wear his wallet on the right and his heart on the left." An orthodox Republican on fiscal policy, he has taken unorthodox positions on a wide range of social issues.

This has not always been the case. Anderson came to Congress in 1961 as a typical Midwestern conservative. Elected on a campaign platform that stressed opposition to "big government" and the expansion of communism, he compiled through most of the 1960s a voting record that was hailed by the Americans for Constitutional Action (ACA) as one of the most conservative of any of the members of Congress.

"He stands firm against the liberal pressures in Washington, the wild spending schemes, and the permissive society offered by the proponents of the Great Society," trumpeted an ACA release that endorsed Anderson for re-election in 1968.

If there was a watershed in Anderson's political odyssey, it came in April 1968 when as a member of the House Rules Committee he cast the deciding vote that sent a controversial open housing bill to the floor. Several days later he argued passionately for its passage and won credit for swinging over several crucial Republican votes for the civil rights bill, which eventually became law.

While Anderson had been lobbied intensively by both sides before the Rules Committee vote, he wrote later that his decision was ultimately made after a careful examination of his evangelical faith.

"There came to bear in my thinking," he said, "the realization that as a Christian, I had to be willing to give up age-old prejudices, even to the point of subordinating something as fundamental as the right of contract to the even more fundamental principle of human rights."

Religious Faith

Anderson's faith always has been an important aspect of his personal life. The son of a Swedish immigrant, he was raised in a predominantly Scandinavian section of Rockford, Ill., where he attended an evangelical church. At age nine he was "born again" at a summer tent meeting.

Anderson vividly described the event and his religious faith in an autobiographical book entitled *Between Two*

Congressional Quarterly Vote Study Scores...

	1961	1962	1963	1964	1965	1966	1967	1968	1969
Presidential[1]									
Support	25%	30%	30%	35%	32%	36%	54%	64%	62%
Opposition	65	60	61	58	46	44	37	26	17
Conservative Coalition[2]									
Support	91	94	80	92	76	68	59	55	42
Opposition	0	0	13	8	4	8	22	37	38
Party[2]									
Unity	86	88	77	77	73	66	70	57	44
Opposition	5	7	10	16	7	11	16	33	36
Voting Participation[2]	89	91	89	89	79	80	85	91	80

NOTE: Failure to vote lowers scores so that total in each category will not be 100% in every year.

[1] *Ground Rules, p. 67.*
[2] *Definitions, p. 67.*

Worlds: A Congressman's Choice (1970). He has written other articles about his faith for Christian publications and in 1964 was named the outstanding layman of the year by the National Association of Evangelicals.

While most evangelicals tend to be politically conservative, Anderson has used his faith, beginning with the 1968 open housing vote, to justify more liberal positions on a wide range of political issues.

On civil rights, he has been in the forefront of Republican opposition to a constitutional amendment that would ban busing to achieve racial integration in schools. The position has helped him win the endorsement of civil rights activist Dick Gregory for his presidential campaign and embellish Anderson's claim that he could run better than any other Republican candidate among black voters.

On women's rights, he was one of the first House members to urge ratification of the ERA, and he opposes a constitutional amendment to ban abortions.

While Anderson's conversion on social issues has made him unpopular with conservatives, he also has veered away from the traditional Republican standard on other issues.

He contends that he does not advocate a "milquetoast" defense policy. But over the past decade, he has criticized the "mad momentum of the arms race" and opposed the development of new weapons such as the B-1 bomber and the neutron bomb. He supported the Panama Canal treaties and has endorsed ratification of the SALT II treaty.

Anderson backed President Richard M. Nixon's plan for a negotiated settlement of the Vietnam War, although in 1970 he denounced the war as "the most tragic error in diplomacy and military policy in our nation's history."

To the chagrin of many Republicans, Anderson has been a leader in the fight to overhaul federal campaign finance law. In recent years he has been a prime cosponsor of legislation to extend public financing to House general election campaigns, a measure that has drawn the fire of most party leaders.

In 1979 Anderson joined with Democratic Rep. Morris K. Udall of Arizona to sponsor an Alaska lands bill that won the endorsement of both environmental groups and the Carter administration. The measure passed the House in May, but the Senate had not acted on it by the end of 1979.

Anderson has labeled the energy problem as one of the major issues in the 1980 campaign and has gone further than most other candidates in warning that it may be time for the American people to be austere. He has proposed a 50-cent per gallon tax on gasoline to reduce consumption. And he was only one of seven Republican House members to vote for President Carter's standby gasoline rationing plan when it was defeated in May.

Personal sacrifice, Anderson has indicated, should be coupled with a massive effort to develop alternative energy sources and the creation of an oil-purchasing cartel to deal with OPEC.

GOP Orthodoxy

In spite of a voting record that deviates significantly from most of his GOP colleagues, Anderson claims to be a "mainstream" Republican in tune with the average Republican voter if not the party leadership.

On bread-and-butter issues he is certainly orthodox. While his views on social issues have undergone a metamorphosis, he has remained a fiscal conservative who abhors budget deficits and lavish spending programs.

Anderson would fight inflation by curbing government spending. "I do not believe in the quick-fix, the $50 rebate, the huge surge of spending as a way of suddenly reversing the economy," he has said. "We cannot launch another spending spree to try to cure inflation."

Anderson has also been very orthodox in his party loyalty, dating from his support for Barry Goldwater in the 1964 presidential election to his frequent digs at Jimmy Carter and the "greedy, parochial, self-interested" Democratic Congress.

As chairman (from 1969 to mid-1979) of the House Republican Conference, the third-ranking position in the GOP hierarchy, Anderson sought to marshal congressional support for the legislative programs of Presidents Nixon and Gerald R. Ford. He was particularly effusive in his

...Covering Anderson's Career in the House

	1970	1971	1972	1973	1974	1975	1976	1977	1978	1979
Presidential[1]										
Support	72%	88%	78%	55%	70%[3]/56%[4]	72%	53%	53%	54%	26%
Opposition	6	7	11	29	19[3]/22[4]	17	25	33	24	8
Conservative Coalition[2]										
Support	57	61	49	44	45	56	43	46	38	9
Opposition	20	30	37	44	45	35	36	38	43	16
Party[2]										
Unity	65	65	60	46	44	56	42	47	38	9
Opposition	18	22	26	39	42	31	36	38	37	20
Voting Participation[2]	80	82	87	75	84	84	76	84	71	28

[3] During President Nixon's tenure in 1974.
[4] During President Ford's tenure in 1974.

praise of Nixon domestic initiatives, hailing the "New Federalism" plan for revenue sharing, welfare reform and manpower retraining as one of the most farsighted proposals presented by a president in the 20th century.

Yet for Anderson, there are limits to party loyalty. He was revolted by the Watergate scandal and was one of the first Republican members of Congress to urge that Nixon step down.

Anderson's disgust with Nixon did not cool even after the president's resignation. In a book published in 1975, Anderson condemned the former president for "moral crassness" and denounced him as "as a man of great duplicity — a man who in public would eschew the use of profane and vulgar language, but whose own language in the Oval Office was not unlike the graffiti on bathroom walls."

Watergate seems to have colored Anderson's view of the presidency. He has lamented the rise of "an imperial presidency" and the growing illusion that the president is "our savior," who possesses the power and wisdom to solve all of our national problems.

Anderson has indicated that his presidency would be less grandiose and more visionary. When he launched his presidential campaign in June 1979, he declared that he would try to use the office to re-establish what he described as the nation's "vital center," appealing to competing interest groups to work together toward a common national purpose.

Anderson claims a trio of Republican heroes — Abraham Lincoln for his compassion, Teddy Roosevelt for his dynamism and Dwight D. Eisenhower for his promotion of the Republican tenets of fiscal responsibility and decentralized government.

For remolding the image of the GOP, the energetic Roosevelt would be his prime model. "I want the Republican Party to be clearly identified in the public mind," Anderson has written, "as a driving force behind the reformation of our political and social structures."

Unlike many of the other Republican candidates, Anderson is not a man of great personal wealth. According to his personal financial disclosure statement that was filed with the Federal Election Commission, Anderson's principal asset is a Washington, D.C., house valued at over $250,000 which he has been renting. He also owns several stocks; his largest holding — Combined Communications — is worth between $15,000 and $50,000.

Honoraria income totaled $12,680 in 1978 and $8,600 for the first half of 1979.

He reported liabilities to three banks — the largest a mortgage valued between $15,000 and $50,000 on his Washington, D.C., house.

Public Career

Anderson launched his political career in 1956 by winning the post of state's attorney of Winnebago County (Rockford). It followed a three-year stint in the Foreign Service in West Germany and a brief law practice in his hometown of Rockford.

Not lacking for ambition, Anderson sought the 16th District U.S. House seat of the retiring Republican Rep. Leo E. Allen just four years later. Decisively carrying the large Swedish-American community in populous Winnebago County, he won a five-way Republican primary contest that was tantamount to election. The area traditionally has voted Republican. *(Election results, see p. 71.)*

Anderson had no trouble winning re-election throughout the 1960s. But he did not gain national attention or even draw the interest of many of his House colleagues until he cast his 1968 vote for open housing.

That one vote earned him a reputation as a man of conscience with the Washington press corps and established him as a leading spokesman for moderate and liberal Republicans in the House.

GOP Conference

Anderson capitalized on his new-found fame by winning the chairmanship of the House Republican Conference in January 1969. He succeeded Rep. Melvin R. Laird, who gave up his House seat to join the Nixon Cabinet.

> ## Anderson's Background
> **Profession:** Lawyer.
> **Born:** Feb. 15, 1922; Rockford, Ill.
> **Home:** Rockford.
> **Religion:** Evangelical Free Church.
> **Education:** University of Illinois, A.B., 1942; J.D., 1946; Harvard Law School, LL.M., 1949.
> **Offices:** State's attorney of Winnebago County (Ill.), 1956-60; U.S. House, 1961- .
> **Military:** U.S. Army, 1943-45.
> **Family:** Wife, Keke; five children.
> **Committees:** Rules; ranking Republican on Rules of the House Subcommittee.

Anderson's election to head the GOP policy committee was probably the high-water mark of his congressional career. The decade of the 1970s has largely been one of frustration.

Not only has his influence in the House been limited by the continuing minority status of the GOP, but on three occasions he has had to fend off conservative challenges to hold his conference chairmanship.

The most serious assault came in 1971 from Samuel L. Devine of Ohio, who came within eight votes of winning. Anderson was re-elected by more comfortable margins in 1974 over Charles E. Wiggins of California and in 1978 over Thomas N. Kindness of Ohio.

But in each case Anderson was forced to defend his record to his colleagues, and the conservative challenger won the support of nearly 40 percent of the Republican House members.

When Gerald R. Ford left the House to become vice president in 1973, Anderson briefly considered a bid for Ford's old post of minority leader. But he abandoned the race, noting that his candidacy would encounter the fierce opposition of conservatives and that he would be unable to provide President Nixon with "total fidelity."

Like his efforts to advance in the House, Anderson's attempts to enter the Senate also were stymied. His first try came in 1969, when he lobbied Republican Gov. Richard B. Ogilvie unsuccessfully to appoint him to the seat left vacant by the death of Republican Everett McKinley Dirksen. Although Ogilvie appointed Illinois House speaker Ralph Tyler Smith to fill the vacancy, Ogilvie is now supporting Anderson's presidential candidacy.

Anderson came close to running against Democratic Sen. Adlai E. Stevenson in 1974 but backed off when he concluded that he could not upset the popular incumbent in the Watergate election year.

His political advancement blocked, Anderson experienced the ultimate political frustration in 1978 when he faced a well-financed conservative primary challenge for his House seat.

Backed by direct mail specialist Richard Viguerie and a phalanx of conservative interest groups, fundamentalist minister Don Lyon mounted an aggressive campaign that sharply criticized Anderson's positions on social issues and lambasted the incumbent for losing touch with the district. Lyon charged that Anderson had become "Washington's representative to the 16th District."

Anderson responded by bringing a host of big-name Republicans into the district to vouch for his party loyalty and influence in Congress. Former President Ford, Henry Kissinger, Republican National Committee Chairman Bill Brock and Rep. Jack F. Kemp of New York all campaigned on behalf of Anderson.

The incumbent won the primary with 58 percent of the vote, but Lyon supporters contended that the victory margin was the result of Democratic crossovers. Anderson carried his home base, populous Winnebago County, by a margin of 2-to-1 but ran behind Lyon in the rest of the district.

While the campaign had not forced him to change his basic political beliefs, Anderson candidly admitted to the *Chicago Sun-Times* that he had moved a bit rightward because of the Lyon challenge. "Like a lot of liberals or moderates," he said, "I may have been overenthusiastic about what government can do . . . I've probably retrenched some."

Presidential Ambition

Against this background of frustrated ambition, Anderson announced his presidential candidacy in June 1979. Declaring that he was as qualified as the other candidates in the large Republican field, he made it plain that it would be the presidency or nothing for him in 1980.

He has ruled out a House re-election campaign next year or a race for the Senate seat being vacated by Stevenson, who is retiring. At age 58, Anderson says, he is too old to become a freshman senator.

While admittedly a long shot for the presidency, Anderson optimistically believes that he has major assets that, if well-publicized, could transform him into a major contender.

Foremost is his reputation as one of Congress' best orators and finest minds. His performance in the House has drawn favorable comment from congressional colleagues on both sides of the aisle as well as from the Washington press corps.

A Republican presidential rival, Sen. Robert Dole of Kansas, has been quoted as calling Anderson "probably the brightest of the Republican candidates." A *Washington*

> ## Anderson Staff
> **National campaign manager:** William G. Bradford, 54, a 30-year Foreign Service veteran who most recently was U.S. ambassador to Chad.
> **Campaign director:** Dan Swillinger, 37, former attorney with the Federal Election Commission and ex-political director with the Ripon Society.
> **Political director:** Kirk Walder, 26, a four-year veteran of Anderson's congressional staff.
> **Press secretary:** Vicky Markell, 29, formerly assistant editor of the *Ripon Forum*.
> **Administrative assistant (congressional office):** Michael MacLeod, 37, former executive director of both the House Republican Conference and the Ripon Society.
> **Legislative assistant (congressional office):** Bruce Post, 32, a three-year veteran of Anderson's staff and a former member of the staff of Rep. James R. Jeffords, R-Vt.
> **Campaign headquarters:** 719 8th Street, S.E., Washington, D.C., and 1100 Talcott Building, Rockford, Ill.

Star editorial referred to him as "one of the truly creative figures in Congress."

Anderson is hopeful that he will receive equally favorable reviews from the local press along the campaign trail. And there is early evidence that he is succeeding.

In a quotation featured in Anderson's campaign literature, the executive editor of the *Des Moines Register*, James P. Gannon, described the candidate as "a man of charm, grace and intellect whose Achilles heel is a passionate attachment to issues and a willingness to argue his viewpoint when it would be shrewder to shut up. . . ."

Although no House member has gone directly to the presidency since James A. Garfield in 1880, Anderson believes that his congressional experience would be a valuable asset. He contends a president in the 1980s can only be effective if he understands and knows how to deal with an activist Congress.

Anderson began the campaign with low name recognition and virtually no support in the polls. A September 1979 Gallup Poll measuring name familiarity showed that barely one-fifth of the respondents recognized Anderson's name, far below all the other major Republican contenders except Rep. Philip M. Crane of Illinois.

In an effort to increase his name recognition in New Hampshire, Anderson ran ads in the state's newspapers simply headed "John Who?" While campaign officials feared the ads might unfavorably remind voters of "Jimmy Who," they claim that they helped double Anderson's name recognition in the state.

The early stages of the Anderson campaign were hampered by a lack of money. During the first four months of his campaign, Anderson raised less than one tenth as much as Connally.

Ironically, Anderson's fund-raising capability has been curtailed by the public financing law that he helped to enact.

Anderson has drawn support within the Republican business community, but with the $1,000 limit on individual contributions he cannot fully tap this source. "We're hoisted on our own petard," says campaign manager Bradford.

Another problem for Anderson is a thin organization. Outside of several early primary states he has no organization, and in more than half of the states there was not even a campaign representative by late October 1979.

Early Primary Strategy

With a limited amount of money available, Anderson planned to concentrate on the early primary states. "We cannot campaign everywhere," says Bradford. "Our strategy is dictated by the calendar and our limited resources."

Thereafter, he would follow a Midwestern strategy, concentrating on winning support in his home region which he points out will have more delegate votes to the 1980 Republican convention than any other region.

Anderson's Interest Group Ratings

Americans for Democratic Action (ADA) — The percentage of the time Anderson voted with or entered a live pair in accordance with the ADA position.

AFL-CIO Committee on Political Education (COPE) — The percentage of the time Anderson voted in accordance with or was paired in favor of the COPE position.

National Farmers Union (NFU) — The percentage of the time Anderson voted in accordance with, was paired for or announced for the NFU position.

Americans for Constitutional Action (ACA) — The percentage of the time Anderson voted in accordance with the ACA position.

Following are Anderson's ratings since he became a member of the House in 1961:

	ADA[1]	COPE[2]	NFU[2]	ACA
1961	0[3]	0[3]	10[3]	95[3]
1962	—	—	—	—
1963	4[4]	9[4]	8[4]	91[4]
1964	—	—	—	—
1965	11	0[5]	13	91
1966	0	—	NA	87
1967	13	17	NA	82
1968	17	50	NA	67
1969	33	60	67	40
1970	28	14	62	67
1971	32	36	14	63
1972	44	36	50	43
1973	36	27	33	46
1974	43	45	64	33
1975	58	41	36	54
1976	50	28	33	29
1977	40	29	45	38
1978	55	39	NA	44

[1] *Failure to vote lowers score.*
[2] *Percentages compiled by CQ from information provided by group.*
[3] *Rating is for entire 87th Congress for all groups.*
[4] *Rating is for entire 88th Congress for all groups.*
[5] *Rating is for entire 89th Congress.*
NA—not available.

The early key for Anderson is whether he can build a liberal base that will withstand forays by Baker and Bush. Because he is the only Republican candidate supporting liberal positions on a variety of social issues, Anderson feels that he can.

"If there were only two candidates" in next year's Republican race, Bradford optimistically declares, "we wouldn't do so well. But there are more than two. We will have our whole slice of the pie. Others will have to cut theirs."

Howard H. Baker

Aiming for the Republican Middle

Howard H. Baker Jr. is a creature of Congress.

The Tennessee senator values the qualities that spell success on Capitol Hill — compromise, shrewdness and caution. He places a premium on the dispassionate, articulate, if verbose, oratory that prevails on the Senate floor.

His smoothly delivered speech, reluctance to offend and middle-of-the-road course have earned him respect from both sides of the aisle.

As Senate minority leader, his conciliatory gifts enabled him to weld together previously feuding GOP factions. While weighted toward the conservative side, his ideologically eclectic alignment on issues, ranging from a liberal position on open-housing legislation to a hard-line stance on military spending, points to the flexibility that helps people get ahead in Congress.

"Government by ideological reflex, left or right, will not bring the unity we need," he declared as he announced his candidacy in the Senate caucus room Nov. 1, 1979. "I can appeal to the broadest range of support."

To counter conservative antipathy to his 1978 support of the Panama Canal treaties, the standard Baker statement on the campaign trail is straight out of the book of legislative give-and-take. Through dickering with other senators, Baker explains, he was able to safeguard the right of U.S. military intervention in the Canal Zone.

Still, it is an open question whether the qualities that make a successful senator will land Baker the Republican presidential nomination or even would help him as president.

The even-keeled speeches that serve Baker well in the Senate sometimes sound flat on a stump he shares with such accomplished campaign orators as former California Gov. Ronald Reagan and former Texas Gov. John B. Connally.

In addition, his past departures from conservative orthodoxy, especially on Panama, may hurt him in a party whose center has shifted rightward. Conservative activists complain that he is too slick and stands for nothing other than his own advancement.

"Baker is suited to accommodating people in the Senate, but that's not leadership," commented Paul M. Weyrich, executive director of the conservative Committee for the Survival of a Free Congress. "He doesn't want to bite the bullet. He doesn't act according to principles. After Jimmy Carter, the country is looking for leadership, and Baker is the wrong man at the right time."

As a member of the Senate Foreign Relations Committee, Baker came out against the Strategic Arms Limitation Treaty (SALT). But his critics on the right charge that was merely an attempt to rehabilitate himself after his Panama vote.

Baker's Senate ties may have hindered him in another way. His active schedule as floor leader prevented him from working early primary and caucus states full time for much of 1979. In Iowa and New Hampshire, for instance, former U.S. Rep. George Bush, one of Baker's main rivals for the moderate Republican vote, began campaigning in the spring of 1979. Bush's strong showing in a straw poll at a GOP fund raiser in Portland, Maine, in November was cited as one reason for a decision by Baker to turn over his Senate duties to others and devote full-time to campaigning. By spending more time on the campaign trail Baker hoped to make up for ground lost to Republican candidates who started their quest for the nomination months earlier.

Baker, who turned 54 on Nov. 15, 1979, has had an eye on national office for some time. In 1976, he angled to become President Ford's running mate but was passed over.

A Moderate's Record

"Henry has never been too overtly conservative or too overtly liberal," Irene Baker, the senator's stepmother, told *The Wall Street Journal*. "He's more like the Tennessee River; he flows right down the middle."

"To hear them talk in the Senate, Howard Henry Baker Jr. could bring together a boll weevil and a cotton grower if he tried," editorialized the Chicago *Sun-Times* as quoted in Baker's campaign literature. "If politics is the art of compromise, Baker has the strokes of a budding Renoir."

What may seem like cynical sail-trimming to others is, to Baker, a virtue. Without it, his adherents say, he would never have been able to knit together the various Republican segments in the Senate. That is a feat of cohesion his two predecessors as Senate Republican floor leader, the late Everett McKinley Dirksen, R-Ill., a conservative as well as Baker's father-in-law, and Hugh Scott, R-Pa., a moderate-to-liberal, could not accomplish.

CQ Vote Study Scores For Baker's Senate Career

	1967	1968	1969	1970	1971	1972	1973	1974	1975	1976	1977	1978	1979
Presidential[1]													
Support	55%	35%	65%	71%	67%	63%	57%	63%[3]/60%[4]	70%	64%	55%	53%	33%
Opposition	27	40	17	19	18	4	25	20[3]/21[4]	14	15	35	27	26
Conservative Coalition[2]													
Support	70	76	77	75	76	57	59	77	70	70	82	64	55
Opposition	9	6	7	10	6	3	9	10	5	12	11	21	16
Party[2]													
Unity	64	72	69	76	72	58	59	72	68	68	71	50	43
Opposition	14	4	12	11	14	3	10	14	10	11	19	33	19
Voting Participation[2]	82	74	83	82	82	51	75	83	82[5]	76	91	79	62

[1] *Ground Rules, p. 67.*
[2] *Definitions, p. 67.*
[3] *During President Nixon's tenure in 1974.*
[4] *During President Ford's tenure in 1974.*
[5] *Absent a day or more in 1975 due to illness, or illness or death in family.*

NOTE: Failure to vote lowers scores so that total in each category will not be 100% in every year.

Even detractors say Baker, who entered the Senate in 1967, is an able legislator. When Dirksen was Republican floor leader, Baker persuaded him to drop his longstanding opposition to open-housing legislation which prohibited racial discrimination in the sale or rental of housing.

Approval of the Panama Canal treaties likely would have been impossible without him. He was a central figure in gaining passage of the Carter administration's Mideast arms package and in securing an end to the Turkish arms embargo. In 1977, he assembled near-unanimous Republican opposition to public financing of senatorial election campaigns, killing the proposal.

Baker claims an overall conservative record in keeping with the mainstream of the Republican Party. He was a Vietnam hawk and is against gun control, for example. But his fidelity to the conservative side is hardly constant as illustrated by his opposition to an anti-abortion constitutional amendment.

Throughout his Senate career, the conservative Americans for Constitutional Action score on him has oscillated. It swung from a high of 89 percent in 1970 to a low of 52 percent in 1977. In 1978, it bounced back up to 79 percent.

"I'm a fiscal conservative, but I'm also humane," explained Baker when he announced his candidacy. "Government should help the poor and the downtrodden."

Due to his political flexibility, Baker's legislative record contains seemingly contradictory elements — something not uncommon among members of Congress but possibly troubling to those for whom consistency is important.

Baker supported the equal rights amendment to the Constitution in 1972 but in 1978 opposed extending the time period in which to ratify it. While he advocates cutting back on government bureaucracy, he voted this fall for creating a separate Department of Education.

He was a key proponent of landmark environmental legislation affecting air, water and coal strip mining. Now, however, he feels government regulation has gone too far.

In 1978, he was instrumental in weakening the Endangered Species Act, which he had voted for in 1973. Under the original law, Tennessee's Tellico Dam could not be operated because that would wipe out a rare fish known as the snail darter.

Political Issues

Here is a review of Baker's stands on the issues:

- **SALT.** Baker believes the treaty, as written, guarantees Soviet strategic superiority. He says he will not vote for it unless there are major modifications, which he has been trying to attach to the pact in the Senate. The Soviet Union's Backfire bomber, for instance, is not covered in the treaty even though it is capable of carrying nuclear weapons, he argues.

While Baker professes a commitment to arms control, he does not accept administration contentions that rejection of SALT would be catastrophic. The Russians are so eager for an agreement that they would hasten back to the negotiating table where the United States could get a better deal by tougher bargaining, he says.

Consideration of the SALT treaty, originally scheduled to be finished by the end of 1979, was postponed until 1980 by Senate majority leader Robert C. Byrd, D-W. Va. As the second session of the 96th Congress began in January, it was uncertain what action would be taken on the SALT treaty.

- **Panama.** When challenged about his advocacy of the canal treaties — the step that alienated many in the party's important conservative wing — Baker emphasizes that he inserted amendments establishing American rights related to the waterway. He also points out that, despite the unpopularity of the treaties in Tennessee, the voters gave him a landslide re-election victory in 1978.

On NBC's "Meet the Press" aired Oct. 7, 1979, he depicted the treaties as necessary "to reduce the tensions in that area." Otherwise, he says, Panama would have turned into another Vietnam for the U.S.

- **Foreign Policy.** Overall, Baker wants America to be more resolute than he thinks it has been in its dealings with the Soviets. Baker claims he would have used harsher retaliatory measures than did Carter after the Russian combat brigade was discovered in Cuba. Halting the SALT ratification process and agricultural shipments to the U.S.S.R. are among the options Baker says the president could have taken.

"I'm afraid what Carter did was nothing at all," Baker commented after the president's television address on the troops in Cuba. "In this case, we stood toe to toe with the Soviet Union and, unlike 1962, we blinked."

Baker advocates a common market for energy and power resources among the U.S., Canada and Mexico. Diplomats of the stature of Henry A. Kissinger should be called on to set it up, he says.

- **National Defense.** Baker has argued for greater defense expenditures to counter growing Soviet might. While saying America has not yet been eclipsed by Russia militarily, he contends that will be the result if present trends continue. Baker favors resumption of draft registration and a beefing up of reserve forces, but does not call for actual conscription.
- **Energy.** Baker supports dismantling oil and gasoline price controls as a spur to domestic production. He favors a windfall profits tax but wants part of it plowed back to energy companies for exploration purposes.

"[An oil price increase] is the only way, painful as it may be in the short run, to let the laws of supply and demand energize the productive genius of American free enterprise to produce its way out of the energy crunch," he said. He was a reluctant supporter of gas rationing.

Synthetic fuels are a short-term answer but more attention should be focused on solar, geothermal and nuclear power, according to Baker. Clusters of atomic reactors should be located away from population centers, he proposes. Baker champions the federal Clinch River breeder reactor project in Tennessee. Carter wants to scuttle it.

- **Inflation.** Baker is for cuts of 30 percent in personal income taxes over the next three years along with reductions in the corporate rate and capital gains taxes. The resulting rise in economic activity would relieve the burden of inflation, he argues.

While Baker believes that federal outlays are not the sole cause of inflation, he feels they are a significant factor. So he backs a constitutional amendment to bar deficit spending. Under his plan, both chambers of Congress would have to approve going into deficit by a two-thirds majority.

Anti-pollution and workplace safety regulations, though commendable in intent, have gotten out of control, Baker charges.

"A moratorium on new regulations may be in order for a period of a year or two while we digest what is on the books," he told the Economic Club of Detroit.

Background

Baker has politics in his blood. He had a grandfather who was a judge and a grandmother who was a sheriff. His father, Howard H. Baker Sr., also a Republican and an attorney, represented the 2nd District of Tennessee in the U.S. House from 1951 to 1964. Upon the father's death in 1964, Baker's stepmother Irene succeeded her husband for the remainder of his term.

The future senator was born in Huntsville, a tiny town in the Cumberland Mountains of Republican Eastern Tennessee.

Baker's Background

Profession: Attorney.
Born: Nov. 15, 1925; Huntsville, Tenn.
Home: Huntsville.
Religion: Presbyterian.
Education: University of the South, 1943-44; Tulane University, 1945; University of Tennessee, 1946-49, LL.B.
Military: Navy, 1945-46; discharged as lieutenant (j.g.).
Family: Wife, Joy; two children.
Offices: U.S. Senate, 1967- , including service as Senate minority leader, 1977-
Committees: Environment and Public Works — Member of subcommittees on Nuclear Regulation, Regional and Community Development and Resource Protection.
Foreign Relations — Member of subcommittees on Arms Control, Oceans, International Operations and Environment and European Affairs.
Rules and Administration.
Joint Library.

He attended public elementary school in Huntsville and then went to the McCallie School, a military academy in Chattanooga. Graduating in 1943, he entered the Navy's V-12 program to study electrical engineering, first at the University of the South in Sewanee, Tenn., and then at Tulane University in New Orleans. Called to active duty before he could finish his studies, Baker served a brief tour aboard a PT boat in the South Pacific and was discharged as a lieutenant (j.g.).

Although he lacked an undergraduate degree, Baker entered law school at the University of Tennessee. He once told a reporter that he wanted to finish engineering school, but the law school line was shorter on registration day. On the way to getting his law degree in 1949, Baker was president of the student body. He joined the Knoxville-based law firm of Baker, Worthington, Crossley & Stansberry, which had been founded by his grandfather in 1885.

Baker, who had won a public speaking contest at age 11, proved himself a skillful courtroom cross-examiner, earning the nickname "Old Two-to-Ten" because of the relatively light sentences he often obtained for his clients. An equally proficient corporate attorney, he won a $1 million settlement for four coal companies he represented in a legal action against the United Mine Workers in the 1950s.

Business Dealings

An adept business sense brought Baker personal wealth. He and several associates bought a controlling interest in the First National Bank of Oneida, Tenn., a lackluster institution that they turned into a highly profitable operation. He also set up a partnership to develop a 40,000-acre parcel rich in coal.

In a Senate financial disclosure statement for 1978, Baker listed assets worth at least $410,000 and at most $940,000. Included in that are a Huntsville office building wholly owned by the senator, interest from shares in the Oneida bank and a real estate partnership in Sevierville, Tenn.

The sole liability reported was a promissory demand note held by the Oneida bank, valued at between $100,000

Baker's Interest Group Ratings

Americans for Democratic Action (ADA) — The percentage of the time Baker voted with or entered a live pair in accordance with the ADA position.

AFL-CIO Committee on Political Education (COPE) — The percentage of the time Baker voted in accordance with or was paired in favor of the COPE position.

National Farmers Union (NFU) — The percentage of the time Baker voted in accordance with, was paired for or announced for the NFU position.

Americans for Constitutional Action (ACA) — The percentage of the time Baker voted in accordance with the ACA position.

Following are Baker's ratings since he became a member of the Senate in 1967:

	ADA[1]	COPE[2]	NFU[2]	ACA
1967	23	33	60	65
1968	21	50	60	80
1969	11	33	44	36
1970	13	20	45	89
1971	4	27	30	55
1972	0	13	40	71
1973	10	22	53	73
1974	14	30	64	72
1975	11	33	60	54
1976	5	14	27	80
1977	15	28	42	52
1978	25	37	67	79

[1] *Failure to vote lowers score.*
[2] *Percentages compiled by CQ from information provided by group.*

and $250,000. His income during the period was a minimum of $277,000 and a high of $405,500.

The investment in the coal-rich land has generated controversy in Tennessee. Environmentalists were angered when 24,000 acres of it were leased for strip mining. He also was criticized when he got an old Tennessee Valley Authority power plant exempted from clean air requirements and the plant burned coal taken from Baker land. A spokesman for Baker explained that the senator had no control over where the coal was sold. It had been mined by a lessee and traded through a broker. Two years ago, Baker sold the property.

A coal and lumber company on whose board Baker served before his election to the Senate later proved a political burden as well. Under a proposal supported by Baker to establish a national recreation area along the Big South Fork of the Cumberland River, the government would purchase land from the Stearns Coal and Lumber Co. Although Baker no longer is connected with Stearns, its chairman, Robert Gable, is a longtime friend and campaign contributor.

Senate Career

Politically, Baker gambled for high stakes from the beginning, becoming the first popularly elected GOP senator in Democratic-dominated Tennessee.

Despite assured election to his father's House seat in 1964 and the doubts of his wife Joy and father-in-law Dirksen, he opted to "break out of the East Tennessee [Republican] beachhead" and ran for the Senate in a special election to fill the unexpired term of the late Estes Kefauver, D.

That year Baker lost to Democrat Ross Bass. But he gained attention by not attacking Bass' pro-civil rights record and by amassing the largest vote total of any Republican in state history.

In 1966 Baker easily defeated Kenneth Roberts, a Goldwater Republican, in the senatorial primary. With campaign help from Richard M. Nixon, he won the general election from Democratic Gov. Frank Clement, who had beaten Bass in the primary.

Baker's cool demeanor came across better on television than Clement's loud style. Further, his advocacy of such liberal legislation as open housing helped him make inroads into the traditionally-Democratic black vote.

In his two subsequent Senate elections, he has maintained a relatively high level of black support for a Republican by similar issue stances. In 1978 he pleased minorities by voting for a constitutional amendment to grant congressional representation to the District of Columbia.

Baker won re-election handily in 1972, beating Democratic U.S. Rep. Ray Blanton, and in 1978, outpolling Democrat Jane Eskind, a Nashville community activist. *(Election results, see p. 71.)*

His ambitions in the Senate showed early. After Dirksen died, Baker ran for the post of minority leader in 1969 and again in 1971, losing narrowly both times to Scott. He finally won the job in 1977 by one vote over Robert P. Griffin, R-Mich., and was unopposed for a second term in 1979.

Watergate

Perhaps the only Republican helped by Watergate was Baker.

The ranking Republican on the 1973 Senate committee investigating the scandal, Baker impressed television viewers as much by his calm, carefully reasoned questioning as by his charm and appearance. His repeated lawyer-like query of "What did the president know and when did he know it?" was tempered by good-natured needling of the Runyonesque cover-up bagman, Tony Ulasewicz: "Who thought you up?"

It is problematical whether Baker actually planned to land a spot on the committee investigating Nixon, a friend of 20 years. He led the Republican drive to ensure equal representation of his party on the panel. Then, at the behest of Minority Leader Scott, he accepted the assignment. Scott told Baker he was a unanimous choice for it in a poll the floor leader had made of Republican senators.

Baker told reporters that, while the job had "its peril," he could not "in good conscience" refuse. Accused by some of helping Nixon behind the scenes and by others of being too hard on the president, Baker protested he was neutral. He called the probe "a bipartisan search for the unvarnished truth."

Whatever his motives, the public liked what it saw. In a Harris Poll taken that year, 57 percent of those interviewed rated Baker's committee performance good or excellent, and just 13 percent thought it fair or poor.

Personal Style

Throughout his career Baker has displayed a low-key style. Baker occasionally displays a temper, yet it is confined to quick bursts of anger at subordinates alone, hardly ever to outsiders.

Noted for his ability to recall names, Baker projects a likable personality that comes across well in small groups.

But he draws mixed reviews about his stump performance. While Baker speeches are invariably thoughtful and articulate, the senator often delivers them with hands stuffed in his pockets and seldom raises his voice — to the dismay of aides who feel he should sound more forceful. The polysyllabic debater's speaking style fails to excite crowds, observers say.

According to one assessment in the political community, Baker lacks the all-out scrapper mentality some think is needed to win the presidency. Although that is dismissed as idle talk by Baker adherents, the senator indeed is not a driven man and maintains a host of outside interests.

A compact fellow who stands five-foot-seven and must fight a tendency to grow pudgy, he enjoys playing tennis, piloting a small plane and riding trail bikes. Photography is his main hobby, and Baker maintains darkrooms in both his Huntsville and Washington homes. He has had several one-man photo exhibits.

The father of two grown children, Baker for years carried the burden of wife Joy's alcoholism. Her condition was cited as one reason Baker was passed over as Ford's running mate in 1976. Joy Baker reportedly has not had a drink for the past three-and-a-half years.

Baker observes the Republican's so-called 11th Commandment ("Thou shalt not speak ill of another Republican") and actually goes beyond it. In joint appearances with other presidential candidates, he habitually espouses congressional-type conviviality by telling audiences, "Any one of these Republicans is better on a bad day than Jimmy Carter or Teddy Kennedy on a good day."

A cynical view of this magnanimity is that he is positioning himself for the vice-presidential nomination as the moderate to balance a ticket led by a conservative such as Reagan. That is a suggestion that Baker followers deny.

Baker decries what he views as "the savagery in American politics" and pledged, when asked Oct. 5, 1979, at the Economic Club of Detroit, that he would never bring up Chappaquiddick. This sentiment, observers speculate, may be motivated as much by whispering about the former alcoholism problem of his wife as by Senate civility.

When he does cut down his Republican opponents, Baker prefers the subtlety used on the Senate floor.

Thus, he did not have to mention Reagan, a 68-year-old presidential hopeful on his third outing, when telling a Florida audience "the party needs a new face.... I don't think the party wants a rerun of 1976."

And after Connally announced a controversial Middle East peace plan, which some branded as unfavorable to Israel, Baker did not have to bring up the Texan's shoot-from-the-hip reputation. The Connally proposal, Baker said, was not "careful" or "prudent." With typical senatorial courtesy, Baker distinguished his criticism of the plan from his personal regard of Connally for whom he professed "admiration."

Strategy

Baker bases his campaign on his "electability." Indeed, some Democratic strategists feel he would be the hardest Republican to beat in the general election because of his broad public recognition, his Southern roots, his strong Washington record and his lack of personal liabilities such as Reagan's age or Connally's wheeler-dealer image.

As a moderate, some Democrats believe he might attract more easily the Democrats and independents needed to win in November 1980 than Reagan or Connally would.

Baker Campaign Staff

Campaign Chairman: Sen. Richard G. Lugar, R-Ind., 47.

National Campaign Manager: Wyatt A. Stewart, 40, formerly director of finance and administration for the National Republican Congressional Committee.

Director of Candidate Services (Advance Work and Scheduling): Don Stansberry, 40, former Baker law partner from Huntsville, Tenn.

Deputy Manager for Convention States: Bill Tucker, 42, formerly caucus state manager for President Ford in 1976 campaign.

Deputy Manager for Primary States: Andrew Lawrence, 34, an Arlington, Va., stockbroker.

Legal Counsel. A. B. Culvahouse, 31, former chief legislative assistant to baker.

Political Consultant: Bill Roesing, 32, formerly with a Washington political consulting firm.

Political Manager: Rob Mosbacher, 28, former Baker Senate staffer.

Deputy Manager for Finance and Administration: Robert Perkins, 32, formerly executive director of the Republican National Finance Committee.

Finance Chairman: Ted Welch, Nashville businessman and former chairman of the Republican National Finance Committee.

Finance Director: Bruce McBrearty, 29, former assistant finance director of both the National Republican Congressional Committee and the Republican National Committee.

Research Chairman: Sen. John C. Danforth, R-Mo., 43.

Press Secretary: Tom Griscom, 30, ex-Tennessee newspaper reporter.

Headquarters: The Baker Committee, 25 K St., N.E., Washington, D.C.

The polls show Baker has a good share of electoral strength nationally. In a CBS News/*New York Times* poll released Nov. 5, 1979, he placed third with 13 percent as the choice for the Republican nomination behind Reagan (37 percent) and Connally (15 percent).

In a September Gallup Poll, 58 percent of the public recognized Baker's name. That was not as good a showing as Reagan or Connally, but it was better than the 38 percent rating of Bush, who is vying with Baker for the centrist position in the Republican contest.

Baker's use of the Watergate hearings, where he first gained national attention, demonstrated his ability to command the news media spotlight. Baker backers contend their man's Senate duties, while hardly as good as day-in-day-out stumping in New Hampshire, at least guaranteed him headlines.

As minority leader and a Foreign Relations Committee member, Baker certainly has made news during the SALT deliberations. Despite their failure to get passed, his bids to amend the treaty in markup sessions — in an attempt, he said, to rectify provisions unfavorable to the United States — generated widespread publicity.

Timing

Baker intends to keep the floor leader title during the campaign, temporarily turning over its duties to Minority

Whip Ted Stevens, R-Alaska. This has caused some grumbling from Sen. Paul Laxalt, R-Nev., the Reagan campaign chairman, who complained Baker was "trying to have his political cake and eat it too."

But the candidate replies that there is precedent for his action. The most recent example is Sen. Lyndon B. Johnson, D-Texas, who stayed on as majority leader while running for president in 1960.

The decision by Baker to devote most of his time until November to the Senate minority leadership was a calculated risk. By staying at his post for so long he "demonstrated leadership and decisive ability," explained Sen. Richard G. Lugar, R-Ind., the Baker campaign chairman.

On the negative side, the delay has cost Baker valuable time on the hustings in the view of some. It has taken a toll organizationally as well.

The major factors in the timing of Baker's announcement of candidacy were SALT and the fiscal 1980 federal budget, whose consideration by the Senate continually has been pushed later into the year. At the beginning of 1979, when it appeared the treaty and the budget would be considered by summer, Baker planned to announce in July. At the urging of aides who argued he could wait no longer, he chose Nov. 1. By that time it was clear SALT would not be considered before Congress adjourned for Christmas.

Catching Up

Baker's object is to catch Reagan, who, although he did not formally announce his candidacy until Nov. 13, 1979, had long been the Republican front runner for the nomination.

When Ford declared he would not run in 1980, barring some extraordinary event, Baker pronounced himself "relieved and delighted." A 1976 Ford backer, the senator hopes to pick up much of the former president's support in the party. That is an ambition shared by Bush.

But on Nov. 3, Baker lost a straw poll at a statewide GOP conference in Maine to Bush. Baker had been expected to win because he had the support of Maine's Republican senator, William S. Cohen.

In the wake of that defeat Baker revised his campaign strategy, dropping plans to actively contest all primaries. The greatest effort will be made in the Northeast and Midwest states, leaving the fight for delegates in Baker's native South to other Republican hopefuls.

Like Bush and several other Republicans, Baker has lined up big-name Republican endorsements. In his camp are former New Hampshire Gov. Walter Peterson, Tennessee Gov. Lamar Alexander and Sens. Lugar, Cohen, John C. Danforth of Missouri, Rudy Boschwitz of Minnesota and John H. Chafee of Rhode Island.

George Bush

Organizing an Uphill Presidential Bid

George Bush, an experienced public official with only a very modest record of electoral success, is targeting his drive for the presidency clearly at the ideological middle of the Republican Party.

With sparse public recognition and a low standing in the public opinion polls, the 55-year-old Bush is faced with the task of establishing his political identity and capturing the party's center. That task is complicated by a public perception of him as a moderate even though his record and campaign rhetoric have been conservative. Bush also is selling himself as a man with wide experience.

Indeed, George Herbert Walker Bush is experienced. He might well be known as the handyman of American politics. In a period of 10 years, Bush held five different government and party posts at the national level.

Beginning in 1967, he served four years in the U.S. House from Texas. He followed that service with stints over the next six years as U.S. ambassador to the United Nations, chairman of the Republican National Committee (RNC), head of the U.S. liaison office in Peking and director of the Central Intelligence Agency.

His electoral success in House contests is balanced by two statewide losses for the U.S. Senate from Texas in 1964 and 1970. *(Election results, see p. 71.)*

Even with his appeal to the GOP center, the record of Bush in politics fundamentally has been a conservative one. Although his congressional career avoided a completely doctrinaire conservative line, his positions were not so unorthodox that his conservative stripes were questioned by the Republican right wing.

Bush himself disdains ideological categories. "I avoid being labeled," Bush said in January 1979 on ABC News' "Issues and Answers" when he was asked whether he was a liberal, moderate or a conservative. "We Republicans — this is our death wish — we try to categorize some person, label them. I don't want to be labeled."

But others are willing to do the labeling. For example, the liberal journal *New Republic* called Bush "one of the more modern and humane Republicans" when President Nixon named him to head the Republican National Committee in December 1972.

Several factors contribute to Bush's moderate image. During the 1960s, he avoided the far right in Texas politics. And he advocated financial disclosure by public officials before the Watergate era made it politically fashionable to do so.

Also, he still looks more like a suave Ivy Leaguer than a Texas oil man. Bush, the son of the late Connecticut Sen. Prescott Bush, transplanted himself to West Texas more than 30 years ago and entered the oil drilling business.

He is a personable and casual man who has been able to get along with the diverse elements of the Republican Party. "One would sooner look for the needle in the haystack than for someone who, having been exposed to Bush, dislikes him," wrote conservative columnist William F. Buckley Jr.

However, as the British magazine *The Economist* pointed out, "his unsullied, almost chaste image" could be a political liability. It might conflict with his effort to portray himself as a strong leader to a public that reputedly is looking for aggressive leadership.

The centrist reputation has been enhanced by his ability to draw campaign workers from all points of the ideological spectrum and to form an ecumenical political organization.

But beneath the moderate image lies a conservative base. "There is probably more Houston oil man in Bush than Connecticut Yankee," noted Robert Healy in the *Boston Globe* Oct. 26, 1979.

Bush has a formidable road ahead of him in his presidential quest. As the *Ripon Forum* commented, "Bush has assembled impressive organizational and financial support without lighting any fires among the party rank and file." Bush's supporters contend that by the early stages of the delegate selection process those assets will have been translated into support among the party faithful.

Centrist Politics

Bush's appreciation of centrist politics is most evident in his brief career in the House. There he avoided extremes,

Bush's Background

Profession: Public official and former oil drilling company executive.
Born: June 12, 1924, Milton, Mass.
Home: Houston.
Religion: Episcopal.
Education: Yale University, B.A., 1948.
Offices: Member of U.S. House, 1967-71; ambassador to the United Nations, 1971-73; chairman of the Republican National Committee, 1973-74; head of the U.S. liaison office in Peking, 1974-75; director of the Central Intelligence Agency, 1976-77.
Military: U.S. Navy, 1942-45.
Family: Wife, Barbara; five children.

shunned shrill rhetoric and often put something in his speeches that appealed to almost everybody.

However, his voting record basically was conservative. And it had to be to please his affluent constituents in suburban Houston's 7th District — still the most Republican congressional district in Texas.

Through his four-year House tenure he generally scored high in the ratings of the conservative Americans for Constitutional Action and low on the scoreboard of the liberal Americans for Democratic Action. On Congressional Quarterly's conservative coalition support score, Bush generally earned a higher score than the average Republican in the House.

But there is evidence of progressive leanings in Bush's congressional record. The most notable is his vote for the Civil Rights Act of 1968 and the open housing requirements it contained.

"I do not want it on my conscience that I have voted against legislation that would permit a Negro, say a Negro serviceman returning from Vietnam, where he has been fighting for the ideals of his country, to buy or rent a home of his choosing if he has the money," Bush told the House.

At the same time, Bush qualified his support, saying that he would like to amend the bill and "remedy some of the inequities in the open-housing section."

Despite his support for the 1968 Civil Rights bill, he was upset at what he saw during the Poor People's March on Washington several weeks later.

Bush said that the march had rapidly deteriorated "into a power struggle at the expense of those honest poor people who made this long and often arduous trip to petition their government."

"This Congress will not buy threats," Bush wrote to civil rights leader Ralph Abernathy. "It will not condone violence. It will not accept legislative goals which are financially impossible and which lack inventiveness and stifle the initiative of the individual."

In 1970 when he was a Senate candidate, Bush bluntly told CQ: "Civil rights legislation has caught up with the conscience of the country. No more major legislation [is] needed now." Also in 1970, Bush signed an anti-busing brief, prepared by Rep. William C. Cramer, R-Fla., that was filed with the U.S. Supreme Court.

Bush's balancing of progressive and conservative approaches also was seen in his reaction to the civil disorders of the late 1960s. In 1967 he supported legislation that would have made interstate travel to incite a riot a federal crime. "There is no place for professional agitators who incite or take part in rioting, no matter what the cause," Bush said.

However, in 1969 Bush opposed legislation that would have withheld federal funds from higher education institutions that did not curb campus disorders. "I do not feel we should pass legislation that will penalize the innocent to get at the guilty," Bush told the House.

Concerning urban disorders, Bush advocated creation of a Neighborhood Action Crusade — volunteer organizations working to ease tensions in urban communities.

Environmental Questions

During his House career, Bush expressed concern for environmental and consumer issues but called for "responsible" action in both areas. He also supported world population control.

In late 1969, as chairman of the House Republican earth resources task force, Bush noted that environmental problems were becoming a top priority among young persons, but warned that little progress could be made if time was spent looking for scapegoats.

"Inherent in this concern for the environment, however, is the danger that some will place an unrealistic overemphasis on problems to the detriment of the interests of the consumer and our national economy," Bush once said.

In 1970 Bush supported creation of the Environmental Protection Agency, while advising against overzealousness.

He also backed legislation proposed in 1969 by President Nixon to establish a consumer protection division in the Justice Department.

Personal Finances

Bush was in the forefront of the movement for procedural reform in politics. He called for full disclosure by public officials of assets, liabilities and sources of income.

He disclosed his own finances, including the expenses of his House office. He also advocated banning foreign travel by House members after they were defeated for re-election.

As a presidential candidate, Bush has continued his emphasis on public disclosure of personal finances. His statement of personal wealth filed with the Federal Election Commission (FEC) goes beyond the requirements of the law, which calls for a listing of assets and liabilities with their value stated only in broad categories. Bush provided exact values for his assets and liabilities as of April 30, 1979, and for his net worth — $1.8 million.

Bush also filed with the FEC his personal income tax returns for the past six years, which was not required by federal law.

Government Structure

He has advocated certain alterations in government institutions such as the Electoral College.

In 1969 Bush voted for a proposed constitutional amendment, passed by the House, that would have abolished the Electoral College and provided for the direct election of the president. Bush told the House his first preference for Electoral College reform was to use the district or proportional plans.

The next year Bush spoke in favor of extension of the Voting Rights Act of 1965, but he objected to a provision that extended the voting franchise in all elections to persons 18 years old or more. Bush said he believed it was improper to attempt that by legislation and preferred to see

18-year-olds receive the right to vote through a constitutional amendment of which he was a cosponsor.

In another constitutional debate, Bush was a cosponsor of the proposed Equal Rights Amendment.

But as RNC chairman, Bush opposed in 1974 a bill that would have established a nationwide postcard voter registration system for federal elections. Consideration of the measure was blocked in the House.

Fiscal Questions

Bush's conservative tendencies were most pronounced on issues involving the role of the federal government and on fiscal policy.

A CQ study of 1967 House votes showed that out of 11 key votes Bush voted four times for expanding the role of the federal government and seven times against, placing him near the middle of House Republicans.

His fiscal outlook was orthodox Republican. In 1967 Bush, a member of the House Ways and Means Committee, cosponsored the Human Investment Act, which was designed to combat poverty through tax incentives rather than categorical grant programs. It did not become law.

Bush also repeatedly made it clear that his idea of tax reform did not mean collecting more from the rich.

On the House floor, Bush spoke periodically in behalf of the domestic oil industry. He had acquired his personal wealth through his oil business in Texas, but he divested himself of his oil interests upon his election to the House in 1966.

In the House, Bush promoted curbs on the amount of oil that could be imported into the United States, favored a higher price for natural gas as a means of stimulating exploration and opposed reductions in the oil depletion allowance.

"I do not consider the oil depletion a tax break," Bush said during the debate on the Tax Reform Act of 1969. "It is not a gimmick; it is not a loophole."

Although Bush said the reform act would provide meaningful tax relief, he voted against the measure and its reduction in the oil depletion allowance.

In June 1970 Bush opposed President Nixon's plan to have all nations renounce their claims over seabed resources beyond a depth of 200 meters because Bush said it would give up access to natural gas and oil resources.

"He [Bush] unloaded his oil stock," columnist Jack Anderson wrote in 1969, "but could not unload a heart that remained with oil."

When asked on NBC's "Meet the Press" in May 1979 about whether his oil background would make it difficult for him to deal with energy problems as president, Bush replied:

"I have never accepted the Washington thesis that if you know something about a problem that should automatically disqualify you.... I sold out of a drilling contracting business ... in 1966, just so cynical people couldn't make the charge against me that I was in it to feather my own nest."

Issue Stands

During his campaign for the presidency, Bush generally has taken conservative positions on various issues:

● **Domestic Economy.** He has proposed a $20 billion tax cut, of which one-half would go to individuals to encourage increased personal savings and to provide tax incentives for home purchases and one-half would go to the business sector for investment tax credits and tax incentives to hire

Bush's CQ Vote Study Scores

Below are Bush's scores in Congressional Quarterly's vote studies since he became a member of the House in 1967:

	1967	1968	1969	1970
Presidential[1]				
Support	54%	53%	64%	46%
Opposition	44	34	34	12
Conservative Coalition[2]				
Support	87	78	78	41
Opposition	13	6	13	14
Party[2]				
Unity	79	67	69	40
Opposition	20	9	18	22
Voting Participation[2]	96	78	90	56

[1] *Ground rules, p. 67.*
[2] *Definitions, p. 67.*

NOTE: Failure to vote lowers scores so that total in each category will not be 100% in every year.

and train young workers. As president, Bush said he would not allow federal spending to grow by more than 7 percent a year.

On CBS' "Face The Nation" in October 1979, Bush said that if he were president he would propose a balanced federal budget for 1982. But he does not want to achieve a balanced budget through higher taxes. Bush acknowledged that his goals of tax cutting and budget balancing would be reached partly by inflation increasing the total amount of taxes collected, but he maintained that inflation would be eased by his tax and budget plan.

While Bush favors a balanced budget through legislation, he is opposed to a mandatory balanced budget amendment to the Constitution. He also has expressed opposition to a constitutional convention on the subject. He is opposed to wage and price controls.

● **Energy.** Bush supports decontrol of oil prices as well as a windfall profits tax on oil companies.

He also favors expansion of nuclear power after taking steps to ensure public safety and to improve weaknesses in the Nuclear Regulatory Commission's procedures. He also advocates increased tax credits for individuals who make energy-saving improvements in their homes.

Bush is opposed to gasoline rationing except in a national wartime emergency.

● **Defense.** Bush has advocated restoration of new weapon systems canceled or delayed by the Carter administration, including the neutron bomb.

"Over the past decade, the Soviets have engaged in a massive, unprecedented buildup in their military arms and with or without SALT, they easily could far outdistance us in the 1980s," Bush said in June 1979 before the World Affairs Council in Philadelphia. "Yet the United States continues to flounder."

- **SALT II.** Bush has said that he opposes the Strategic Arms Limitation Treaty in its originally negotiated form.

"The SALT treaty is seriously defective and should be corrected before it leaves Capitol Hill," Bush said in a speech at the National Press Club in Washington in early September 1979.

Bush believes the treaty should be renegotiated and be made more verifiable.

- **Russian Combat Troops in Cuba.** Bush has been critical of the Carter administration's handling of the revelation that Russian combat troops were located in Cuba, although he has stated that he does not believe they are a threat to the United States.

"The question is," Bush said on "Face the Nation" in October 1979, "this president knows that the troops are there, in this force — an offensive force — and what's he going to do about it? He says the status quo is unacceptable and two weeks later he accepts the status quo. That is not strong, convincing presidential leadership."

- **Intelligence.** The former CIA director believes the American intelligence system should be strengthened but with stringent protections for the rights of U.S. citizens. He has criticized Carter for stopping in 1977 SR-71 flights over Cuba as a weakening of U.S. intelligence.

- **Middle East.** In a meeting Oct. 18, 1979, with the American Jewish Community, Bush disputed the views of John B. Connally on the Middle East. Bush, who visited Egypt and Israel in July 1979, said one "way not to lower oil prices is to trade Israel's security for price cuts." At that October meeting, a Bush statement comparing the Palestinian Liberation Organization to the Ku Klux Klan was distributed.

- **China.** The former envoy to Peking has been critical of the manner in which the Carter administration established diplomatic relations with the People's Republic of China. "For the first time in our history, a peacetime American government has renounced a treaty with an ally [Taiwan] without cause or benefit," Bush wrote in *The Washington Post* in late December 1978.

- **Chrysler.** Bush took a cautious approach toward federal relief for financially-ailing Chrysler Corp. "I want to reduce government involvement in business, not strengthen it," Bush said. "And bailing out Chrysler through federal financial assistance gets the government more deeply involved."

Early Career

Bush's roots are deeply in New England. He was born in Milton, Mass., and graduated from Phillips Academy in Andover, Mass.

After serving as a World War II Navy pilot — at 18 he reportedly was the youngest at the time — he attended Yale University in New Haven, Conn. Following graduation in 1948 he moved to Texas to enter the oil business.

He first took a job as a warehouse sweeper and then a supply salesman with the Odessa, Texas firm of Dresser Industries, an oil field supply company of which his father was a director. In 1951 he helped start the Bush-Overby Development Company. Two years later he co-founded Zapata Petroleum Corporation and in 1954 became president of the Zapata Off-Shore Company, first based in Midland and then Houston.

In Houston Bush became active in Republican affairs and eventually became chairman of the GOP organization in Harris County. In 1964 he sought the Republican Senate nomination. Against three other contenders, Bush was forced to overcome the stigma of being from the East and the handicap of not being well known. Avoiding the party's far right wing, he finished first in the initial GOP primary with 44 percent of the vote. A month later he won the nomination in a runoff with 61.6 percent over the better-known Jack Cox who had come within 132,000 votes of upsetting Connally for governor in 1962.

Against Democratic Sen. Ralph Yarborough, Bush won a respectable 43.6 percent of the vote, losing to Yarborough by 330,000 votes while Lyndon B. Johnson was carrying his native state by 704,000 votes in the presidential election.

In 1966 Bush won a newly-created House seat in the Houston suburbs against a right-wing Democrat with 57.1 percent of the vote. *(Election results, see p. 71.)*

In 1968 Bush was mentioned as a vice-presidential possibility, but Nixon bypassed the one-term representative. That year he won re-election to his House seat without opposition.

Two years later Bush made another bid for the Senate. He was preparing to run against the liberal Yarborough, but his plans were upset when the incumbent was defeated in the Democratic primary by Lloyd Bentsen. So in November 1970, as the *Texas Observer* put it, "the main question seems to be whether the next conservative senator from Texas should be a Republican or a Democrat."

Bush received indirect aid from the liberal wing of the Texas Democratic Party which found Bentsen unacceptable. Liberal economist John Kenneth Galbraith and ex-Sen. Ernest Gruening, a liberal Democrat from Alaska, wrote letters in behalf of Bush. The conservative Americans for Constitutional Action endorsed Bush over Bentsen.

But that assistance and campaign appearances by Nixon and Vice President Spiro Agnew were not enough for Bush, who conducted a sophisticated television advertising campaign. He lost by nearly 160,000 votes, receiving 46 percent of the vote.

Bush's Interest Group Ratings

Americans for Democratic Action (ADA) — The percentage of the time Bush voted with or entered a live pair in accordance with the ADA position.

AFL-CIO Committee on Political Education (COPE) — The percentage of the time Bush voted in accordance with or was paired in favor of the COPE position.

National Farmers Union (NFU) — The percentage of the time Bush voted in accordance with, was paired for or announced for the NFU position.

Americans for Constitutional Action (ACA) — The percentage of the time Bush voted in accordance with the ACA position.

Following are Bush's ratings since he became a member of the House in 1967:

	ADA[1]	COPE[2]	NFU[2]	ACA
1967	7	8	90	83
1968	0	25	NA	77
1969	7	0	47	69
1970	12	0	50	58

[1] *Failure to vote lowers score.*
[2] *Percentages compiled by CQ from information provided by group. NA—not available.*

Bush Campaign Staff

Campaign chairman: James A. Baker III, 49, former under secretary of commerce and chairman of President Ford's general election campaign in 1976.

Finance chairman: Robert Mosbacher, 52, national finance chairman of the President Ford Committee in 1976.

Deputy chairman for political operations: David A. Keene, 34, former national chairman of the Young Americans for Freedom and southern coordinator of Ronald Reagan's 1976 presidential campaign.

Communications director: Peter E. Teeley, 39, former press secretary to Republican Sens. Robert P. Griffin (Mich.) and Jacob K. Javits (N.Y.) and to the President Ford Committee in 1976 and communications director of the Republican National Committee.

Media consultant: Robert Goodman, 50, founder and president of a Baltimore-based advertising firm that has handled the election campaigns of several Republican U.S. senators.

Campaign headquarters: 732 N. Washington St., Alexandria, Va., and 710 N. Post Oak Road, Houston, Texas.

Executive Career

In December 1970 Bush entered the second phase of his political career when Nixon announced he would appoint the Texan as ambassador to the United Nations. The selection drew praise from both Republicans and Democrats in the House, but the appointment was criticized in other quarters because of Bush's lack of foreign policy experience. The Senate confirmed his appointment by a voice vote in February 1971.

At the U.N. Bush pushed unsuccessfully for keeping Taiwan in the United Nations while seating the People's Republic of China. By advocating the U.S. policy of representation for both Chinese governments, Bush displayed a shift from his 1964 campaign statement that the United States should leave the U.N. if the Peking government were admitted.

His efforts in behalf of the Taiwan government silenced the complaints of most of his critics that he knew nothing about diplomacy.

Republican Leader

In December 1972 Nixon selected Bush to be the Republican national chairman. His tenure in that post covered the turbulent last year and a half of Nixon's presidency.

Bush faced the difficult task of defending the interests of the party while Nixon was under fire in the Watergate scandal. "We've struggled mightily to make it clear that the party is separate from Watergate, but I don't know that I've been overly successful," Bush said at the end of 1973.

Bush attempted to be loyal to Nixon while criticizing Watergate. "You don't see pictures of Gordon Liddy [on the walls of the party headquarters]; you see them of Nixon....," Bush told Congressional Quarterly in early 1974. "I don't feel inhibited from criticizing Watergate. I do believe in supporting the president. I don't think that's contradictory."

That approach didn't satisfy everyone. Columnist George Will wrote in November 1975 that "in spite of all the available evidence, he [Bush] never expressed independent judgments inconvenient to Richard Nixon."

When Bush's appointment as CIA director was pending, Sen. Barry Goldwater, R-Ariz., defended Bush, saying "I think Bush was the first man ... who let the president know he should go."

"In some ways Nixon was a good president; in some ways he was flawed," Bush remarked in October 1979.

Ford Years

In August 1974, after Gerald R. Ford succeeded Nixon as president, Bush was mentioned as a possible choice when Ford filled the vacant vice president's post. Instead Ford picked Bush as the U.S. envoy to Peking. The appointment did not require Senate confirmation.

Bush received little public attention while serving in Peking. Slightly more than a year after his appointment, Ford fired William E. Colby as CIA director and named Bush to replace Colby.

Bush's selection to head the CIA met with opposition from Sen. Frank Church, D-Idaho, chairman of the Senate Select Intelligence Committee. Critics objected to his past political roles, particularly as RNC chairman, and the possibility he would be Ford's vice-presidential running mate in 1976. Bush told the Senate Armed Services Committee in December 1975 that he would not forswear acceptance of the number two spot on the 1976 GOP national ticket, but he promised to actively discourage any campaign in his behalf.

On Jan. 27, 1976, the Senate confirmed Bush by a 63-27 vote after Ford gave assurances that he would not propose Bush as his 1976 running mate.

At the end of his tenure as CIA director in early 1977, several of his Democratic detractors in the Senate praised Bush's stewardship of the intelligence agency.

Strategy

Bush outlined his plans for pursuing the GOP presidential nomination in an interview in January 1979 on ABC's "Issues and Answers":

"The strategy is going to be to go up into New Hampshire and other early primary states. Right after that is Massachusetts, Vermont, Connecticut and Alabama, go in there, work my heart out, not with a large entourage, not with a lot of public attention, going one on one in small towns, in counties and at the same time trying to peel away from what now is a strong Reagan in-cadre up there."

Bush said he also was "trying to get people that were for President Ford for me."

That statement described the essentials of a strategy that is designed to make Bush, rather than Tennessee Sen. Howard H. Baker Jr., the more moderate alternative to Ronald Reagan.

It is a strategy that faces considerable obstacles. A Gallup Poll in December 1978 showed that Bush was less well known among Republicans than either Reagan or Baker and trailed both of them as the presidential preference.

In January 1979, Bush said "I am back where Jimmy Carter was at this time in 1975."

By September 1979 Bush still had a low standing in the polls. A Gallup Poll released Sept. 23 showed he was the choice of 3 percent of the Republicans and independents interviewed. But he had increased his recognition to 38 percent from the 33 percent standing in 1978.

The most notable gain for Bush has been in Maine, where he won a Nov. 3 straw ballot of delegates chosen to attend a statewide Republican conference. Baker had been expected to win the straw poll because he had the support of the state's popular GOP senator, William S. Cohen.

Some attributed Bush's success in Maine to his forceful speech to the delegates. But there was speculation that Reagan's supporters, knowing the former California governor would not do well in Maine and seeking to embarrass Baker, threw their votes to Bush.

Both Bush and Baker received a boost Oct. 19 when Ford took himself out of the presidential competition. "I think you're going to see a lot of those people who were holding back because of respect for [Ford] go forward now, and I hope I will get far more of those than others," Bush said.

Long Quest

Bush has been preparing his campaign for the presidency since shortly after the end of the Ford administration. His first vehicle was the Fund for a Limited Government, which he formed to pay for his travel expenses while he was campaigning for Republican congressional candidates and which contributed money to those candidates. In early January 1979, he formed the George Bush for President committee.

At the end of the third quarter of 1979, the Bush committee had raised about $2.4 million. Among Republicans, that put him behind Reagan, Connally and Rep. Philip M. Crane in total funds raised.

In line with Bush's efforts to appeal to politically disparate elements, Bush has assembled a campaign staff that is diverse in its background.

His campaign chairman ran Ford's general election campaign in 1976. Bush's political operations director was a key leader in Reagan's 1976 presidential campaign. His campaign press secretary is a former communications director for the Republican National Committee, and the deputy press secretary was the Democratic National Committee's communications director.

Several aides of former Alabama Gov. George C. Wallace, a Democrat, are working in the field for Bush.

John B. Connally

Making the Move for the Top Office

After nearly 20 years as a high-level adviser to presidents of both parties, John B. Connally has decided he would like to have the top job himself.

In January 1979, Connally, a former Democrat, announced that he was officially in the race for the 1980 Republican presidential nomination.

As with Sen. Edward M. Kennedy, Connally evokes an element of nostalgia in his campaign. His ebullient evocation of strength — a strong American economy and a strong American military and foreign policy — harks back to an attitude prevalent after World War II when America held unquestioned primacy in the world.

Connally expresses this theme when he tells audiences, "This nation can do whatever we want to do.... The days of glory of America are not past; they are ahead of us.... We don't have to live with shortages and sacrifices.... There isn't any problem we can't lick."

Connally also is a survivor. He narrowly missed death during the assassination of President John F. Kennedy in Dallas on Nov. 22, 1963, sustaining severe wounds that required several months to heal. He jumped from one political party to another and within seven years became one of the leading candidates for his new party's highest position. He fought successfully against an indictment of accepting an illegal gratuity and was found innocent by a Washington, D.C., jury in 1975.

Perhaps more adjectives — both admiring and pejorative — have been attached to Connally's name than any other of this year's presidential candidates.

Connally's admirers constantly use such words as "bold," "sure," "strong," "decisive," "forceful" and "active" when referring to his qualities. His detractors see him in different terms — "wheeler-dealer," "reckless," "slick," "opportunist" or "hot-tempered."

Connally has had a long time to build up legions of friends and enemies. He has been connected with the political world off and on longer than any of his major rivals for the presidency, starting with his service 40 years ago as secretary to Rep. Lyndon B. Johnson of Texas.

During that time, Connally not only served as an administrative and political aide to Johnson but as Navy secretary under President Kennedy and treasury secretary under President Richard M. Nixon. And he was elected to three two-year terms as governor of Texas in the 1960s.

Political Outlook

Connally always has been identified on the conservative side of the political spectrum, although he is a conservative of a very particular type.

Connally's political philosophy includes a strong belief in the positive results of cooperation between business and government. It is not the traditional laissez-faire philosophy often identified with the Republican Party of the mid-20th century.

Rather, Connally's economic philosophy appears akin to 19th century Republicanism and ultimately to the Whigs and Hamiltonian Federalists. All three groups were intent on building up the economic power of the country through stimulating commerce and industry. Federalists, Whigs and early Republican administrations stimulated the building of an industrial society through tariffs, land grants, public works and other aid. During that era there was a partnership between the federal government and expanding American industry.

After the Civil War and during the first half of the 20th century, Texas — and the South in general — found themselves in roughly the same economic position as Hamiltonian America — an economically underdeveloped region dependent on agriculture. The region longed to catch up with the more prosperous North. It was natural that Southern leaders would look to business for the economic salvation of the area and would do everything they could to promote its growth. Business would provide the jobs, economic development and prosperity that the South hungered after, they believed.

It was out of this tradition that John Connally emerged. Connally saw cooperation between business and government build Texas from a relatively backward agricultural and ranching state to a wealthy and booming industrial state.

He also saw his own personal fortunes transformed from a member of a family sometimes on the edges of poverty to a millionaire.

Connally's robust belief in a dynamic business climate forms one of the main elements of his campaign. In speech after speech, he pounds home the theme that business creates jobs and needs help to reverse what he argues is a decline in investment and productivity. He says that current U.S. policy is discouraging trade and capital formation.

In a June 1979 Mississippi speech, Connally argued that workers benefit when business booms. He also called for fewer environmental restrictions on the use of coal, an end to "demagogic" attacks on oil companies, increased exploration for oil on federal lands and faster construction of nuclear plants.

Connally also has talked about a modern-day Reconstruction Finance Corporation, a government financing agency established during the Depression to aid business. And he discussed a form of energy mobilization board long before President Carter proposed one in July.

Other Connally economic proposals include slashing government spending, sharp cuts in taxes of from $50 billion to $100 billion dollars during his term and giving more incentives to business to expand their plants.

His plan to create a better business climate involves a "halt of irresponsibility in government spending, a balanced budget and curbing the bureaucracy to let Americans lead their own lives their own way," Connally told an Albuquerque audience. He often adds that the country should "stop taking our advice from Ralph Nader and Jane Fonda" on economic and energy policy.

The candidate's position on business has brought him both benefits and problems. On one side, it has helped him gain a sizable financial war chest for his campaign. Between January and October 1979, Connally had raised a total of $4.3 million — more than any other candidate — and had more than $1 million of that amount on hand. Much of the money came from the American business establishment, although he also has received thousands of contributions from ordinary citizens. In December 1979 he became the first presidential candidate to refuse federal matching funds since they became available in 1976.

Connally's stance also has won him support from many conservatives who are concerned by the country's economic climate and appreciate Connally's aggressive championing of the business community's interests.

But Connally's pro-business positions also have led to his being labeled by some as "corporate America's candidate" or the candidate of big business. Like other politicians, Connally rejects those labels.

He recently told a Republican governors' meeting, "some people say I'm a defender and advocate of big business. I'm not at all." He added that in order to win in 1980, the Republican Party must "show a different face."

Connally appears to believe that he can surmount any negative repercussions from his pro-business image by his forceful style and position on other issues.

Even some conservatives are not comfortable with Connally's philosophy of business-government cooperation. Some of them call him a "corporate statist" who would build up federal powers through his belief in government activism. Thus the government would encroach even more on the private sphere, these conservatives feel.

Military Position

The second major strand in Connally's campaign is his belief that America needs to revitalize its military strength and foreign policy.

Connally's Background

Profession: Attorney.
Born: Feb. 27, 1917, Floresville, Texas.
Home: Houston, Texas.
Religion: Methodist.
Education: University of Texas Law School, LL.B., 1941.
Offices: Secretary of the Navy, 1961; governor of Texas, 1963-69; treasury secretary, 1971-72; special adviser to the president, 1973.
Military: U.S. Navy, 1941-46; naval reserve, 1946-54.
Family: Wife, Idanell; four children, one deceased.

He has harsh words for the Carter administration's international policy. In September 1979, he told a Kentucky audience, "If appeasement were an art form, this [Carter] administration would be the Rembrandt of our age."

Connally's complaint is that the Democrats have not spent enough on national defense. They have allowed the Soviet Union to build up its own strength to the point where the Russians are threatening to overshadow American military power, Connally contends.

In March 1979, Connally voiced his concern with the Strategic Arms Limitation Treaty (SALT). He said that the United States should consider calling off the talks. That would be more of a contribution to world peace than continuing them because U.S. weakness was inviting Soviet aggression, he asserted.

While expressing support for the goal of arms limitation, Connally did not feel the United States was in a good position to negotiate at that time. He also called for a resumption of the draft.

The assertion of American power should come in nonmilitary ways as well, Connally contends. For example, he feels that the United States is being taken advantage of in international trade. A strong and bold United States under his leadership would end that, he asserts.

What Connally would say to the Japanese, whom he sees as one of the principal offenders of fair trade, has become much-quoted: "I'd tell the Japanese that unless they opened up to more American products they'd better be prepared to sit on the docks of Yokohama in their Toyotas watching their Sony sets, because they aren't going to ship them here."

In another foray into the field of international relations, Connally proposed on Oct. 11, 1979, a comprehensive Middle East settlement including provisions for stationing U.S. military forces in the area to guarantee the settlement. Included in Connally's proposal were Israeli withdrawal from occupied Arab lands, Palestinian self-determination including the possibility of the creation of an independent Palestinian state if they so choose, the recognition by the Arab states of Israel's right to exist within secure boundaries and an agreement for a stable supply of Middle East oil at reasonable prices.

It is unusual for a presidential candidate to present such a detailed program on such a controversial issue. Such a stance exposes a candidate to attack from his rivals who do not have to defend any elaborate plans of their own.

Predictably, Connally soon became the target of attacks from many sides. Republican Sens. Howard H. Baker

Jr. of Tennessee and Robert Dole of Kansas and ex-Rep. George Bush of Texas, all aspirants for their party's presidential nomination, said Connally's plan sought to trade Israeli security for Arab oil. Many leaders of the Jewish community reacted strongly against the plan, and two Jewish members of Connally's national campaign committee resigned in protest.

What the long-term effect of Connally's Middle East plan will be is not clear, but in the short term it gave his opponents a target to shoot at and an opportunity to try to cut into the momentum of Connally's campaign.

Connally aides contended the speech was part of an effort to deal specifically with a tough issue, gain more national attention and do something dramatic to break away from the pack of Republican candidates.

American Crisis

A third important theme Connally has been propounding is that America is entering a major crisis in its history — and by implication that Connally is the best man to handle the situation.

Outlining this theme in his announcement speech, Connally presented what he saw as the "four major periods of extraordinary crisis" in American history. The first three were the Revolution, the Civil War and the Depression of the 1930s. The fourth is occurring today, he believes.

He described its components in stark terms: "We are a nation becoming lethargic from problems before which Washington seems helpless. Inflation is as yet unchecked.... The American dollar has lost its position as the symbol of strength around the world.... Annual budget deficits of $30 [billion] to $60 billion have become the norm, feeding inflation and eroding the dollar. Our national energy program, which ought to produce more energy, produces nothing but more regulation and more federal spending. Anti-American forces are on the move around the world, encouraged by our loss of resolve. In a dangerous world where our enemies have no rules, America's counterintelligence is in a straightjacket."

Connally concluded that "the leadership we so desperately need has not evolved from this administration and it is growing increasingly clear that it never will." No one was under any illusion as to who Connally thought could provide the needed leadership.

A no-nonsense assertion of what he sees as America's national interests is integral to Connally's conception of presidential leadership. He showed his confidence in his ability to move the federal bureaucracy and, indeed, the world, when he answered questions in Iowa about his policies.

When asked how he would balance the federal budget, he said "I'd insist on it." When queried on how he expected the Japanese to agree to take more American exports, he replied, "I'd make 'em." And he tells audiences, "If I am elected, I can change the whole complexion of this country in the first 48 hours."

It is this sort of shoot-from-the-hip response that bothers many people about Connally. The Texan plans to develop detailed proposals to counter this impulsive image.

Background

John Connally's career was closely intertwined with that of another major figure of Texas politics — former President Johnson.

From the day Connally volunteered to work in Johnson's 1938 House campaign to the moment 35 years later when he spoke at Johnson's funeral in a little cemetery on the banks of the Pedernales River, Connally and Johnson continually weaved in and out of each other's lives.

Connally followed Johnson to Washington and served as an aide from 1939 to 1941. Johnson was best man at Connally's wedding in 1940. After World War II, Johnson helped Connally get started in business by aiding him and other veterans in establishing radio station KVET in Austin.

Connally managed Johnson's successful 1948 Senate campaign, then served as the newly-elected senator's administrative assistant from January to October of 1949. In 1956, while in private law practice, he helped Johnson capture control of the statewide Texas Democratic Party.

When Johnson tried for the Democratic presidential nomination in 1960, he again turned to Connally to be his manager. At the Democratic National Convention that year, Connally was criticized for spreading the story that Kennedy was suffering from Addison's disease and therefore should not be trusted with the presidency.

Johnson again played a major role in Connally's career in 1961 when, along with House Speaker Sam Rayburn, he sponsored Connally for Navy secretary in Kennedy's administration. However, Connally served only until December because he had his eye on a more attractive office.

Connally entered the race for governor of Texas as a Johnson ally and served three terms from 1963 to 1969. Recovered from his wounds in Dallas, he made the nominating speech for President Johnson at the 1964 Democratic National Convention.

Connally performed his last service for his old ally in 1968 by holding the Texas delegation to the Democratic National Convention for Vice President Hubert H. Humphrey and helping Humphrey carry Texas that November, the only Southern state in Humphrey's column.

Personal Differences

And yet, despite their sometimes being portrayed as virtual twins, Connally and Johnson were really very different people.

Johnson, though not from a wealthy family, came from local gentry. His father was a state legislator for ten years during Johnson's youth, and his maternal grandfather was secretary of state of Texas during the 1880s. In contrast, Connally came from a poor rural Southern background, with his father working variously as a tenant farmer, butcher, barber and bus driver to support his family of eight children.

The personalities of the two also were at opposite poles. Johnson had a compulsive need to be liked and praised, and he spent much of his energy trying to generate those responses in other people.

Connally, on the other hand, wastes little time in trying to ingratiate himself to those whom he believes are against him. In July 1979, he told *Washington Post* reporter Sally Quinn, "Basically, I don't set out to please everyone 'cause if you do you don't please anyone. I try to make fast friends and I try to make strong enemies...."

Nor did Johnson and Connally see eye to eye on many political issues. Even allowing for the fact that the two had different constituencies when they held executive office in the 1960s — Connally in Texas and Johnson in the nation as a whole — and therefore might be expected to behave differently, they still had basic philosophic differences.

Johnson was a faithful New Deal liberal during his House service (1937-49). He became somewhat more conservative when he represented the state of Texas in the Senate (1949-61), but when he took over the presidency he fought for and won some of the widest-ranging social legislation in the history of the country.

Connally had a more conservative outlook than Johnson on social programs, tending to concentrate on stimulating economic development. The one social area that interested him was education, which he championed while serving as governor. But even in that field, he tended to see education as an adjunct to economic advancement, concentrating on vocational and technical educational facilities. He had little sympathy with the student and civil rights demonstrations of the 1960s, although he was never identified as a segregationist.

During the 1950s, Connally took time out from political life to make money. After serving as manager and president of KVET in the late 1940s, he practiced law in Austin and Fort Worth from 1949 to 1952. In 1952, he became attorney for oil tycoon Sid W. Richardson, who eventually made Connally the administrator of his vast business holdings. He became one of the executors of the Richardson estate.

By the end of the 1950s, Connally was a millionaire with vast land holdings and investments in several large businesses. He also was serving on the boards of directors of many major corporations.

Governorship

Entering the 1962 Texas gubernatorial race as a Johnson protege, Connally had to campaign hard to win the office.

He was forced into a runoff for the Democratic nomination with the hero of Texas liberals, Don Yarborough, and beat him by only 26,000 votes out of over 1,100,000 cast (51.2 to 48.8 percent).

Connally then was faced with the first major effort by the Republicans since Reconstruction to take the governor's office. He was caught in a vise formed on one side by angry liberals who threatened not to vote and on the other by conservatives attracted to the Republican nominee Jack Cox.

Treading carefully between the two, Connally managed to win in November by an unimpressive 54 percent of the vote, the smallest percentage received by a Democratic gubernatorial nominee in the state in the 20th century up to that time.

But for the adventitious events in Dallas on Nov. 22, 1963, Connally may have faced a major challenge to renomination in 1964. But the new governor's popularity soared following the wounds he received in the assassination of President Kennedy. When Yarborough challenged him for renomination in 1964, Connally ran away with the vote, receiving 69.1 percent of the ballots. In both 1964 and 1966, he won over 70 percent of the vote against his Republican opponents. *(Election results, see p. 71.)*

Connally's record as governor centered around his efforts to promote the state's prosperity. He claims to have helped create a climate that brought 1,500 new industrial plants into the state and expanded 1,900 others. He continued the state's policy of no income tax — corporate or personal — but added to the state sales tax. He also promoted tourism.

The governor's other major interest was education. When he came to office, the state had more adult functional illiterates than any other state except New York.

Connally Campaign Staff

Campaign chairman: Winton Blount, former postmaster general of the United States (1969-71).

Chief administrative official: Charles Keating, formerly a businessman in Arizona.

Campaign director: Eddie Mahe Jr., executive director of the Republican National Committee (RNC), 1974-77.

Director of special services: Maxine Cooper Brand, formerly with The Management Group, a Washington, D.C. political fund raising firm.

Director of communications: Julian Read, president of Read Poland Inc., an advertising agency.

Press secretary: Jim Brady, formerly press secretary to Sen. William V. Roth Jr., R-Del., and to Donald Rumsfeld while he was defense secretary.

General Counsel: Michael Gardner, a partner in Bracewell & Patterson, a Washington, D.C., law firm.

Campaign treasurer: Presley Werlein, member of the accounting firm of Storms and Werlein.

Headquarters: Connally for President, 901 South Highland St., Arlington, Va.

Connally felt this was a major obstacle to industries wanting to move into the state, and he initiated an across-the-board improvement in the state's educational system. He raised teachers' salaries and increased junior college, technical and vocational enrollments with emphasis on providing industry with more skilled workers. He also established three new state schools for the mentally retarded and pushed through a new program of community-oriented mental health care.

Critics claimed that Connally favored big business during his governorship at the expense of the general public. The increase in the sales tax was retrogressive, they said, and business should have been made to bear more of the tax burden.

One of the most publicized events Connally's liberal critics point to is his confrontation in 1966 with striking South Texas farm workers. After Texas Rangers broke up a rally, the farm workers marched on Austin, the state capital, to ask for a state minimum wage of $1.25 an hour. Connally met with them before they reached Austin, but he did not support the minimum wage demands. He was not available to them when they arrived at the capital.

Connally's opponents felt the incident reflected his lack of concern for a more equitable distribution of the state's growing wealth. They claimed that Connally had forgotten what it was like to be poor.

But Connally has tried to rebut that charge. "We're going to have to show a care and a concern and a compassion for people," Connally told the nation's Republican governors in Austin in November 1979. "We must not deny the needy the sustenance they require. We must show how we can deliver aid and assistance more efficiently."

National Politics

While Connally had helped Humphrey carry Texas in 1968 as a favor to his old friend Johnson, he also aided Republican candidate Nixon make contacts for fund-raising purposes among the state's leading political gift-givers. Nixon remembered Connally's help and in 1970 enticed him into his administration as treasury secretary.

Taking office in 1971, Connally soon became a dominant force in Nixon's domestic policy-making apparatus. In June 1971, Nixon announced that Connally would be the administration's "chief economic spokesman."

In this role, Connally played a major role in formulating the dramatic new economic program announced by Nixon in August 1971, which included wage and price controls, tax reductions to stimulate economic growth and reduce unemployment, a tax credit for business investment, suspension of the $35 fixed price for an ounce of gold and a 10 percent surcharge on imports.

During the little more than one year he served at the Treasury Department, Connally supported two controversial subsidies to major American corporations. In March 1971, he backed using government funds to develop the supersonic transport airplane (SST). He claimed building the SST would produce a gain of billions of dollars in the U.S. foreign trade account over the next twenty years. The SST also was supported by organized labor which coveted the expected 150,000 jobs the project was expected to create. But in a serious defeat for the administration, Congress voted in 1971 to halt government funding for the project, effectively killing it.

Connally and the Nixon administration were more successful the same year in fighting for a federal loan guarantee for the Lockheed Corporation. Lockheed had been assessed large penalties by the government for cost overruns on military projects and claimed it needed the credit guarantee to stay in business. The loan guarantee passed the Senate by one vote and the House by three votes.

Connally resigned his treasury post in May 1972, and there was immediate speculation that he would replace Vice President Spiro T. Agnew as Nixon's running mate.

Only a few days before his resignation, Connally had criticized liberal Democrats' opposition to Nixon's Vietnam policy, saying their criticism raised doubts about "the basic stability and essential commitment [the liberal Democrats] have to act always . . . in the best interests of the nation."

However, Agnew was retained on the ticket, and Connally became head of the Democrats for Nixon Committee. He worked hard for Nixon's re-election, including speaking on a paid national political telecast in which he charged that Democratic presidential nominee George McGovern's defense budget proposal was "the most dangerous document ever seriously put forth by a presidential candidate in this century."

As the Watergate scandal worsened in the spring of 1973, Connally formally switched from the Democratic Party to the Republicans. He argued that the Democrats had moved too far left and the Republicans were more responsive to the real needs of the people. He also pointed out that he was joining the Republican Party in a time of adversity, demonstrating that his switch was more a matter of principle than opportunism.

A few days later, Connally was named a special adviser to President Nixon on domestic and foreign affairs. The move was an attempt on Nixon's part to beef up the White House staff after the resignations of chief of staff H. R. Haldeman and John D. Ehrlichman, Nixon's chief domestic adviser.

Only a month after his appointment Connally resigned his White House position, complaining that he had not been used effectively as an adviser and that he had no real responsibilities.

In the fall of 1973, when Vice President Agnew resigned, Connally's name came up as a possible replacement. But President Nixon was in such a weak political position that he dared not risk choosing a controversial nominee for vice president who might be defeated in a bitter confirmation battle. So he chose the non-controversial and universally-liked House Republican leader, Gerald R. Ford of Michigan.

Indictment

On July 29, 1974, the political world was jarred when John Connally was indicted by a federal grand jury on charges of perjury, conspiracy to obstruct justice and accepting an illegal gratuity. The government alleged that Connally took $10,000 from the Associated Milk Producers Inc. after persuading President Nixon to back a controversial 1971 hike in milk price supports. Connally vehemently denied the charges.

The result was an April 17, 1975, acquittal of the charges of accepting a gratuity and the dropping of the other charges the next day.

Despite his acquittal, Connally's indictment has continued to dog him on the campaign trail, even though the subject has seemed to come up less and less as 1979 has progressed.

Connally has developed a forceful counter when the indictment is raised. He notes that he was found innocent by a Washington, D.C., jury composed of ten blacks and two whites.

"I'm the only certified not guilty candidate running in either party," he asserts. "They said I'm not guilty, not guilty. What more do you want?"

Strategy

Connally's activities throughout 1979 revealed a three-step strategy for winning the Republican presidential nomination.

He spent much of the first half of the year appearing at Republican Party gatherings, letting the faithful of his new party have a close look at him and confirming his Republican credentials. He usually was received with great enthusiasm that often included standing ovations following his stem-winding speeches.

The second step was to woo business groups, delivering his evangelical message of the necessity for a more dynamic use of America's talent for enterprise. The businessmen also responded enthusiastically. And from a practical standpoint, Connally amassed a large campaign war chest, much of it collected from corporate executives.

The third phase of Connally's campaign will consist of attempting to broaden his base of support among the voters. But Connally has problems in widening his appeal. One is his "wheeler-dealer" image that has resulted from his association with Lyndon Johnson, his indictment and his personal brash style.

But Connally is trying to turn this image to his advantage by linking it to two key issues of 1980 — leadership and competence. He tells audiences that if "wheeler-dealer" means "somebody who can deal with Congress, then I'm going to plead guilty. . . . If you mean somebody smart enough not to get caught in a shell game, I'm that smart."

Connally's image problem is reflected in the public opinion polls, where he consistently has high negative ratings. For example, in an October 1979 NBC News-Associated Press poll 34 percent of those interviewed had an unfavorable opinion of Connally, while 25 percent had a favorable attitude. In contrast, the same interviewees were favorable toward Reagan 51 percent to 28 percent and favorable toward Tennessee Sen. Howard H. Baker Jr. 28 percent to 7 percent.

Connally is trying to reverse that large negative perception through personal campaigning and large expenditures on media advertising.

But he appears to be having trouble advancing in the polls. A Gallup Poll conducted in early November 1979 among Republicans showed Connally running a relatively poor third behind Reagan (41 percent) and Baker (18 percent). Connally received 13 percent.

In addition, Connally was disappointed by the outcome of the Florida Republican straw vote on Nov. 17. Connally had hoped to upset Reagan in the balloting, but he ran second by 10 percentage points.

Along with other Republican candidates, Connally's main task is to knock Reagan out of first place. He will have to run strongly against the former California governor in early primaries, especially in the South, then overcome him in a major state. If he replaces Reagan as the candidate of the right, then Connally will have to fight it out with whomever survives the scramble among the rest of the candidates.

Connally announced Dec. 12, 1979 he would not seek federal matching funds to help finance his primary campaign. That decision meant Connally would not be bound by any spending limits, either overall or for the individual primaries. No candidate had rejected public funds since the system was instituted in 1976.

A major consideration in rejecting the funds, according to some observers, was the feeling that the only way to knock out Ronald Reagan in an early primary would be to outspend him. If Reagan accepted public funds, as was expected, his expenditures in the early primary states would be severely limited. Connally on the other hand could spend as much as he liked. This would be particularly important if he wanted to mount a massive media blitz.

Connally has not had any difficulty raising money on his own. By the end of 1979 he had raised in excess of $8 million.

A spokesman for the Federal Election Commission said that although Connally would not be taking matching funds he still would be required to follow reporting requirements. He also would be bound by the limits on contributions of $1,000 for individuals and $5,000 for qualified political action committees.

In refusing public money for the primary campaign Connally did not rule out the possibility of accepting public financing for the general election if he wins the Republican nomination.

Sen. Edward M. Kennedy's entrance into the presidential sweepstakes could have various implications for Connally.

Connally argues that only he can match Kennedy in a political slugfest and only he among potential Republican nominees has the strong leadership qualities Americans also see in Kennedy.

But others argue that Connally's high negative rating among voters could lessen Republicans' ability to take advantage of any negative reaction to Kennedy's past, including Chappaquiddick.

Philip M. Crane

Fighting For Traditional Political Ideals

For Philip M. Crane, things started to go badly for the United States about 50 years ago.

That was when the New Deal, in its efforts to alleviate the ills of the Depression, began taking the country down the road to big government and restricted personal liberty, the Illinois Republican believes.

The 49-year-old Crane sees much of American political history as a struggle against the encroachment of the federal government on the states and individual citizens. It is a struggle he is carrying on through his long-shot presidential campaign.

To some Crane is like a modern Don Quixote, charging at the windmills of the federal government at every opportunity. At times, he seems to be a man from another era off on a personal crusade to restore the old virtues that he feels are vanishing from American life.

Philosophical Roots

His speeches frequently invoke the Founding Fathers, the Constitution and the Declaration of Independence as the wellsprings for his analysis of what is wrong with the country. That array serves as a source of inspiration, security and rigidity for Crane.

The Constitution, especially, is a kind of secular Bible for Crane. As a professional historian he has studied it, and as a political officeholder he has had to grapple with its implementation.

On most political questions, Crane goes back to the principles stated in the documents of the Founding Fathers.

For example, in a discussion of the Alaska lands bill in the House in 1979, Crane harked back to the Northwest Ordinance of 1787, passed by the Continental Congress. The Northwest Ordinance guaranteed each state that would be admitted from the Northwest Territory the right of ownership of the land within its boundaries.

"But times have changed since 1787," Crane lamented, "and the omnipotence of the federal government has again interfered in states' rights."

Crane supported Alaska's right to control publicly-owned land within its boundaries instead of the federal government having the authority to determine how it was managed.

In a 1974 House speech opposing a government mandate to the auto industry to install seat and shoulder harnesses, Crane stated his basic philosophy of minimal government:

"It was the belief of the Founding Fathers that the primary function of government was to provide an atmosphere in which men and women would be able to make the important decisions in their own lives without outside interference. One man's right, they believed, ended where another man's right began. Government's function was, in effect, to be a negative one, to oppose those who would interfere with freedom. Today, however, the most significant interferences with freedom in our society come from government itself. Today, government believes that it is its responsibility to look out for the 'good' of its citizens and coerce them into acting in a manner which government believes is appropriate."

Crane's attitude toward the federal government was clear in his opposition to the creation of the Department of Education. "Two hundred years of our system of government have provided many reasons to believe that the federal government is certainly a no wiser depository of the public interest than the citizens themselves and is undoubtedly less safe and honest," he said in June.

Free Marketplace

Second only to the reverence for the Founding Fathers in Crane's political philosophy is the principle of the free marketplace.

The free functioning of the marketplace — both for products and ideas — is fundamental to the prosperity and preservation of the nation, Crane believes. For Crane a free economic marketplace is closely connected to personal liberty.

To the extent that the government interferes in the economy, it will inevitably infringe upon individual rights, he believes.

Crane repeatedly has endorsed the free market as a better alternative than the government to guide the econo-

CQ Vote Study Scores For Crane's House Career

	1969	1970	1971	1972	1973	1974	1975	1976	1977	1978	1979
Presidential[1]											
Support	38%[5]	54%	60%	35%	60%	60%[3]/37%[4]	61%	71%	23%	9%	12%
Opposition	62[5]	29	33	46	26	28[3]/43[4]	33	20	67	60	49
Conservative Coalition[2]											
Support	100[5]	66	83	83	78	77	91	87	89	79	60
Opposition	0[5]	9	6	12	6	6	4	4	3	2	2
Party[2]											
Unity	89[5]	82	74	80	77	75	84	84	87	73	54
Opposition	11[5]	4	12	15	9	4	6	7	4	4	2
Voting Participation[2]	100	81	87	82	85	84	90	86	88	72	54

[1] *Ground Rules, p. 67.*
[2] *Definitions, p. 67.*
[3] *During President Nixon's tenure in 1974.*
[4] *During President Ford's tenure in 1974.*
[5] *Not eligible for all roll calls in 1969.*

NOTE: Failure to vote lowers scores so that total in each category will not be 100% in every year.

---

my. His support of the free market runs the gamut from energy to metric conversion.

Discussing the energy situation in 1975, Crane said, "If the free market is permitted to work, the energy problems we face, while not disappearing, would hardly appear the 'crisis' they now seem to be."

He urged the government to stop controlling energy prices and allocations and let the market work its will. In that way, the market would promote both conservation and production, Crane argued.

But Crane does not reserve his endorsement of the free market just for the big issues. In August 1978, he introduced an amendment to delete funds for the U.S. Metric Board, objecting to any coercion in converting to the metric system.

During the House debate, he argued that "since any move toward the metric system is to be voluntary [according to the Metric Conversion Act of 1975] a costly government entity is simply unnecessary.... If such a conversion is to take place at all, it should come naturally, as demanded by the marketplace, not in response to pressure from a government agency."

On a few occasions, Crane's devotion to the Constitution and personal liberty has led him into alliance with liberals. One of the most notable instances came in 1978 when he introduced a bill to protect the confidential sources of newspaper reporters.

Reintroducing the bill in January 1979, he said it reflected the "pure, straightforward and absolute terms found in the First Amendment."

Crane's bill was in response to the jailing of a *New York Times* reporter for refusing to reveal his sources of information. Crane argued, "We must act to preserve the most essential ingredient of self-government — an informed electorate — by protecting our most efficient means of informing the electorate. We must, before it is too late, reaffirm the freedom of the press that our forefathers established."

His use of the phrase "before it is too late" is symptomatic of the urgency Crane feels about combating the wrongheaded way in which he sees the country moving.

Crane has tried to counter the image of an inflexible ideologue by attempting to make his philosophy relevant to current problems.

In the spring of 1978, he and U.S. Rep. Mickey Edwards of Oklahoma, another conservative Republican, visited Youngstown, Ohio, whose steel industry was in serious trouble. The two conservatives met with local labor union chiefs to see if they could find some common political ground.

They talked about jobs, taxes, federal regulations and anti-dumping rules. Out of the meetings came three legislative proposals that Crane introduced in the House in March 1978. They included tax incentives to encourage capital investment, job creation and economic growth; a requirement that all federal agency regulations be preceded by economic and environmental cost-benefit analyses to ensure that the affected industries were not hurt, and an acceleration of procedures designed to prevent dumping of foreign products at unreasonably low prices in the United States.

While none of his bills was enacted, Crane felt that he had confirmed his belief that conservative Republicans and working people had much in common and that the latter could be attracted to a conservative Republican ticket, including one led by himself.

Background

Crane's political philosophy was formed early, and the principal catalyst was his father, Dr. George W. Crane III, a psychologist and writer.

For the past 44 years, the elder Crane has written a syndicated newspaper column of psychological and medical advice called "The Worry Clinic." The column's advice is heavy on such ideas as hard work and self-reliance.

It was at his father's table that Crane learned those same virtues. He also was taught there to cherish the wisdom of the Founding Fathers. He never has deviated from those early lessons.

The Cranes sometimes are compared to the Kennedy family — "the Kennedys of the Right" *Newsweek* labeled them in 1978. Indeed, there are some striking comparisons. Each family had a strong father, whose authority was unquestioned and who molded his children to be disciplined and committed.

In both families, the eldest son, named after the father, was killed in an air accident. George W. Crane IV died in 1956 when his plane crashed during a Marine air show near Chicago. Joseph P. Kennedy Jr. was killed in an air accident during World War II.

And the three remaining brothers in both families all have entered politics. Philip's younger brother Daniel Crane, a dentist, was elected to the U.S. House from the 22nd District of Illinois in 1978 after an unsuccessful try for the Republican nomination in Indiana's 7th Congressional District in 1966. Their brother David, a psychiatrist and lawyer, has lost two House races — in 1976 and 1978 — in Indiana's 6th District. The Cranes show the same determination as the Kennedys to carry on and serve their country.

But there also are significant differences between the two families. In contrast to the Kennedys, the Cranes were relatively poor, with the children growing up in a working-class neighborhood on the South Side of Chicago. Their Protestant Calvinist rigor contrasts with the Kennedys' more boisterous lifestyle. And on political philosophy, the two families are at opposite ends of the spectrum — the wealthy Democratic liberals versus the poorer Republican conservatives.

After his brother's death, Philip Crane abandoned his early career of advertising and went back to school, earning a doctorate in history from Indiana University. He then went into teaching, first at Indiana University and then at Bradley University in Peoria, Ill. In 1967-68, he served as director of Westminster Academy, a private conservative-oriented school north of Chicago.

Electoral Politics

In 1969, Crane entered the Republican primary in a special election held to fill a U.S. House vacancy caused by Donald Rumsfeld's resignation to become head of the Office of Economic Opportunity (OEO) in the Nixon administration. Although Crane had worked in both Barry Goldwater's 1964 presidential campaign and in Richard M. Nixon's 1968 campaign, this was the first time he had run for elective office.

In a field of seven Republican candidates, Crane emerged victorious with only 22.8 percent of the vote. His meticulous organization of dedicated conservative activists, though a minority in the party, was enough to win the nomination for Crane in a crowded field.

Although the district was traditionally Republican, it had a significant minority of Democrats in the Evanston and Skokie areas. With Crane's reputation for rigid conservatism, Democrats thought they had a chance to win the district, and they put up a strong candidate in state Rep. Edward A. Warman.

Warman turned the election into a referendum on the Vietnam War, calling for complete withdrawal of American troops by the end of 1970 and endorsing that November's anti-war demonstrations. Crane supported Nixon's policy of turning over conduct of the war to the South Vietnamese.

Crane's Interest Group Ratings

Americans for Democratic Action (ADA) — The percentage of the time Crane voted with or entered a live pair in accordance with the ADA position.

AFL-CIO Committee on Political Education (COPE) — The percentage of the time Crane voted in accordance with or was paired in favor of the COPE position.

National Farmers Union (NFU) — The percentage of the time Crane voted in accordance with, was paired for or announced for the NFU position.

Americans for Constitutional Action (ACA) — The percentage of the time Crane voted in accordance with the ACA position.

Following are Crane's ratings since he became a member of the House in 1969:

	ADA[1]	COPE[2]	NFU[2]	ACA
1969[3]	0	0	0	100
1970	8	0	15	100
1971	14	0	13	96
1972	0	18	14	100
1973	8	18	5	100
1974	9	0	0	92
1975	0	5	10	100
1976	5	14	9	96
1977	5	14	18	96
1978	5	6	0	100

[1] *Failure to vote lowers score.*
[2] *Percentages compiled by CQ from information provided by group.*
[3] *Did not serve for entire period covered by ratings.*

Crane offset Warman's attempt to paint him as an extreme right-winger by claiming he was really a "moderate" and by his soft-spoken and articulate manner. In the end, Crane won with 58.4 percent of the vote — a substantial victory, though not an overly impressive one in view of the district's overwhelming Republican voting history.

In an unusual move, U.S. House officials waived the formalities of receiving an official certificate of election so Crane could take his seat in time to vote in favor of a congressional resolution expressing support for President Nixon's war policy.

Crane was re-elected in 1970. Then in 1972, his district was divided in two and he ran in the more Republican part, gaining 72.8 percent of the vote. He has had a safe seat ever since. *(Election results, see p. 71.)*

Crane's career in Congress has been more one of arguing for conservative political principles rather than gaining passage of any substantive legislation.

He has been in the minority party during his entire congressional service so his power to affect events has been limited. Also, he has chosen consciously to be a conservative spokesman rather than concentrate on the nitty-gritty legislative process. Although he has been a member of the House Ways and Means Committee since 1975, he has not made an important mark on the committee's work, and there have been complaints about his absenteeism.

Presidential Campaign

Crane's deeply held convictions about America's problems apparently led him to seek the presidency, the position from which he could most effectively enact his princi-

Crane's Background

Profession: History professor and school administrator.
Born: Nov. 3, 1930, Chicago, Ill.
Home: Mount Prospect, Ill.
Religion: Methodist.
Education: Hillsdale College, B.A., 1952; Indiana University, M.A., 1961; Ph.D., 1963.
Offices: U.S. House, 1969- .
Military: U.S. Army, 1954-56.
Family: Wife, Arlene; seven daughters and one son.
Committees: Ways and Means; ranking Republican on Health Subcommittee.

ples. On Aug. 2, 1978, Crane became the first candidate to enter the 1980 presidential sweepstakes.

For the first eight months, Crane seemed to be making headway in his campaign. He created his usual careful organization centered around activist conservative groups. He concentrated on Iowa, where the Jan. 21 caucuses begin the delegate selection process, and the early primary states of New Hampshire and Florida. He basically was following Jimmy Carter's 1975-76 strategy of announcing early, traveling constantly and building up a loyal core of followers.

Crane's service as chairman of the American Conservative Union from 1977 to 1979 helped make him known in conservative circles. In addition, Crane hired the renowned conservative fund-raiser Richard Viguerie to bring in the finances needed for an effective campaign.

By February 1979, political observers were beginning to take him seriously. *Washington Star* political writers Jack W. Germond and Jules Witcover declared, "Crane is no longer just a fringe candidate." They saw him breaking into former California Gov. Ronald Reagan's conservative strength and attracting respectable audiences in New Hampshire.

Campaign Crises

Germond and Witcover were not the only ones to notice Crane's increasing strength in New Hampshire. William Loeb, publisher of the *Manchester Union-Leader* and a Reagan supporter, also noticed. He did not like what he saw — a division of the conservative vote to the detriment of Reagan — and this led to one of a series of crises in Crane's campaign in the spring of 1979.

In a series of articles, the *Union-Leader* charged that Crane was a womanizer and that he and his wife Arlene were heavy drinkers and inveterate partygoers. Crane charged that the articles were "gross violations of the ethics of the journalistic profession and of Western civilization." In March, the New Hampshire House passed a unanimous resolution condemning the articles. But Crane apparently was damaged politically, with such gossip difficult to squelch despite Crane's denials.

Loeb's articles were only the first of several damaging blows to Crane, however. Many leaders of the so-called New Right, who originally had been attracted to Crane's campaign, began to abandon him because they felt he was not stressing their favorite issues enough. They envisaged a campaign concentrating on such social issues as abortion, pornography, gun control and right-to-work, which eventually would build a new conservative coalition with blue-collar Democrats.

Instead, Crane, while agreeing with the New Right position on most of these issues, insisted on talking mainly about economic, energy and national security issues. One of Crane's most important losses was Paul Weyrich, chairman of the Committee for the Survival of a Free Congress and one of the chief figures in the New Right.

Crane suffered another major blow early in May when much of his campaign staff resigned or was fired. In quick succession, he lost his campaign chairman, executive director, pollster and press secretary. Shortly afterward, the fund-raiser Viguerie also left to join John B. Connally's campaign. The aides left under confused circumstances, but there apparently was a combination of differences involving ideology, strategy and personalities. There were complaints about Crane's wife Arlene being too involved in running the campaign and interfering in relations between the staff and the candidate.

Still another problem developed for Crane when it became widely known in mid-1979 that his campaign was in debt despite the fact that he had raised more money than any other contender. Much of the money had gone to pay Viguerie's fund-raising expenses, leaving a relatively small amount for the actual campaign. Solving the money problem put a further crimp on Crane's presidential efforts. In late 1979 Crane's financial position still was shaky.

Nevertheless, Crane was still plugging ahead by counting on a loyal band of followers to turn out for straw polls and caucuses to re-establish his credibility as a serious candidate.

He has tried to develop eye-catching proposals such as one for the decentralization of the federal bureaucracy. Under this plan, he would move the headquarters of the

Crane Campaign Staff

Campaign manager: Jerry Harkins, 50, chairman of the board and president of the Citizens State Bank of Donnellson, Iowa; administrative assistant to Crane (1969-70); Missouri state representative (1963-65); Midwest coordinator for Ronald Reagan's 1968 presidential campaign; Missouri coordinator for 1964 presidential campaign of Barry Goldwater.

Assistant campaign manager and northeast field coordinator: Jack Stewart, 31, staff member of the National Republican Congressional Committee, 1974-77; administrative assistant to Rep. Arlan Stangeland, R-Minn., 1977-78.

Assistant field director: Kathy Kish, 24, staff member in Jeffrey Bell's 1978 campaign for the U.S. Senate in New Jersey.

Chief accountant: Victoria Tigwell, 28, controller of a Washington, D.C. political consulting firm; accountant for the National Republican Congressional Committee, 1977-79.

Director of communications: James P. Flowers, president of a New York advertising firm; media consultant and speech writer for New York Gov. Nelson A. Rockefeller's re-election campaign in 1970; press aide and writer for Richard M. Nixon's presidential campaign in 1960.

Campaign headquarters: 5600 Columbia Pike, Baileys Cross Roads, Va. and 4416 Woodson Road, Woodson Square Center, St. Louis, Mo.

Agriculture Department to Iowa and the main offices of the Social Security Administration to St. Petersburg, Fla., shifting the bureaucrats closer to the constituencies they are supposed to serve. Crane envisages moving all the departments out of the Washington D.C. area except State, Justice, Treasury and Defense.

Crane will have to do well in the early caucuses and primaries, coming within shooting distance of the two leading conservative contenders, Reagan and Connally, if he is to gain any momentum.

His campaign received a small boost when he finished fourth in a presidential straw poll of delegates to the Florida state Republican convention Nov. 17. In a separate ballot to determine the delegates' second choice for the GOP presidential nomination, Crane finished ahead of all the other contenders.

Robert Dole

Looking for an Opening on the Right

A slicing wit, a conservative record and a nationally-known name are some of the qualities Robert Dole brings to his long-shot quest for the Republican presidential nomination.

Far back in the polls and troubled by organizational and fund-raising problems, the Kansas senator is hoping for the GOP front-runner, former California Gov. Ronald Reagan, to falter. This, Dole reasons, would give him a better shot at the party's conservative wing.

To rescue his flagging presidential bid, Dole is banking heavily on successes in the early primary and caucus states. If he has to drop out of the race, Dole can always return to Kansas and run for a third term as senator in 1980.

A member of Congress since 1961, Dole first gained national visibility as the sarcastic, fiercely partisan Republican national chairman in the early 1970s.

He brought his combative style to the Republican national ticket in 1976 as Gerald Ford's vice presidential running mate and stirred controversy with his comment that Democrats were to blame for the country's 20th century wars.

Since then, Dole has been less acerbic. But he still cannot resist taking pokes at others. An example is his assessment of Jimmy Carter's presidency: "The difference between the way the White House is run and the way the Boy Scouts are run is that the Boy Scouts have adult leadership."

Political Philosophy

Dole follows a generally conservative line. Exceptions are his support of farm subsidies and other agriculture-related programs, as well as his advocacy of legislation to help the handicapped. Dole himself lost use of his right arm from a war injury.

Also, he has maintained an uncommitted stance on the pending Strategic Arms Limitation Treaty (SALT) at a time when other Republican presidential candidates are running hard against it.

In both the House and Senate, he never dipped below a 50 percent rating from the conservative Americans for Constitutional Action (ACA). Conversely, the liberal Americans for Democratic Action has given him low marks throughout his congressional career. He consistently received higher ratings on Congressional Quarterly's conservative coalition support score than the average Republican in the House or Senate.

In a seeming paradox Dole, who styles himself as the farmer's friend, has gotten a mixed review from the National Farmers Union, which gave him an 80 percent support score in 1978 but only 36 percent in 1976.

The reason is that the National Farmers Union is a fairly liberal organization, and its voting yardstick measures a legislator on more issues than just farm-oriented votes.

During his eight years in the House, Dole looked out for the interests of his wheat-growing state from a seat on the Agriculture Committee.

Like many farm state conservatives, he found little problem embracing government subsidies for growers. Although Dole in 1964 voted against legislation setting up the food stamp program, he later changed his position when farmers found the program to be a boon to agricultural production. Dole went on to back subsidized school lunch plans and other seemingly liberal social legislation involving agriculture.

Otherwise, Dole took a conservative stance on most issues. While he favored the Civil Rights Act of 1964, the Voting Rights Act of 1965 and the Civil Rights Act of 1968, he opposed programs such as Medicare and the Equal Employment Opportunity Act.

He declared the Johnson administration's plans to rehabilitate the cities to be of "doubtful necessity." The conservative ACA gave him a distinguished service award for his votes in the 89th Congress (1965-66).

In recent years in the Senate, Dole has softened his hatchet man image.

"Bob Dole is a mellower individual these days, and he's a good personal friend," said Sen. George McGovern, D-S.D., the recipient of much verbal abuse from Dole during the 1972 presidential campaign. "Of all the people I know in the Senate, he has grown the most."

Congressional Quarterly Vote Study Scores...

	1961	1962	1963	1964	1965	1966	1967	1968	1969
Presidential[1]									
Support	15%	33%	23%	27%	34%	37%	40%	42%	75%
Opposition	83	65	76	73	63	63	53	46	21
Conservative Coalition[2]									
Support	100	94	93	100	98	100	91	88	87
Opposition	0	0	7	0	2	0	4	0	7
Party[2]									
Unity	88	93	100	94	91	90	84	79	80
Opposition	12	5	0	6	7	10	7	6	12
Voting Participation[2]	99	98	99	99	99	99	94	85	94

Note: Failure to vote lowers scores so that total in each category will not be 100% in every year.

* *Dole became a member of the Senate in 1969.*
[1] *Ground Rules, p. 67.*
[2] *Definitions, p. 67.*

Dole observers agree that the senator has shed much of his slashing, snide partisanship since the days of the Nixon administration. On the campaign trail he is trying to emphasize his compassionate side by advocating aid for the handicapped and welfare reform.

As a senator, he lacks the skill at forming voting coalitions that Sen. Howard H. Baker Jr., the minority leader and a 1980 presidential rival, has. But Dole has given signs of working easily with some of his committee colleagues.

As ranking Republican on the Finance Committee, he has developed a cooperative relationship with Chairman Russell B. Long, D-La., on tax issues. On the Agriculture Committee, he also gets along with Chairman Herman E. Talmadge, D-Ga., and Nutrition Subcommittee Chairman McGovern.

Dole was a major ally this year of McGovern when the Senate voted to remove the spending cap on the food stamp program. He also worked with Sen. Birch Bayh, D-Ind., in the unsuccessful move to abolish the Electoral College in 1979. In addition, he was a figure in the 1979 oil windfall profits tax debate.

But he has not forgotten his roots. Remaining a steadfast advocate of agricultural aid, Dole welcomed protesting farmers when they came to Washington the last two years to push for larger federal subsidies.

Campaign Issues

As a presidential candidate, Dole has taken a generally right-of-center position on a variety of issues:

• **Taxes.** Dole favors indexing the federal income tax to prevent inflation from pushing people into higher tax brackets. In a rewritten tax code, savings account interest should be excluded from taxation and a 10 percent tax credit granted for research and development spending, he says.

• **Federal Spending.** Like many other conservatives, the Kansas Republican believes that an amendment to the U.S. Constitution is the only realistic way to balance the federal budget.

He has introduced a measure in the Senate (S J Res 5) mandating a balanced budget in five out of every nine years. Should a deficit be incurred to fight a war or alleviate an economic downturn, the amount borrowed must be repaid within four years under the Dole plan.

• **Energy.** To Dole, phased decontrol of domestic petroleum is needed to spur production and lessen the nation's dependence on foreign oil. While he backs a windfall profits tax on the proceeds, he would like to see a tax savings granted to the oil companies if they plowed some of their extra revenue back into production.

He does not want to close nuclear plants but prefers to enhance their safety until new forms of energy are available.

Gasohol development, Dole contends, is one way to lessen the energy dependence of the United States on foreign countries. That is a popular position in his home area, where the grain is grown to make the gasoline-stretching blend.

• **SALT.** By the end of 1979 Dole was one of the few senators still undecided on the arms reduction treaty, which has become a litmus test for conservatism. In mid-1979 he seeming to be leaning in favor of SALT by saying that the Republican Party could not afford to defeat the arms pact when polls showed the public for it.

Later, he adopted a more neutral posture, explaining that he wanted to be sure that the treaty could be verified and that it would not weaken America militarily. "I voted for SALT I [in 1972] and would like to be able to vote for SALT II," he told Congressional Quarterly.

Consideration of the SALT treaty was postponed indefinitely in early January 1980 in response to a Soviet invasion of Afghanistan during the final week of 1979. President Carter notified Senate majority leader Robert Byrd, D-W.Va., that consideration of the treaty in a time of international crisis was unlikely to produce positive results.

• **Foreign Policy.** Dole opts for orthodox Republican views on foreign policy as a whole. "We've cut old friends in a naive belief that good intentions prevail over cold strength," he wrote in a *Washington Post* Op-Ed piece Nov.

...Covering Dole's House and Senate Career*

	1970	1971	1972	1973	1974	1975	1976	1977	1978	1979
Presidential[1]										
Support	81%	80%	87%	71%	63%[3]/34%[4]	75%	66%	53%	32%	39%
Opposition	15	13	4	27	33[3]/37[4]	16	17	44	65	57
Conservative Coalition[2]										
Support	86	87	88	89	76	90	77	89	83	85
Opposition	7	4	1	10	17	5	7	8	14	14
Party[2]										
Unity	88	80	87	83	71	86	71	85	77	78
Opposition	8	9	3	14	21	8	12	12	19	16
Voting Participation[2]	94	86	92	96	89[5]	93	78	97	95	93

[3] During President Nixon's tenure in 1974.
[4] During President Ford's tenure in 1974.
[5] Member absent a day or more in 1974 due to illness, illness or death in the family.

4. "...[W]e've reversed Teddy Roosevelt's old maxim to read: 'Speak loudly and carry a toothpick.'"

Dole has called for creation of a special commission to study American military needs for the rest of the century. He feels America's defense capabilities have slipped but does not dwell on this to the degree some other Republicans in the race do.

● **Health.** On national health insurance, Dole has a plan to cover catastrophic care alone. Under the Dole proposal, just major medical expenses would be included and would be paid for by the government and private insurers. This is billed as less costly than the more comprehensive plans offered by the Carter administration and Sen. Edward M. Kennedy, D-Mass.

● **Agriculture.** As a senator from a grain-growing state, Dole wants to see higher federal agricultural subsidies because he thinks prices for wheat and corn are too low and farm income is inadequate. Dole favors such liberal social spending programs as food stamps, school lunches for poor children and meal-on-wheels for the elderly and handicapped — all indirect government subsidies to agriculture.

He also has sponsored legislation to stem the flow of cheap imported beef into this country, which he says hurts cattle producers and consumers alike by contributing to price fluctuations. Proponents of meat imports say Dole's bill would be inflationary if enacted.

Background

Regarded as the foremost political figure in his state, Robert Joseph Dole has combined conservative beliefs, a heroic war record and support for agriculture to bring off an unbeaten streak in Kansas elections.

The only electoral loss for Dole came in 1976 as Ford's running mate. The Republican national ticket carried Dole's native Kansas with a less than overwhelming showing — 52.5 percent to 44.9 percent for Jimmy Carter.

Dole attended public schools in Russell, Kan., where he was born, and went to Kansas University for two years before joining the Army for World War II service.

As a combat platoon leader in Italy, he was wounded severely when he led an infantry assault on a machine gun nest. His right shoulder bone was shattered and several vertebrae were cracked. Doctors thought he never would walk again, but after three years in hospitals he regained the use of his legs. Today, his right arm is useless except to hold small objects, and he has difficulty dressing himself.

In 1948, he married Phyllis Holden, the physical therapist who had attended him when he was bedridden. After his discharge, he studied at the University of Arizona and received his bachelor's degree from Washburn University of Topeka, Kan., in 1949. He went on to get a law degree from Washburn, graduating *magna cum laude* in 1952. During his studies, his wife took notes for him. Dole later learned to write with his left hand.

Dole was divorced from his first wife in January 1972 after 23 years of marriage. Four years later, the senator married Elizabeth Hanford, then a member of the Federal Trade Commission. A Phi Beta Kappa at Duke University and one-time campus beauty queen, the new Mrs. Dole has acquired a reputation as an effective speaker while campaigning for her husband.

Political Career

Even before completing his law degree in 1952, Dole entered politics. He was elected to the Kansas House in 1950 and served one two-year term. Next he won the Russell County prosecuting attorney's post, a job he held for four terms from 1953 to 1960. Dole came to Washington in 1961, representing Kansas' 6th District, which later became the 1st District. *(Election results, see p. 72.)*

The hard hitting partisanship that became the Dole hallmark first showed up in the House when he served as chairman of a Republican group investigating the Bobby Baker scandal in 1964. Baker, a Lyndon B. Johnson protege, had used his post as secretary to the Senate majority to amass a personal fortune.

In 1968, Republican Sen. Frank Carlson announced his retirement, and Dole ran to replace him. He easily beat former Kansas Gov. William H. Avery in the primary and

Dole Campaign Staff

Political director: Pat Roberts, a Texas management and political consultant.

Administrative director: John W. Crutcher, 62, former Kansas lieutenant governor and ex-administrative assistant to Dole.

Treasurer: Anne McLaughlin, 37, vice president of McLaughlin Co., a political consulting firm.

Assistant treasurer: Joann McSorley, 32, former audit manager for the Federal Election Commission.

Finance director: Rick Brown, 31, fund raiser for the 1978 Senate campaign of William S. Cohen, R-Maine, and for the 1979 gubernatorial campaign of Republican Gil Carmichael in Mississippi.

Press secretary: Janet Bradbury, at one time press secretary in Dole's Senate office.

Staff director: Mari Masing, formerly press secretary for Sen. Strom Thurmond's, R-S.C., reelection campaign.

Campaign headquarters: The Dole Campaign, 104 St. Asaph St., Alexandria, Va.

---

coasted to a comfortable victory in November over Democrat William I. Robinson, a Wichita attorney.

Entering the Senate in the midst of the Vietnam War and the turmoil of the late 1960s, Dole quickly made a name for himself with his razor-tongued defenses of the Republican president, Richard Nixon.

The Kansas senator offended many of his senior colleagues with his sardonic humor and personal attacks against other senators, which violated the Senate code of cordiality. At one point in 1971, after Sen. Edmund S. Muskie, D-Maine, criticized the Federal Bureau of Investigation for domestic spying, Dole compared "Muskieism" with "the McCarthyism of the 50s."

When floor debates had finished, Dole would buttonhole other senators in the corridors to continue arguing — a practice also frowned upon in the Senate.

So acid-tempered had he become that Sen. William Saxbe, R-Ohio, in 1971 called Dole "a hatchet man" who "couldn't sell beer on a troopship."

As a diehard Republican, Dole backed completely the Nixon and Ford administrations' Vietnam policies. He helped lead GOP fights for confirmation of Nixon's controversial nominations of G. Harrold Carswell and Clement F. Haynsworth to the Supreme Court and for building the Safeguard anti-ballistic missile system.

Party Chairman

This loyalty to Nixon was rewarded in 1971 when the president made Dole chairman of the Republican National Committee (RNC) over the protests of Senate Minority Leader Hugh Scott, R-Pa., who thought the Kansan was too abrasive for the job.

As party spokesman, Dole had a national audience for his cutting sense of humor. An example is his comment following an incident in the 1972 New Hampshire primary contest where presidential candidate Muskie appeared to be crying due to attacks on his wife by a local newspaper.

"I don't blame Muskie," Dole remarked. "If I had to run against Nixon, I'd do a lot of crying too."

During the 1972 election, Dole launched polemical counterattacks against the Democrats over the Watergate break-in. In the Senate, he introduced a resolution to scuttle the Senate Watergate Committee hearings, arguing that the public was tired of them and that the matter should be settled in court.

He accused *The Washington Post*, which exposed some of the scandal, of mounting a "rescue operation" for the sagging campaign of Nixon's opponent, Sen. McGovern. He assailed "the brazen manner in which, without benefit of clergy, *The Washington Post* has set up housekeeping with the McGovern campaign."

This blistering rhetoric began to discomfit even some in his own party. During 1972 several GOP governors urged him to tone down.

Dole often found himself the lightning rod for the discontent of state and local Republican Party organizations, which felt that the Committee to Re-elect the President was denying them campaign funds despite a sure Nixon victory.

By relaying these complaints and by his own criticism of Nixon's lack of active stumping for other Republican candidates, Dole came into disfavor at the White House. Although he wanted to stay on, he was replaced as chairman in January 1973 by former U.S. Rep. George Bush of Texas, currently a rival for the 1980 GOP nomination.

In 1974, weighted down with Watergate, Dole barely won a second Senate term, turning aside a strong challenge from Rep. William R. Roy, D-Kan., an obstetrician who harped on the senator's ties to Nixon.

To little avail, Dole attempted to distance himself from the scandal by rebuking President Ford for pardoning Nixon. Dole turned to television, using a series of spots that

Dole's Background

Profession: Attorney.
Born: July 22, 1923, Russell, Kan.
Home: Russell.
Religion: Methodist.
Education: University of Kansas; University of Arizona; Washburn University, Topeka, Kan., B.A. 1949, LL.B., 1952.
Military: Army, discharged as captain; Bronze Star, Purple Heart.
Family: Married Phyllis E. Holden, 1948; divorced, 1972; one child; married Mary Elizabeth Hanford, 1975.
Offices: Kansas House, 1951-53; Russell County prosecuting attorney, 1953-60; U.S. House, 1961-69; Senate, 1969- ; Republican national chairman, 1971-73; Republican vice presidential nominee, 1976.
Committees: Agriculture — Member of subcommittees on Agricultural Research and General Legislation, Foreign Agricultural Policy, and Nutrition.

Finance — Member of subcommittees on Health, International Trade, and Private Pension Plans and Employee Fringe Benefits.

Judiciary — Member of subcommittees on Administrative Practice and Procedure, Improvements in Judicial Machinery, and Jurisprudence and Governmental Relations.

Senate Republican Personnel Committee — chairman.

Joint Taxation.

featured a poster of him being splattered with mud and wiped clean. The media tactic helped Dole win with 50.9 percent of the vote. His victory margin was 13,500 out of nearly 795,000 votes cast.

Vice Presidential Candidate

Having jettisoned Nelson Rockefeller for the vice presidential spot on the 1976 ticket and having edged out Reagan for the nomination, Ford needed a running mate acceptable to the conservative wing of the party. He found that in Dole, whose selection also was part of a strategy that would allow Ford to campaign by acting aloofly presidential while the vice presidential nominee hit the Democrats hard.

"We couldn't have two people running from the Rose Garden," Dole said, "so I went to the briar patch."

Jimmy Carter felt the full force of the Dole sarcasm. At one point, Dole said, "We've had the New Deal and the Fair Deal and the fast deal, and we're about to have the ordeal if Carter is elected."

Many observers agree that Dole went too far in his nationally televised debate with the Democratic vice presidential candidate, Walter F. Mondale of Minnesota, in blaming the other party for the nation's wars.

"If we added up the killed and wounded in Democrat wars in this century, it would be about 1.6 million Americans, enough to fill the city of Detroit," he said.

According to Carter's pollster, Patrick Caddell, Dole's negative rating surged following the debate. In appearances and through his television advertisements, Carter began to compare Dole unfavorably to Mondale.

Whether Dole ended up as a net plus or minus to Ford in 1976 is an open question. To suggestions that he became a drag on Republican chances after the debate, Dole insists that he was a key factor in whittling Ford's 30 percentage point poll deficit in late summer to a close race by November.

"Dole was a minor plus in the farm belt," said Kevin Phillips, a conservative political analyst and newsletter publisher. "But the make-up in the polls was Carter's fault, not Dole's doing."

Personal Style

Quick on his feet, Dole possesses an irrepressible wit that these days is somewhat more good-natured than in the past.

Here is a sampler of Dole wisecracks. On the job of vice-president: "It's not so bad. It's inside work and no heavy lifting." On his ties as RNC chairman to the Watergate-tainted Nixon: "The night of the break-in was my night off." On his post-1976 activities: "Since the election, I've been working with the handicapped — the Republican Party."

On Carter's encounter with a swimming rabbit: "The poor thing was simply doing something a little unusual these days — trying to get aboard the president's boat. Everyone else seems to be jumping ship." On Ronald Reagan's age: "The rest of us would never dream of making an issue of it. Of course, we are planning a big birthday party for him in February. There'll be a cake with 69 candles."

Work consumes Dole, and he regularly logs 12-hour days. Dole also drives his staff hard.

Some who know Dole, however, criticize his ability to organize and plan long-range. "He switches signals at the last minute," said one former member of Dole's Senate staff. "One big reason his campaign has done so poorly is that he is difficult to schedule for. He's never sure where he wants to go next. He's had [campaign] staff turnover because he doesn't pay the attention he should to them, and no one is sure what is going on."

Financial Worth

In a Senate financial disclosure statement for 1978, Dole listed assets worth at least $395,000 and at most $915,000. Holdings include stock in a North Carolina bank, the Wachovia Corp.; a blind trust set up for his wife, and two Washington cooperative apartments, one of which is rented out. Dole has two outstanding mortgages held by the John Hancock Mutual Life Insurance Co.

During the period, Dole listed income between a minimum of $112,700 and a high of $173,000. Apart from salary and stock dividends, he received substantial income from speaking engagements — earning $22,500 in honoraria, mainly from addresses to agricultural groups.

Dole's Interest Group Ratings

Americans for Democratic Action (ADA) — The percentage of the time Dole voted with or entered a live pair in accordance with the ADA position.

AFL-CIO Committee on Political Education (COPE) — The percentage of the time Dole voted in accordance with or was paired in favor of the COPE position.

National Farmers Union (NFU) — The percentage of the time Dole voted in accordance with, was paired for or announced for the NFU position.

Americans for Constitutional Action (ACA) — The percentage of the time Dole voted in accordance with the ACA position.

Following are Dole's ratings since he became a member of the House in 1961 and Senate in 1969:

	ADA[1]	COPE[2]	NFU[2]	ACA
1961	0[3]	0[3]	0[3]	91[3]
1962	—	—	—	—
1963	4[4]	9[4]	4[4]	—
1964	—	—	—	95[5]
1965	0	0[6]	25	89
1966	0	—	20	93
1967	7	9	8	96
1968	0	25	50	90
1969	0	18	25	64
1970	13	17	43	76
1971	4	17	33	71
1972	0	10	56	84
1973	10	27	56	82
1974	19	18	35	84
1975	17	24	78	67
1976	10	16	36	87
1977	5	11	55	70
1978	20	22	80	58

[1] Failure to vote lowers score.
[2] Percentages compiled by CQ from information provided by group.
[3] Rating is for the entire 87th Congress.
[4] Rating is for the entire 88th Congress.
[5] Rating is based on the ACA "consistency index" on selected issues since 1957.
[6] Rating is for entire 89th Congress.

Strategy

While he admits that his candidacy has not gone very far, Dole says that he can turn his fortunes around by making a good showing in the early party caucuses and primaries.

Dole also is counting on his high name recognition to help him. A Gallup Poll released Sept. 23, 1979, found him the fourth best-recognized among GOP presidential possibilities. Sixty percent of the public knew Dole. He was surpassed by former President Ford, Reagan and former Texas Gov. John B. Connally.

Among Republicans, however, Dole is far back in the pack as a choice for president. According to a Gallup Poll released Nov. 25, he was the preference of only 3 percent, far behind Reagan, Baker and Connally with Ford not included in the survey.

Dole spent much of 1979 occupied in the Senate while other candidates were out campaigning. Partly as a result, he is behind organizationally.

Dole says he kept his Senate attendance high out of devotion to his voting record. His critics say this demonstrates an inability to establish priorities wisely.

"I've had bad management," Dole said when asked to explain his organizational problems. He fired the Washington consulting firm that was handling his campaign — Response Marketing — in August and slowly has been building a new staff. Meanwhile, key field operatives have drifted away.

For the Florida Republican convention Nov. 17, Dole made few advance preparations and ended up tied for fifth with only nine first place votes in the straw balloting after spending $5,000.

Unable to afford an in-state phone bank, the Dole national headquarters staff in Alexandria, Va., was reduced to making sporadic long-distance calls and sending mailgrams to Florida delegates, asking for votes.

Dole concedes that for him to succeed Reagan has to fade, permitting the Kansas senator to attract the conservative votes claimed by the front-runner. The major problem with that approach is that Connally and U.S. Rep. Philip M. Crane, R-Ill., also are bidding for conservatives' support.

"Dole can't make any headway when the conservative field is blanketed by Reagan, and he can't get the moderates because they see him as a guy who goes to the jugular," said M. Staunton Evans, former chairman of the American Conservative Union.

"Reagan has peaked," Dole said. "But then again, maybe it's just that I'm hard to discourage."

Ronald Reagan

Working to Protect His Early GOP Lead

In the autumn of 1964 Ronald Reagan arrived on the American political scene in a nationwide television speech. He spoke of the United States as "the only island of freedom that is left in the whole world."

Reagan was trying to revive Barry Goldwater's slumping presidential campaign. Instead, sounding a theme that has remained his rhetorical signature for the last 15 years, the Hollywood actor embarked on the beginning of a new career as a politician.

At every critical juncture in the political career of the former Republican governor of California, Reagan has turned to television — the medium where he found his greatest success as an actor. Perhaps more than any other political figure Reagan can claim the title of the original television candidate.

"Reagan developed a mastery of the television medium in the days when he was host for 'GE Theatre'," Lou Cannon, a journalist who has watched Reagan's entire political career, wrote several years ago. Cannon noted that Reagan as governor would resort to a televised speech to appeal directly to the voters whenever his programs were blocked by the Democratic legislature.

In March 1976 after he had lost five straight primaries and his hopes for capturing the 1976 presidential nomination were fading quickly, Reagan again turned to television.

According to Reagan's campaign manager, John Sears, the 30-minute televised speech was the turning point in the campaign. It brought in about $1 million in campaign contributions and spurred Reagan to present President Ford with the most serious challenge to an incumbent Republican president since Theodore Roosevelt challenged William Howard Taft in 1912.

More recently, Reagan used his skills as a television actor when he launched his third try for the GOP presidential nomination on Nov. 13, 1979. None of the commercial networks would sell Reagan a half-hour of prime time, so his campaign committee bought the time on 98 individual stations covering about 70 percent of the nation's households.

Adam Clymer of *The New York Times* wrote following Reagan's announcement that the former actor demonstrated that he is "still the most accomplished politician in the country in using television as a campaign medium."

Moving easily around a set that included a desk, a globe, flags and other symbolic trappings of the presidency, Reagan evoked emotions ranging from strength and determination to compassion and tenderness. Tears welled up in his eyes as he spoke about a Depression Christmas when, instead of a bonus check, his father received a notice that he had lost his job.

Actor and Politician

Although Reagan never had any formal training as an actor, the skills he acquired during 28 years in the movies and television have influenced all aspects of his political life.

He is a quick study and learns his lines easily. But critics complain that Reagan's knowledge of issues is very limited. A former Republican California state senator, Peter Behr, once remarked of Reagan, "He's a man able to absorb facts readily, but if you walked through his deepest thoughts, you wouldn't get your feet wet."

Another trait Reagan developed in the movie industry was an ability to delegate responsibility. Just as cameramen, prop people and directors go about their tasks with little interference from the actor, Reagan believes he should hire responsible people for campaign and government work and then not get in their way.

Surrounded by a competent staff, Reagan has been praised for his adept political moves and his relatively trouble-free years as California's governor. The negative consequence of Reagan's penchant for delegation, however, is that it prompts charges that he is lazy and led around by a staff that does all his thinking for him.

Rus Walton, Reagan's chief issue's adviser in the governor's office, told journalist Cannon, "We had a saying in the Air Force that you had to fly the plane or the plane would wind up flying you. There was always a suspicion in Sacramento that the plane was flying Ronnie."

Reagan's approach to issues and the way he discusses them also reflect his years as an actor.

Most problems are reduced to their basic elements by Reagan. The solutions are just as simple for him. Reagan's rhetoric is clear and easily understood. Throughout his previous campaigns, Reagan has given essentially the same set speech over and over. The same startling statistics, the same catch phrases, the same lines denouncing Democrats all come from small index cards Reagan clutches behind the rostrum.

But Reagan does not apologize for simplifying his political discourse. In his 1967 California inaugural address, Reagan remarked, "We have been . . . told there are no simple answers to complex problems. . . . Well, the truth is there are simple answers, just not easy ones."

Reducing the size of the federal government is the simple answer Reagan gives to a host of the country's problems in areas ranging from inflation to education to welfare.

Opposition to big government has been the central tenet of Reagan's philosophy for nearly two decades. It first was developed during speeches he gave to employees of General Electric, when as the host of "GE Theatre" he toured the company's plants around the country.

Inflation is Reagan's favorite target in his campaign against the burgeoning federal government. Reducing the issue to what he considers its most fundamental element, Reagan says "inflation comes from the government spending more than the government takes in. It will go away when the government stops doing that." Inflation, Reagan goes on to assert, "threatens the very structure of family life itself as more and more wives are forced to work."

'Planned, Orderly Transfer'

Reagan's proposal to reduce inflation and limit the federal government's role in citizens' lives is simply to give back many government functions to the states and local governments. That was the central theme of his 1976 campaign. In announcing his candidacy for the 1980 nomination, Reagan made it clear he had not deviated from that approach.

"The federal government has taken on functions it was never intended to perform and which it does not perform well," Reagan told the television audience. "There should be a planned, orderly transfer of such functions to states and communities."

He now is quick to add that the federal money used for these programs also should be turned over to the state and local governments. In his last campaign, Reagan made the political mistake of putting a $90 billion price tag on the transferred programs. Only after a storm of editorial criticism did Reagan realize he had been too specific and would have a difficult time actually meeting that goal. This year he refuses to put a dollar amount on the federal savings.

Only "national" programs dealing with defense, space exploration, veterans' affairs, energy and the environment should remain under federal government control, Reagan believes. Welfare, education, housing, food stamps, Medicaid and community development all are federal programs Reagan would like to see in state and local hands.

Beginning in January 1980 Reagan planned to release issue papers that would go into more detail about the "planned, orderly transfer" and other subjects. But the debate continued among Reagan-watchers over whether there was a "new Reagan" emerging for the 1980 campaign or whether voters would find the same conservative hard-liner they saw in 1976 and in his late-starting presidential campaign in 1968.

Since losing to Ford in 1976, most political analysts believe Reagan has sought to soften his conservative image, while trying not to lose the activist conservative base that in the past has provided his organizational strength.

As the early front-runner for the 1980 Republican nomination, Reagan feels he must demonstrate he is "responsible," a carefully chosen word that neither denies nor endorses the claim that he has become more moderate.

"What we are correcting is a misconception [of Reagan as an extreme conservative], not creating a new perception," Reagan said recently.

"Frankly, every time I read those things [about Reagan softening his conservatism] I get madder than hell because I'm not changing and no one is trying to change me," Reagan told the American Conservative Union's magazine, *Battle Line*.

Another misconception Reagan is hoping to combat is that he has no new ideas. By giving essentially the same speech for years Reagan has furthered that perception. To counter this his aides have been talking about what they call "conservative activism," which they say will pervade the 1980 Reagan campaign. "It's not enough for conservatives just to stop every new idea that comes along," a Reagan aide commented.

Reagan campaign strategist Sears believes that after years of coming up with new ideas, liberals now have run dry and are busy trying to protect 40 years of liberal legislation. The burden to develop innovative approaches to government has fallen to the conservatives, Sears thinks.

One of the first fresh ideas Reagan has advanced is one that eludes classification on the political spectrum. In his November announcement Reagan suggested establishing closer economic cooperation with Mexico and Canada. His so-called "North American accord" would "work toward the goal of using the assets of this continent, its resources, technology and foodstuffs in the most efficient ways possible for the common good of all its people."

Although such an idea is a newcomer to the lexicon of presidential campaigns, it long has been pushed by Michigan Gov. William G. Milliken. He is a moderate Republican, who Reagan has been courting in recent months.

In a November 1979 letter to Reagan, Milliken said the idea was "the kind of innovative and forward-looking approach Republicans need to take in the 1980s." Although the "North American accord" did not meet such enthusiasm everywhere and Milliken has not endorsed Reagan, the governor's response was an early indication that Reagan's effort to broaden his ideological base was having some impact.

Some critics, however, see the idea of forming a partnership with Canada and Mexico as just another in a series of poorly researched and ill conceived plans to come from Reagan over the last several years.

Reagan has a reputation for saying things on the campaign trail before they have been thought out completely. During a 1976 visit to Tennessee he suggested selling the Tennessee Valley Authority to a private power company. He began backtracking as soon as he realized the mistake of attacking one of the most locally popular power-generating concerns in the country.

During an appearance on NBC's "Today" show Reagan made a verbal misstep concerning his age. He mistakenly observed that "as president, I would be younger than all the heads of state I would have to deal with except Margaret Thatcher." In fact, virtually every major head of state is younger than Reagan, who will be 70 in 1981.

The only major exception is Leonid I. Brezhnev of the Soviet Union, who is four years older than Reagan.

Gallup and the GOP Presidential Candidates

Percent of Republicans Interviewed

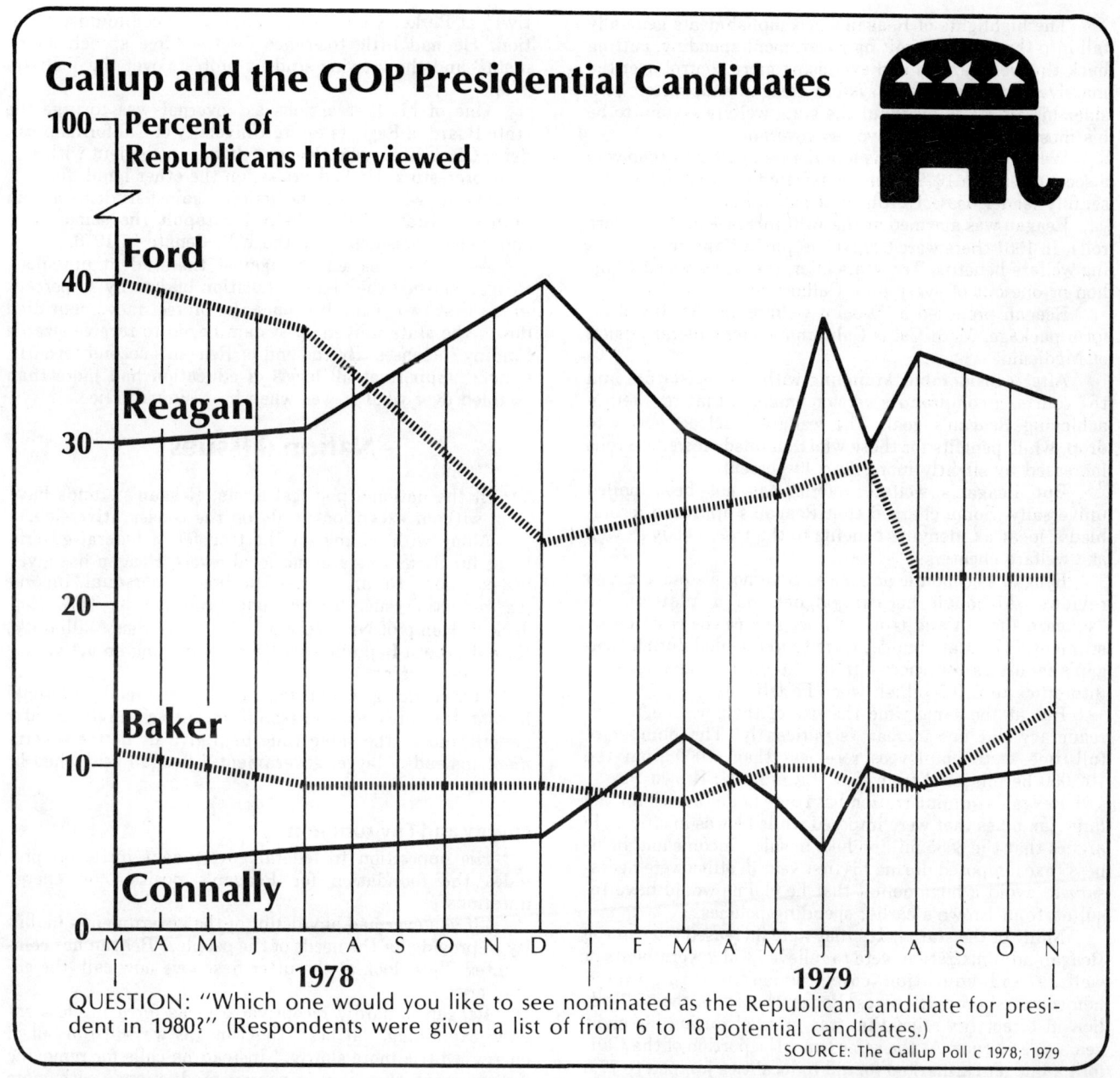

[Line chart showing polling percentages for Ford, Reagan, Baker, and Connally from March 1978 through November 1979. Y-axis ranges from 0 to 100 percent (with break), showing gridlines at 10, 20, 30, 40. Ford starts around 40% in early 1978 and declines to about 22% by late 1979. Reagan starts around 30%, rises to a peak of 40% in late 1978, dips, then rises again to around 37% in mid-1979 before settling near 33%. Baker remains around 10% throughout, rising slightly to 14% by end. Connally starts near 4%, peaks around 12% in early 1979, then settles near 10%.]

QUESTION: "Which one would you like to see nominated as the Republican candidate for president in 1980?" (Respondents were given a list of from 6 to 18 potential candidates.)

SOURCE: The Gallup Poll c 1978; 1979

Reagan's Governorship

One way to judge what kind of a president Reagan would be is to examine his eight years running the country's largest state.

Reagan moved into the governor's mansion in 1967 with no political or governmental experience. Reagan's only previous elective victory was winning six terms as the president of the Screen Actors Guild.

Those who watched Reagan campaign in 1966 assumed they would get a very hard-line conservative governor. He spoke against high taxes, wasteful government spending, the growth of bureaucracy, a rising crime rate, escalating welfare costs and the student unrest at the University of California in Berkeley.

However, the general consensus is that Reagan's actions as governor were more moderate than his rhetoric.

Ed Salzman, the editor of the *California Journal* and a veteran Reagan observer, remarked, "What [Reagan] did once in office didn't always match what he said on the dinner circuit. As governor, Reagan was a pragmatic compromiser."

As president, Salzman concluded, Reagan would run an efficient White House in which the president would serve as the chairman of the board, in much the same way he acted in Sacramento.

Judson Clark of the California Research Institute agrees. "Reagan was essentially a presider, not an administrator," Clark said. "He generally didn't roll up his sleeves and get deeply involved." Instead, as governor Reagan preferred to receive one-page summaries of issues from which he could make a decision.

For all but two of Reagan's eight years in the governor's office, he faced a Democratic-controlled legislature. He had very little interest in dealing with the legislature. But in the few places where Reagan demonstrated a personal involvement, he eventually met with success.

The highlights of Reagan's accomplishments generally fall into three areas: limiting government spending, cutting back the welfare rolls and exercising more control over the massive state educational system. Reagan's supporters consider his efforts to overhaul the state welfare system to be his most successful endeavor as governor.

Welfare reform became a major issue after Reagan won a second term in 1970 when he defeated the Democratic assembly leader Jesse Unruh by a half million votes.

Reagan was alarmed at the swift increase in the welfare rolls. In 1961 there were 620,000 people in California receiving welfare benefits. Ten years later, the figure was 2.4 million or one out of every nine Californians.

Reagan proposed a 70-point welfare and Medi-Cal reform package. Medi-Cal is California's more liberal version of Medicaid.

After considerable wrangling with the legislature and the courts, a compromise version emerged that resulted in achieving Reagan's goal. The welfare caseload began to drop, while benefits for those who remained on welfare rolls increased by slightly more than 40 percent.

But Reagan's welfare reform has not been hailed universally. Some charged that Reagan's approach resembled a meat ax, denying benefits to the truly needy as well as "welfare cheaters."

Reagan's economic actions as governor also met mixed reviews. Although he campaigned on a platform to "squeeze and cut and trim until we reduce the cost of government," the state budget more than doubled during Reagan's tenure as governor — from $4.6 billion when he came into office to $10.2 billion when he left.

But at the same time the size of the government bureaucracy did not increase significantly. The number of full-time state employees rose less than 6,000 from the 102,000 he inherited from Gov. Edmund G. Brown Sr.

Reagan's administration has come under attack for the large tax hikes that were imposed while he was in office. He argues that the $885 million hike in sales, income and business taxes imposed during his first year in office were necessary to avoid a huge deficit that he claims would have resulted from Brown's earlier spending policies.

Many of the state taxes that were increased later in the Reagan administration were to relieve local governments of welfare and education costs, which in turn lowered homeowners' property taxes. Reagan boasts of the $5.7 billion in direct tax relief that was granted during his eight years as governor. At the same time, the portion of the California budget earmarked for aid to localities jumped to $7.8 billion from $2.8 billion.

Five years before tax-cutting Proposition 13 passed in 1978, Reagan proposed a constitutional limitation on government expenditures and taxation. Reagan's proposal was a close relative of Howard Jarvis' 1978 property tax limit and the grandfather of the government spending limitation that California voters overwhelmingly approved in November 1979.

But Reagan's 1973 initiative failed miserably at the polls, due in part to a low voter turnout and complicated ballot language. Later when Jarvis' Proposition 13 was on the ballot, Reagan gave it only lukewarm support.

Reagan's third major interest as governor was the state's public higher education system, the largest in the country.

Reagan's political development in the 1950s was keyed to a fervent anti-communist zeal, which he carried with him to the state capital. He viewed much of the student activity at Berkeley and other campuses as communist agitation. He had little tolerance for the "free speech movement" and the growing student protests over the Vietnam War.

One of his first actions as governor was to urge the state Board of Regents to fire University of California president, Clark Kerr, who Reagan felt was too lenient with student protestors. He had praise, on the other hand, for S. I. Hayakawa, whose hard-line actions against students at San Francisco State College helped catapult the semanticist and college president into the U.S. Senate in 1976.

As part of his actions against the student uprisings, Reagan slashed the higher education budget by 27 percent in his first two years. But once the protest movement died down, the state university system began to receive sizable funding increases. By the end of Reagan's second term, financial support at all levels of education had more than doubled over what it was when he assumed office.

National Issues

In the national political arena, Reagan's stands have been without exception firmly on the conservative side.

Along with calling for the transfer of federal government functions to state and local levels, Reagan has given his support to an across-the-board personal income tax reduction such as the one proposed by U.S. Rep. Jack F. Kemp of New York and Delaware Sen. William V. Roth Jr., both Republicans. Kemp is playing an active role in Reagan's campaign.

"By reducing federal tax rates ... especially personal income tax rates, we can restore incentives, invite greater growth and at the same time help give us better government instead of bigger government," Reagan said when he announced his candidacy.

Energy and Environment

His opposition to federal government intrusion provides the foundation for Reagan's position on energy questions.

"If you ever had any doubt of the government's inability to provide for the needs of the people," Reagan has commented, "just look at the utter fiasco we now call 'the energy crisis.'"

Reagan is hardly receptive to pleas for using less energy, explaining, "at best [that] means we will run out of energy a little more slowly." Instead he calls for removing "government obstacles to energy production," with more exploration and development of U.S. oil and natural gas. He supports all price decontrol efforts, saying "it is not government's function to allocate fuel or impose unnecessary restrictions on the marketplace."

Reagan is a strong supporter of developing nuclear power with "strict safety rules."

Although he says he does not want to place undue burdens on industries, Reagan as governor supported environmental protection measures and once moved to preserve a wilderness area from highway developers. However, he believes the federal Environmental Protection Agency often makes hasty and erroneous judgments that are harmful to industrial development.

Foreign Policy and National Defense

Reagan's foreign policy and national defense positions are shaped in large part by his strong anti-communist

Reagan Campaign Staff

Campaign chairman: Sen. Paul Laxalt, 57, of Nevada, who was Reagan's campaign chairman in 1976.

Chairman for policy development: U.S. Rep. Jack F. Kemp, 44, of New York.

Executive vice chairman: John P. Sears, 39, a Washington lawyer in corporate and administrative practice, who managed Reagan's 1976 campaign and was executive director of Richard M. Nixon's 1968 presidential campaign.

Director of legal and financial affairs: Ed Meese, 48, director of the Center for Criminal Justice Policy and Management, who was executive assistant and later chief of staff in Reagan's gubernatorial administration.

Press secretary: Jim Lake, 42, Reagan's 1976 New Hampshire campaign manager and later campaign press secretary, who directed California's Washington office during Reagan's administration.

Director of research and policy coordination: Gary L. Jones, 35, vice president for administration of the American Enterprise Institute, who formerly served on the staff of Sen. Robert P. Griffin, R-Mich.

National political director: Charlie Black, 32, director of campaign operations for the Republican National Committee in 1978, chairman of National Conservative Political Action Committee from November 1976 through April 1977 and Midwest coordinator for the 1976 Reagan campaign.

National finance chairman: Daniel J. Terra, 68, president of United Republican Fund of Illinois and chief executive officer of Lawter Chemicals, Inc., an Illinois-based international chemical firm.

Headquarters: Reagan for President, 1828 L Street N.W., Washington, D.C., and 9841 Airport Blvd., Suite 1430, Los Angeles, Calif.

stance. His involvement in partisan politics began during the Cold War era of the late 1940s and 1950s. That has colored his views toward world politics ever since.

He sees the Soviet Union as an "expansionist" power that has "never retreated from their Marxist dream of one communist world."

Reagan believes the Strategic Arms Limitation Treaty (SALT) is "fatally flawed." He has stated that the Senate should shelve the current treaty and renegotiate with the Soviet Union "a treaty that fairly and genuinely reduces the number of strategic nuclear weapons."

"One of the Carter administration's principal arguments for ratifying SALT II is that no one will like us if we don't," Reagan has said in his campaign speeches. "Their principal argument for giving away the Panama Canal was, no one will like us if we don't. Isn't it about time that we stop worrying whether someone likes us and decide we're again going to be respected in the world?"

The debate on the Panama Canal treaties in 1978 provided Reagan with perhaps his most visible foreign policy issue. Traveling around the country to stir up opposition, Reagan's declaration became a rallying cry for treaty foes: "We built it. We paid for it. It's ours, and we're going to keep it."

Generally an advocate of more defense spending, Reagan supported the building of the B-1 bomber and in 1978 criticized the "dilly-dallying with regard to the neutron bomb."

Domestic Policy

On domestic issues, Reagan takes a strict point of view. Opposing abortion, decriminalization of marijuana and lenient court sentencing, Reagan has complained in the past of a "virus of permissiveness [that] spreads its deadly poison."

He opposes busing of school children to achieve racial integration, saying it is misconceived. During the height of the civil rights struggles, Reagan opposed California's 1963 open housing law and the 1964 U.S. Civil Rights Act. But he denied allegations made during his 1966 gubernatorial campaign that he was racially biased.

He supports capital punishment and has suggested mandatory jail sentences for persons who use weapons in crimes.

Background

Reagan's conservative political outlook closely matches his personality. He doesn't smoke, only occasionally drinks wine and prefers a night at home watching television with his second wife, Nancy, to going out. Often Reagan boasts of his love for the hard, physical work he does on his ranch near Santa Barbara, which is heated only by the firewood he chops. His personality mirrors his upbringing.

Reagan grew up in modest surroundings in several small towns in rural northern Illinois. He was the youngest of two sons of an alcoholic Irish-Catholic father, who had trouble keeping a job, and a Protestant mother of Scottish descent who loved the theater. When Reagan was nine the family settled in Dixon, Ill., where he did his first acting in high school.

After graduating from a small liberal arts college near his home, Reagan began working as a sports announcer for WOO, a Davenport, Iowa, radio station. He developed a national reputation when the station and its sister station, WHO in Des Moines, joined the NBC network. Over the network "Dutch" Reagan did football and baseball play-by-play broadcasts throughout the Midwest.

He was covering a 1937 baseball spring training session in California when an agent from Warner Brothers signed him up to play a radio announcer in his film debut, "Love Is On The Air." That marked the beginning of an acting career that included more than 50 films over 33 years.

Few of his films received much attention; fewer still won Reagan much acclaim. His favorite and best known roles were as George Gipp, a Notre Dame football player, in "Knute Rockne — All American," and a small-town playboy who has both legs cut off in "Kings Row." Reagan probably would prefer to forget parts in other films, such as "Bedtime for Bonzo," where he played opposite a chimpanzee, and "The Killers," his only villainous role.

After a three-year tour in the Army, where he made training films, Reagan's career centered less on acting and more on the political aspects of his profession.

In 1947 Reagan was elected president of the Screen Actors Guild, one of the major labor unions representing Hollywood talent. During his six one-year terms in that post, Reagan successfully negotiated several contract agreements.

But he received more notoriety for his support of blacklisting Hollywood actors and writers who were thought to have communist affiliations. He engaged in purging from the guild actors who failed to clear themselves of charges they were communists. In October 1947, Reagan appeared before the House Un-American Activities Committee as a friendly witness in its investigation of communism in the movie industry.

Reagan's eight-year marriage to actress Jane Wyman ended during that period, when she claimed he was too involved in politics.

The political beliefs Reagan held while he was growing up began to change rapidly in the 10 years after he left the Army in 1946. In his 1965 autobiography, Reagan characterized himself in the late 1940s as "a near-hopeless hemophiliac liberal. I bled for 'causes.'"

But the one-time member of the liberal Americans for Democratic Action soon became disillusioned with his political associates, sensing communist infiltration in the groups of which he was a member.

Reagan grew up as a Democrat, reflecting his parents' partisan ties. In 1948 he supported Harry S Truman. Two years later he campaigned for Democrat Helen Gahagan Douglas in her Senate contest against Richard M. Nixon. But in 1952 and 1956 Reagan worked, still as a Democrat, for Dwight D. Eisenhower's presidential campaigns. Two years after he supported Nixon's 1960 presidential campaign, Reagan changed his party registration.

By that time Reagan had all but abandoned his movie career in favor of television. Reagan's position as the host for "GE Theatre" from 1954 until 1962 gave him a political forum. It was an opportunity for Reagan to develop his set speech that has been the main ingredient of his political diet ever since. In the early 1960s he crusaded for many right-wing causes, most of which were in line with his strong anti-communist attitude.

Following Reagan's "island of freedom" speech for Goldwater in 1964, several California businessmen approached Reagan, then the host of "Death Valley Days," with a suggestion he run for governor. In a state where parties have traditionally held little influence, Reagan easily was able to transform his image from that of a television personality into a successful political figure.

In the same way that Reagan was catapulted to the top of California's political hierarchy, the decline of party influence on the national level is one of the factors that has made Reagan a viable national figure. Like Democratic Gov. Brown in 1966, many Republican Party officials long have underestimated Reagan's appeal with the voters.

In his 1970 book *Reagan and Reality*, Brown said "We thought the notion was absurd" that he could be thrown out of office by the host of "Death Valley Days."

But in 1966 Reagan first defeated the moderate former mayor of San Francisco, George Christopher, by more than a two-to-one margin in the GOP primary. He then went on to clobber Brown with a plurality that had been surpassed in earlier California gubernatorial contests only by Republican Earl Warren in 1950. *(Election results, see p. 72.)*

Almost immediately Reagan assumed national political stature. In 1968, his name came up repeatedly as a possible presidential candidate. He made a few tentative campaign swings but didn't shift from his favorite son status to a full-fledged candidate until two days before the Republican convention balloting in Miami Beach. Reagan garnered 182 delegate votes, including 86 from California.

When Reagan's second term was ending in 1974, he spurned the pleas of some California Republicans to seek a third term. Instead he prepared for a more determined try for the presidency.

Reagan's Background

Profession: Actor.
Born: Feb. 6, 1911, Tampico, Ill.
Home: Pacific Palisades, Calif.
Religion: Christian Church.
Education: Eureka College, Eureka, Ill., B.A. 1932.
Office: California governor, 1967-75.
Military: Army Air Corps, 1942-46.
Family: Wife, Nancy Davis, married 1952; four children, including two by previous marriage to Jane Wyman.

Unlike his current bid for the White House, Reagan was the challenger for the nomination in 1976. He was the candidate who was forced to shake things up in order to attract attention. His surprise selection of a running mate, Pennsylvania Sen. Richard S. Schweiker, three weeks before the convention was just such a move. It was a scheme hatched by campaign manager Sears to attract delegates from the Northeast to Reagan's candidacy.

In the end neither the Schweiker gambit nor any later Reagan maneuverings on the convention floor could pry enough delegates from Ford. Reagan fell 60 votes short of becoming the first candidate since 1884 to wrest the nomination from an incumbent president.

Strategy

With Ford's announcement Oct. 19, 1979, that he would not be an active candidate in 1980, Reagan's status as the early, undisputed GOP front-runner was assured.

That role presents the Reagan campaign with a strategic problem that is diametrically opposite the one they faced in 1976. The quieter the GOP political scene is the better it is for Reagan's cautious 1980 pursuit of the presidency.

Reagan's advisers realize one failing in the 1976 election was that their candidate was considered too conservative by the party regulars.

Although Reagan's base always has been the party's right wing, he is making a clear attempt in his third bid for the presidency to attract the centrist element of the party.

Campaign staff shake-ups in 1979 have led observers to conclude that the 1980 Reagan campaign, under the careful guidance of strategist Sears, will avoid the shrill conservative rhetoric of past campaigns.

Although Sears was involved in the 1976 campaign, he is clearly aware of the differences between running as a challenger and campaigning as a front-runner. Three long-time aides — Lyn Nofziger, Mike Deaver and issues adviser Martin Anderson — were moved out of major roles in the early stages of the campaign. All three were closely associated with Reagan's image as a hard-line conservative. They were believed to be opposed to Sears' efforts to tone down Reagan's right-wing image.

Sears is trying hard to attract President Ford's supporters from 1976. The skillful and pragmatic manager believes that if Reagan can be made acceptable to them his position in November against a Democrat will be much stronger than if he wins the GOP nomination on the strength of only his conservative support.

When campaign chairman Paul Laxalt, a conservative senator from Nevada, announced the formation of Reagan's campaign committee in February 1979, he made special note of the members of Ford's administration who appeared on the 23-page list of those endorsing the former California governor.

The list also included 28 senators or representatives, which had grown to at least 36 by late 1979. When Reagan began his 1976 campaign, Laxalt was the only member of either chamber willing to support him.

Reagan's newly won support on Capitol Hill can be traced, in part, to his diligent work on behalf of GOP candidates during 1978. After the 1976 campaign, Reagan used a million-dollar surplus to begin Citizens for the Republic (CFTR), a political action committee dedicated to helping Reagan by helping other Republicans.

During the 1978 elections Reagan's group gave $615,385 to federal, state and local candidates and various party organizations. Reagan's contributions to candidates far exceeded efforts by other GOP presidential hopefuls who also established similar committees. Reagan's group gave to 234 candidates running for the House, 25 for the Senate, 19 for governor and 122 running for other offices ranging from lieutenant governor to county clerk.

Many of Reagan's contributions to House candidates were made in contests where the Republican had little chance of winning. But Reagan's interest in their races established valuable political IOUs that he hopes to cash in in 1980.

Reagan held off formally entering the campaign as long as possible. His delay in starting allowed him to continue to be paid for speaking engagements, produce his radio commentaries and write a syndicated newspaper column — his three major sources of income. Being unannounced also exempted him from the equal time provisions that apply to announced candidates.

Since he left the governor's mansion in 1974, Reagan's radio and newspaper work and speaking engagements, which average about $5,000 an appearance, have allowed him to live comfortably. From January 1978 through June 1979 Reagan earned $138,000 from his radio commentaries, which were carried by about 200 stations, and $30,000 from his newspaper column. His other income totaled $650,000 — primarily from speeches.

During his last campaign Reagan revealed his net worth to be $1.5 million. His main property holdings are the ranch in Santa Barbara, which he bought in 1974 for $526,000, and a home in fashionable Pacific Palisades near Los Angeles. He also holds stock in Continental Illinois Properties and several banking concerns.

As the Republican front-runner, the burden is on Reagan not to lose his lead. He is acutely aware of the fate that befell previous early front-runners, such as Democratic Sen. Edmund S. Muskie in 1972 and Republican George Romney in 1968.

To avoid potential criticism that he is holding back and ducking difficult contests, Reagan is forced to vie for delegates in all the primaries and caucus states. Other candidates can pick and choose and marshal their resources more selectively.

Reagan cannot afford to lose many states without seeing his position erode. "He can survive a loss here or there," said Nofziger, "but he can't survive two in a row."

Reagan's age is the major liability that his campaign must overcome. If he is elected he will turn 70 a few weeks after the inauguration. After less than four months in office he would be older than the nation's oldest president, Eisenhower, who was 70 at the end of his second term.

Reagan tries to make light of the issue by joking about his excellent physical condition. "Maybe I'll have to take my opponents on in arm-wrestling," he jests. The other part of the "age issue" strategy is to maintain a vigorous campaign schedule to demonstrate the candidate can handle the physical stress of a campaign and, therefore, of the presidency.

But aides agree that there is little that they can do to eliminate the problem. Sears commented "often you can get people to support you if they can't think of a reason not to." But, he notes, Reagan's age could serve as a "convenient excuse for people not to support you."

Other Candidates

Benjamin Fernandez

Republican presidential hopeful Benjamin Fernandez is used to playing the odds and winning.

The little-known California millionaire thinks he can parlay his personal determination and luck into the 1980 GOP presidential nomination.

Fernandez, the son of Mexican migrants, is the first Hispanic to run for the presidency. He has been campaigning hard for the nomination since last November.

But as a Mexican-American vying for the top spot in a party that traditionally has garnered its strongest support from middle-class white Americans, observers rate Fernandez as a clear long shot. Moreover, he is trying to build his base of support among the nation's 16 million Hispanics who generally have not been attracted to the kind of conservative positions he has taken on most issues.

Fernandez says he supports the free enterprise system and a balanced federal budget. He also would rearrange U.S. foreign policy priorities to stress Latin American countries, he says.

Fernandez is totally serious about his candidacy. Saying he hasn't "the slightest doubt" he will be president in 1981, Fernandez claims that his own rags-to-riches history will attract upwardly mobile Hispanics and other minorities to his campaign.

"I am the American dream personified, from a boxcar to the White House in one generation," he says.

Fernandez was born Feb. 25, 1925, in a converted boxcar in Kansas City, Kan. He worked his way through the University of Redlands in California where he received a B.A. in economics. In 1951 he went to work at the General Electric Company. While working there he received his M.B.A. degree from New York University. In 1960, he started his own management consulting firm in Los Angeles.

Fernandez is no newcomer to national politics. He was a co-chairman of the Committee to Re-elect the President in 1972 and headed the GOP's National Hispanic Assembly from 1975 to 1978.

Still, despite his party ties, Fernandez' long shot candidacy has made it difficult to raise money. David Miller, Fernandez' campaign manager, said the campaign has received about $140,000 in contributions by the end of 1979, far short of its original $7 million goal.

Fernandez has announced plans to compete in all the Republican primaries.

Harold Stassen

The old political warrior Harold Stassen is running for president again. This will be the seventh time he has sought the office.

The 1980 campaign is a far cry from the halcyon days of the 1940s when Stassen, a Republican, was the "boy wonder" of American politics and his future seemed to hold unlimited possibilities.

Stassen was elected governor of Minnesota at the age of 31, keynoted the 1940 Republican National Convention at the age of 33 and was the youngest delegate participating in the drafting of the United Nations Charter in 1945.

A major contender for the Republican presidential nomination in 1948 along with New York Gov. Thomas E. Dewey and Ohio Sen. Robert A. Taft, Stassen won four presidential primaries that year but lost the crucial Oregon primary to Dewey.

In 1948 Stassen moved his political base to Pennsylvania where he served as president of the University of Pennsylvania from 1948 to 1953. In 1952, he again entered the presidential lists but threw his support to Dwight D. Eisenhower at the Republican convention.

He served in top positions under President Eisenhower — in charge of the foreign aid program from 1953 to 1955 and as a special assistant to the president with Cabinet rank for disarmament questions from 1955 to 1958. In 1956, he tried to lead a movement to get Vice President Richard M. Nixon off the ticket but was unsuccessful.

Over the next 23 years, Stassen slowly became transformed into a standard political joke as he ran losing races for public office time after time. He lost bids for the Pennsylvania Republican gubernatorial nomination in 1958 and 1966 and for Philadelphia mayor in 1959. He has sought the Republican presidential nomination in every election since 1948 except when Republican Presidents Eisenhower and Nixon were seeking renomination (1956 and 1972).

Through all his political meanderings, Stassen has achieved something that very few perennial candidates manage — he has kept his dignity and his sense of humor. He still makes a good speech, urging a moderate Republican position and accusing the Carter administration of failing to stop inflation.

Stassen is a successful lawyer and is probably a millionaire. He has said that he is prepared to devote a substantial portion of his wealth to the 1980 presidential campaign.

Explanation of Vote Studies on Members of Congress

In an attempt to provide students of Congress with a meaningful but nonpartisan analysis of record voting, Congressional Quarterly conducts several annual studies. Following are the ground rules for the studies included in this book's chapters on members of Congress who are prospective presidential candidates in 1980.

Presidential Support and Opposition

CQ tries to determine what the President personally, as distinct from other administration officials, does and does not want in the way of legislative action by analyzing his messages to Congress, press conference remarks and other public statements and documents.

By the time an issue reaches a vote, it may differ from the original form on which the President expressed himself. In such cases, CQ analyzes the measure to determine whether, on balance, the features favored by the President outweigh those he opposed or vice versa. Only then is the vote classified.

Occasionally, important measures are so extensively amended on the floor that it is impossible to characterize final passage as a victory or defeat for the President.

Votes on motions to recommit, to reconsider or to table often are key tests that govern the legislative outcome. Such votes are necessarily included in the presidential support tabulations.

Generally, votes on passage of appropriation bills are not included in the tabulation, since it is rarely possible to determine the President's position on the overall revisions Congress almost invariably makes in the sums allowed. Votes on amendments to cut or increase specific funds requested in the President's budget, however, are included.

In tabulating the support or opposition scores of members on the selected presidential-issue votes, CQ counts only "yea" and "nay" votes on the ground that only these affect the outcome. Most failures to vote reflect absences because of illness or official business. Failures to vote lower both support and opposition scores equally.

All presidential-issue votes have equal statistical weight in the analysis.

Presidential support is determined by the position of the President at the time of a vote, even though that position may be different from an earlier position, or may have been reversed after the vote was taken.

Conservative Coalition

As used in this study, the term "conservative coalition" means a voting alliance of Republicans and southern Democrats against the northern Democrats in Congress. This meaning, rather than any philosophic definition of the "conservative" position, provides the basis for CQ's selection of coalition votes.

A conservative coalition vote is defined as any vote in the Senate or the House on which a majority of voting southern Democrats and a majority of voting Republicans oppose the stand taken by a majority of voting northern Democrats. Votes on which there is an even division within the ranks of voting northern Democrats, southern Democrats or Republicans are not included.

For the purposes of this study the southern states are Alabama, Arkansas, Florida, Georgia, Kentucky, Louisiana, Mississippi, North Carolina, Oklahoma, South Carolina, Tennessee, Texas and Virginia. The other 37 states are grouped as the North. The support score represents the percentage of conservative coalition votes on which a member votes "yea" or "nay" *in agreement* with the position of the conservative coalition. Failures to vote, even if a member announces a stand, lower the score.

The opposition score represents the percentage of conservative coalition votes on which a member votes "yea" or "nay" *in disagreement* with the position of the conservative coalition.

Party Unity

Party Unity Votes are defined as recorded votes in the Senate and House that split the parties, a majority of voting Democrats opposing a majority of voting Republicans. Votes on which either party divides evenly are excluded.

Party Unity Scores represent the percentage of party unity votes on which a member votes "yea" or "nay" *in agreement* with a majority of his party. Failure to vote, even if a member announced a stand, lowers the score.

Opposition-to-Party Scores represent the percentage of party unity votes on which a member votes "yea" or "nay" *in disagreement* with a majority of his party. A member's party unity and opposition-to-party scores add up to 100 percent only if a vote was cast on all party unity votes.

Voting Participation

Voting Participation is a compilation of the percentage of recorded votes on which a member voted "yea" or "nay." Failures to vote "yea" or "nay" lower scores — even if the member votes "present," enters a live pair, announces a stand in the *Congressional Record* or answers the CQ Poll. Only votes of "yea" or "nay" directly affect the outcome of a vote. Voting participation is the closest approach to an attendance record, but it is only an approximation. A member may be present and nevertheless decline to vote "yea" or "nay" — usually because a live pair has been formed with an absent member.

Appendix

**Candidates' Races for Governor,
House and Senate**..................... 71
1976 Presidential Primaries................ 73
Key Votes 1977.......................... 79
Key Votes 1978.......................... 89
Key Votes 1979.......................... 99
Selected Bibliography.................... 109
Index................................... 111

Candidates' House, Senate, Gubernatorial Races

The following list contains results of races by presidential candidates for governor, U.S. House of Representatives and U.S. Senate. The source for all returns before 1976 is Congressional Quarterly's *Guide to U.S. Elections;* 1976 returns are from Congressional Quarterly's *Guide to 1976 Elections;* 1978 returns are from Congressional Quarterly's *Politics in America.*

John B. Anderson

House (Ill.) - 16th District

1960	John B. Anderson (R)	115,693	62.3%
	Edwin M. Nelson (D)	69,944	37.7
1962	John B. Anderson (R)	78,594	66.9
	Walter S. Busky (D)	38,853	33.1
1964	John B. Anderson (R)	93,051	56.4
	Robert E. Brinkmeier (D)	71,992	43.6
1966	John B. Anderson (R)	89,990	73.0
	Robert M. Whiteford (D)	33,274	27.0
1968	John B. Anderson (R)	111,037	67.4
	Stan Major (D)	53,838	32.7
1970	John B. Anderson (R)	83,296	66.8
	John E. Devine Jr. (D)	41,459	33.2
1972	John B. Anderson (R)	129,640	71.9
	John E. Devine Jr. (D)	50,649	28.1
1974	John B. Anderson (R)	65,175	55.5
	Marshall Hungness (D)	33,724	28.7
	W. John Schade Jr. (IND)	18,580	15.8
1976	John B. Anderson (R)	114,324	67.9
	Stephen Eytalis (D)	54,002	32.1
1978	John B. Anderson (R)	76,752	65.4
	Ernest W. Dahlin (D)	40,471	34.5

Howard H. Baker

Senate (Tenn.)

Special Election

1964	Ross Bass (D)	568,905	52.1%
	Howard H. Baker Jr. (R)	517,330	47.4
1966	Howard H. Baker Jr. (R)	483,063	55.7
	Frank G. Clement (D)	383,843	44.3
1972	Howard H. Baker Jr. (R)	716,539	61.6
	Ray Blanton (D)	440,599	37.9
1978	Howard H. Baker Jr. (R)	642,644	55.5
	Jane Eskind (D)	466,228	40.3

Jerry Brown

Governor (Calif.)

1974	Edmund G. Brown Jr. (D)	3,131,648	50.2%
	Houston I. Flournoy (R)	2,952,954	47.3
1978	Edmund G. Brown Jr. (D)	3,878,812	56.0
	Evelle J. Younger (R)	2,526,534	36.5

George Bush

Senate (Texas)

1964	Ralph Yarborough (D)	1,463,958	56.2%
	George Bush (R)	1,134,337	43.6

House (Texas) - 7th District

1966	George Bush (R)	53,756	57.1%
	Frank Briscoe (D)	39,958	42.4
1968	George Bush (R)	110,455	100.0

Senate (Texas)

1970	Lloyd Bentsen (D)	1,193,814	53.5%
	George Bush (R)	1,036,045	46.4

Jimmy Carter

Governor (Ga.)

1970	Jimmy Carter (D)	620,419	59.3%
	Hal Suit (R)	424,983	40.6

President

1976	Jimmy Carter (D)	40,830,763	50.1%
	Gerald Ford (R)	39,147,793	48.0

John B. Connally

Governor (Texas)

1962	John B. Connally (D)	847,036	54.9%
	Jack Cox (R)	715,025	45.6
1964	John B. Connally (D)	1,877,793	73.8
	Jack Crichton (R)	661,675	26.0
1966	John B. Connally (D)	1,037,517	72.8
	T. E. Kennerly (R)	368,025	25.8

Philip M. Crane

House (Ill.) - 12th District*

Special Election

1969	Philip M. Crane (R)	68,418	58.4%
	Edward A. Warman (D)	48,759	41.6
1970	Philip M. Crane (R)	124,649	58.0
	Edward A. Warman (D)	90,364	42.0
1972	Philip M. Crane (R)	152,938	74.2
	E. L. Frank (D)	53,055	25.8
1974	Philip M. Crane (R)	70,731	61.1
	Betty C. Spence (D)	45,049	38.9
1976	Philip M. Crane (R)	151,899	72.8
	E. L. Frank (D)	56,644	27.2
1978	Philip M. Crane (R)	110,503	79.5
	Gilbert Bogen (D)	28,424	20.5

* Crane represented the 13th District in 1969 and 1970; he ran in the 12th District in 1972 as a result of redistricting.

71

Candidates' Races - 2

Robert Dole

Senate (Kan.)

1968	Bob Dole (R)	490,911	60.1%
	William I. Robinson (D)	315,911	38.7
1974	Bob Dole (R)	403,983	50.9
	William R. Roy (D)	390,451	49.1

Edward M. Kennedy

Senate (Mass.)

Special Election

1962	Edward M. Kennedy (D)	1,162,611	55.4%
	George C. Lodge (R)	877,669	41.9
1964	Edward M. Kennedy (D)	1,716,907	74.3
	Howard Whitmore Jr. (R)	587,663	25.4
1970	Edward M. Kennedy (D)	1,202,856	62.1
	Josiah A. Spaulding (R)	715,978	37.0
1976	Edward M. Kennedy (D)	1,726,657	69.3
	Michael Robertson (R)	722,641	29.0

Ronald Reagan

Governor (Calif.)

1966	Ronald Reagan (R)	3,742,913	57.6%
	Edmund G. (Pat) Brown (D)	2,749,174	42.3
1970	Ronald Reagan (R)	3,439,664	52.8
	Jess Unruh (D)	2,938,607	45.1

1976 Primaries*

Republican | Democratic

	Votes	%		Votes	%
February 24 New Hampshire					
Gerald R. Ford (Mich.)	55,156	49.4	Jimmy Carter (Ga.)	23,373	28.4
Ronald Reagan (Calif.)	53,569	48.0	Morris K. Udall (Ariz.)	18,710	22.7
Others[1]	2,949	2.6	Birch Bayh (Ind.)	12,510	15.2
			Fred R. Harris (Okla.)	8,863	10.8
			Sargent Shriver (Md.)	6,743	8.2
			Hubert H. Humphrey (Minn.)[1]	4,596	5.6
			Henry M. Jackson (Wash.)	1,857	2.3
			George C. Wallace (Ala.)[1]	1,061	1.3
			Ellen McCormack (N.Y.)	1,007	1.2
			Others	3,661	4.8
March 2 Massachusetts					
Ford	115,375	61.2	Jackson	164,393	22.3
Reagan	63,555	33.7	Udall	130,440	17.7
None of the names shown	6,000	3.2	Wallace	123,112	16.7
Others[1]	3,519	1.8	Carter	101,948	13.9
			Harris	55,701	7.6
			Shriver	53,252	7.2
			Bayh	34,963	4.8
			McCormack	25,772	3.5
			Milton J. Shapp (Pa.)	21,693	2.9
			None of the names shown	9,804	1.3
			Humphrey[1]	7,851	1.1
			Edward M. Kennedy (Mass.)[1]	1,623	0.2
			Lloyd Bentsen (Texas)	364	—
			Others	4,905	0.7
March 2 Vermont					
Ford	27,014	84.0	Carter	16,335	42.2
Reagan[1]	4,892	15.2	Shriver	10,699	27.6
Others[1]	251	—	Harris	4,893	12.6
			McCormack	3,324	8.6
			Others	3,463	9.0
March 9 Florida					
Ford	321,982	52.8	Carter	448,844	34.5
Reagan	287,837	47.2	Wallace	396,820	30.5
			Jackson	310,944	23.9
			None of the names shown	37,626	2.9
			Shapp	32,198	2.5
			Udall	27,235	2.1
			Bayh	8,750	.7
			McCormack	7,595	.6
			Shriver	7,084	.5
			Harris	5,397	.4
			Robert C. Byrd (W.Va.)	5,042	.4
			Frank Church (Idaho)	4,906	.4
			Others	7,889	.6
March 16 Illinois					
Ford	456,750	58.9	Carter	630,915	48.1
Reagan	311,295	40.1	Wallace	361,798	27.6
Lar Daly (Ill.)	7,582	1.0	Shriver	214,024	16.3
Others[1]	266	—	Harris	98,862	7.5
			Others[1]	6,315	.5

73

1976 Primaries - 2

	Republican			Democratic	
	Votes	%		Votes	%

March 23 North Carolina

	Votes	%		Votes	%
Reagan	101,468	52.4	Carter	324,437	53.6
Ford	88,897	45.9	Wallace	210,166	34.7
None of the names shown	3,362	1.7	Jackson	25,749	4.3
			None of the names shown	22,850	3.8
			Udall	14,032	2.3
			Harris	5,923	1.0
			Bentsen	1,675	.3

April Wisconsin

	Votes	%		Votes	%
Ford	326,869	55.2	Carter	271,220	36.6
Reagan	262,126	44.3	Udall	263,771	35.6
None of the names shown	2,234	.3	Wallace	92,460	12.5
Others[1]	583	—	Jackson	47,605	6.4
			McCormack	26,982	3.6
			Harris	8,185	1.1
			None of the names shown	7,154	1.0
			Shriver	5,097	.7
			Bentsen	1,730	.2
			Bayh	1,255	.2
			Shapp	596	.1
			Others[1]	14,473	2.0

April 27 Pennsylvania

	Votes	%		Votes	%
Ford	733,472	92.1	Carter	511,905	37.0
Reagan[1]	40,510	5.1	Jackson	340,340	24.6
Others[1]	22,678	2.8	Udall	259,166	18.7
			Wallace	155,902	11.3
			McCormack	38,800	2.8
			Shapp	32,947	2.4
			Bayh	15,320	1.1
			Harris	13,067	.9
			Humphrey[1]	12,563	.9
			Others	5,032	.3

May 4 District of Columbia

[2]

	Votes	%
Carter	10,521	31.6
Walter E. Fauntroy (unpledged delegates)	10,149	30.5
Udall	6,999	21.0
Walter E. Washington (unpledged delegates)	5,161	15.5
Harris	461	1.4

May 4 Georgia

	Votes	%		Votes	%
Reagan	128,671	68.3	Carter	419,272	83.4
Ford	59,801	31.7	Wallace	57,594	11.5
			Udall	9,755	1.9
			Byrd	3,628	.7
			Jackson	3,358	.7
			Church	2,477	.5
			Shriver	1,378	.3
			Bayh	824	.2
			Harris	699	.1
			McCormack	635	.1
			Bentsen	277	.1
			Shapp	181	—
			Others	2,393	.5

1976 Primaries - 3

	Republican			Democratic		
		Votes	%		Votes	%
May 4 Indiana						
	Reagan	323,779	51.3	Carter	417,480	68.0
	Ford	307,513	48.7	Wallace	93,121	15.2
				Jackson	72,080	11.7
				McCormack	31,708	5.2
May 11 Nebraska						
	Reagan	113,493	54.5	Church	67,297	38.5
	Ford	94,542	45.4	Carter	65,833	37.6
	Others	379	.1	Humphrey	12,685	7.2
				Kennedy	7,199	4.1
				McCormack	6,033	3.4
				Wallace	5,567	3.2
				Udall	4,688	2.7
				Jackson	2,642	1.5
				Harris	811	.5
				Bayh	407	.2
				Shriver	384	.2
				Others[1]	1,467	.8
May 11 West Virginia						
	Ford	88,386	56.8	Byrd	331,639	89.0
	Reagan	67,306	43.2	Wallace	40,938	11.0
May 18 Maryland						
	Ford	96,291	58.0	Edmund G. Brown Jr. (Calif.)	286,672	48.4
	Reagan	69,680	42.0	Carter	219,404	37.1
				Udall	32,790	5.5
				Wallace	24,176	4.1
				Jackson	13,956	2.4
				McCormack	7,907	1.3
				Harris	6,841	1.2
May 18 Michigan						
	Ford	690,180	64.9	Carter	307,559	43.4
	Reagan	364,052	34.3	Udall	305,134	43.1
	Unpledged delegates	8,473	.8	Wallace	49,204	6.9
	Others[1]	109	—	Unpledged delegates	15,853	2.2
				Jackson	10,332	1.5
				McCormack	7,623	1.1
				Shriver	5,738	.8
				Harris	4,081	.6
				Others[1]	3,142	.4
May 25 Arkansas						
	Reagan	20,628	63.4	Carter	314,306	62.6
	Ford	11,430	35.1	Wallace	83,005	16.5
	Unpledged delegates	483	1.5	Unpledged delegates	57,152	11.4
				Udall	37,783	7.5
				Jackson	9,554	1.9
May 25 Idaho						
	Reagan	66,743	74.3	Church	58,570	78.7
	Ford	22,323	24.9	Carter	8,818	11.9
	Unpledged delegates	727	.8	Humphrey	1,700	2.3
				Brown[1]	1,453	2.0
				Wallace	1,115	1.5
				Udall	981	1.3
				Unpledged delegates	964	1.3
				Jackson	485	.7
				Harris	319	.4

1976 Primaries - 4

Republican / Democratic

May 25   Kentucky

Republican	Votes	%	Democratic	Votes	%
Ford	67,976	50.9	Carter	181,690	59.4
Reagan	62,683	46.9	Wallace	51,540	16.8
Unpledged delegates	1,781	1.3	Udall	33,262	10.9
Others	1,088	.8	McCormack	17,061	5.6
			Unpledged delegates	11,962	3.9
			Jackson	8,186	2.7
			Others	2,305	.8

May 25   Nevada

Republican	Votes	%	Democratic	Votes	%
Reagan	31,637	66.3	Brown	39,671	52.7
Ford	13,747	28.8	Carter	17,567	23.3
None of the names shown	2,365	5.0	Church	6,778	9.0
			None of the names shown	4,603	6.1
			Wallace	2,490	3.3
			Udall	2,237	3.0
			Jackson	1,896	2.5

May 25   Oregon

Republican	Votes	%	Democratic	Votes	%
Ford	150,181	50.3	Church	145,394	33.6
Reagan	136,691	45.8	Carter	115,310	26.7
Others[1]	11,663	3.9	Brown[1]	106,812	24.7
			Humphrey	22,488	5.2
			Udall	11,747	2.7
			Kennedy	10,983	2.5
			Wallace	5,797	1.3
			Jackson	5,298	1.2
			McCormack	3,753	.9
			Harris	1,344	.3
			Bayh	743	.2
			Others[1]	2,963	.7

May 25   Tennessee

Republican	Votes	%	Democratic	Votes	%
Ford	120,685	49.8	Carter	259,243	77.6
Reagan	118,997	49.1	Wallace	36,495	10.9
Unpledged delegates	2,756	1.1	Udall	12,420	3.7
Others[1]	97	—	Church	8,026	2.4
			Unpledged delegates	6,148	1.8
			Jackson	5,672	1.7
			McCormack	1,782	.5
			Harris	1,628	.5
			Brown[1]	1,556	.5
			Shapp	507	.2
			Humphrey[1]	109	—
			Others[1]	492	.1

June 1   Montana

Republican	Votes	%	Democratic	Votes	%
Reagan	56,683	63.1	Church	63,448	59.4
Ford	31,100	34.6	Carter	26,329	24.6
None of the names shown	1,996	2.2	Udall	6,708	6.3
			None of the names shown	3,820	3.6
			Wallace	3,680	3.4
			Jackson	2,856	2.7

June 1   Rhode Island

Republican	Votes	%	Democratic	Votes	%
Ford	9,365	65.3	Unpledged delegates	19,035	31.5
Reagan	4,480	31.2	Carter	18,237	30.2
Unpledged delegates	507	3.5	Church	16,423	27.2
			Udall	2,543	4.2
			McCormack	2,468	4.1
			Jackson	756	1.3
			Wallace	507	.8
			Bayh	247	.4
			Shapp	132	.2

Republican

Democratic

	Votes	%		Votes	%
June 1 South Dakota					
Reagan	43,068	51.2	Carter	24,186	41.2
Ford	36,976	44.0	Udall	19,510	33.3
None of the names shown	4,033	4.8	None of the names shown	7,871	13.4
			McCormack	4,561	7.8
			Wallace	1,412	2.4
			Harris	573	1.0
June 8 California			Jackson	558	1.0
Reagan	1,604,836	65.5	Brown	2,013,210	59.0
Ford	845,655	34.5	Carter	697,092	20.4
Others[1]	20	—	Church	250,581	7.3
			Udall	171,501	5.0
			Wallace	102,292	3.0
			Unpledged delegates	78,595	2.3
			Jackson	38,634	1.1
			McCormack	29,242	.9
			Harris	16,920	.5
			Bayh	11,419	.3
			Others[1]	215	—
June 8 New Jersey					
Ford	242,122	100.00	Carter	210,655	58.4
			Church	49,034	13.6
			Jackson	31,820	8.8
			Wallace	31,183	8.6
			McCormack	21,774	6.0
			Others	16,373	4.5
June 8 Ohio					
Ford	516,111	55.2	Carter	593,130	52.3
Reagan	419,646	44.8	Udall	240,342	21.2
			Church	157,884	13.9
			Wallace	63,953	5.6
			Gertrude W. Donahey (unpledged delegates)	43,661	3.9
			Jackson	35,404	3.1
TOTALS					
Ford	5,529,899	53.3	Carter	6,235,609	38.8
Reagan	4,758,325	45.9	Brown	2,449,374	15.3
None of the names shown	19,990	0.2	Wallace	1,995,388	12.4
Unpledged delegates	14,727	0.1	Udall	1,611,754	10.0
Daly	7,582	0.1	Jackson	1,134,375	7.1
Others[3]	43,602	0.4	Church	830,818	5.2
			Byrd	340,309	2.1
	10,374,125		Shriver	304,399	1.9
			Unpledged delegates	248,680	1.5
			McCormack	238,027	1.5
			Harris	234,568	1.5
			None of the names shown	93,728	0.6
			Shapp	88,254	0.5
			Bayh	86,438	0.5
			Humphrey	61,992	0.4
			Kennedy	19,805	0.1
			Bentsen	4,046	—
			Others[4]	75,088	0.5
				16,052,652	

Footnotes, see p. 78.

Source: Richard M. Scammon, *America Votes 12* (Washington, D.C.: Congressional Quarterly Inc., 1977).

1976 Primaries - 6

*Delegate selection primaries were held in Alabama, New York and Texas. In **America Votes**, Scammon did not record vote totals if the primary was strictly for delegate selection and there was no presidential preference voting.

1. Write-in.
2. Ford unopposed. No primary held.
3. In addition to scattered write-in votes, "others" include Tommy Klein, who received 1,088 votes in Kentucky.
4. In addition to scattered write-in votes, "others" include Frank Ahern who received 1,487 votes in Georgia; Stanley Arnold, 371 votes in New Hampshire; Arthur O. Blessitt, 828 votes in New Hampshire and 7,889 in Georgia; Frank Bona, 135 votes in New Hampshire and 263 in Georgia; Billy Joe Clegg, 174 votes in New Hampshire; Abram Eisenman, 351 votes in Georgia; John S. Gonas, 2,288 votes in New Jersey; Jesse Gray, 3,574 votes in New Jersey; Robert L. Kelleher, 87 votes in New Hampshire, 1,603 in Massachusetts and 139 in Georgia; Rick Loewenherz, 49 votes in New Hampshire; Frank Lomento, 3,555 votes in New Jersey, Floyd L. Lunger, 3,935 votes in New Jersey; H. R. H. "Fifi" Rockefeller, 2,305 votes in Kentucky; George Roden, 153 votes in Georgia; Ray Rollinson, 3,021 votes in New Jersey; Terry Sanford, 53 votes in New Hampshire and 351 votes in Massachusetts; Bernard B. Schechter, 173 votes in New Hampshire.

1977 Key Votes

Ethics, Energy Top List Of Key Votes for 1977

After years of suffering under criticism of its behavior, Congress in 1977 responded by approving strong new codes of conduct for its members.

Votes related to ethical matters dominated Congressional Quarterly's annual selection of "key votes." *(Key vote definition, box, this page)*

Besides adopting the ethics codes, Congress began the process of writing the standards into law that applied throughout the federal government, including the judiciary.

The new requirements included sweeping financial disclosure, limits on conflicts of interest and provision for appointment of a temporary special prosecutor to investigate allegations of wrongdoing by top-level government officials. The Senate rolled all these provisions, and more, into a bill that the House had not acted on by the end of 1977.

That legislation, however, was based in part on the new ethics codes that both chambers adopted. Although those codes were approved by substantial margins, the new requirements provoked controversy and much unhappiness among members.

Important votes resulted. In the Senate, members decided not to kill a limit on the amount of money senators could earn outside their official jobs, even though many of them earned substantial sums from speeches and articles.

In the House, members voted against a move to knock out a ban on unofficial office accounts and a $5,000 increase in official office allowances. The accounts, usually secret, had long been criticized as slush funds that created potential conflicts of interest when the money came from special interest groups.

However, the two chambers were not so consistent on other reform proposals. The Senate reorganized its committee system after restricting the number of chairmanships a senator could hold. But the House refused even to formally debate a package of proposals that would have set a committee reform study in motion.

Energy

Of all the vote showdowns on President Carter's controversial energy program, three key votes illustrate best what happened.

A determined challenge to Carter's plan was mounted by House members favoring an end to federal regulation of natural gas prices. The House rejected an amendment to that effect, which if passed would have been a major defeat for Carter.

Later, just before House passage of the Carter plan virtually as proposed, Republicans led a charge to knock out Carter's proposed tax on crude oil, which the administration termed the "centerpiece" of its energy program. The attempt failed narrowly.

Proponents of ending federal regulation over natural gas pricing succeeded in the Senate, which voted 50-46 for deregulation.

Defense

Almost every session of Congress in recent years has had a fight over a controversial weapons system. This year's was on the $100-million-a-copy B-1 bomber promoted by the Nixon and Ford administrations, but ordered halted by President Carter.

Congress took several votes on whether to go along with the President's decision, but the session ended with the issue still unresolved.

Other important defense votes for Carter included the Senate's confirmation—despite the overwhelming opposition of the Armed Services Committee—of Paul C. Warnke to head the strategic arms limitation (SALT) negotiations with the Russians, Senate rejection of an effort in Congress to prohibit the Pentagon from developing a neutron bomb and congressional acceptance generally of Carter's defense spending levels for fiscal 1978.

Economy and Labor

Three key economic votes in 1977 involved tax issues, and two were major tests of the clout of organized labor.

The House rejected a Republican effort to scuttle President Carter's proposed $50 tax rebates in favor of a tax cut, but the closeness of the vote was a key factor in an administration decision to withdraw the rebate plan. After the withdrawal, Senate Republicans took up the fight for permanent tax cuts and lost in an April vote.

By the end of the year, the focus had shifted to a major tax increase, which was widely accepted as necessary to restore the Social Security system to financial health. The Senate narrowly defeated a Republican effort to maintain the traditional equality between employers and employees in Social Security contributions in favor of a Finance Committee plan to require higher contributions from employers. Later, a conference committee restored the principle of equal contributions.

Organized labor suffered a stinging defeat in March, when the House rejected its long-cherished goal of legalizing common-site picketing in the construction industry.

How Votes Were Selected

Congressional Quarterly each year selects a series of key votes on major issues.

Selection of Issues. An issue is judged by the extent it represents one or more of the following:
- A matter of major controversy.
- A test of presidential or political power.
- A decision of potentially great impact on the nation and lives of Americans.

Selection of Votes. For each series of related votes on an issue, only one key vote is ordinarily chosen. This vote is the Senate roll call, or House recorded vote, that in the opinion of Congressional Quarterly was important in determining the outcome.

In the descriptions of the key votes, the designation ND denotes northern Democrats and SD denotes southern Democrats.

But labor won a narrow victory in September, when the House rejected a proposal to create a lower minimum wage for teenagers.

Abortion

The use of taxpayers' money to pay for abortions was one of the most divisive matters before Congress in 1977. Opponents of abortion focused on the Medicaid program, which had financed between 250,000 and 300,000 such operations a year, and pushed for federal funding restrictions.

Congress in 1976 had enacted a provision barring federal funds for abortion except where the life of the mother was endangered. In 1977, however, the Senate held out for something less harsh, that would permit poor women to obtain Medicaid abortions in cases of rape, incest and for other medical reasons.

The House in June revived the abortion controversy by voting for a flat ban on federal funds for abortions—with no exceptions. Nearly five months later, after several fruitless efforts at compromise, the Senate voted to sharply narrow its list of exceptions. Though the House did not buy it then, the proposal laid the groundwork for a final agreement in December.

Senate Key Votes

1. **SENATE COMMITTEE CHAIRMANSHIPS.** The first major business of the Senate in 1977 was a major reorganization of the committee structure. Certainly the most far-reaching of the changes mandated by the reform resolution (S Res 4) were those that placed limits on the number of committees and subcommittees on which a senator could serve and which a senator could chair.

Under the existing Senate committee system, the average senator served on 18 committees and subcommittees and some served on far more. In the 94th Congress, for example, one senator chaired 10 committees and subcommittees and another senator served on 31 committees and subcommittees.

As S Res 4 came to the Senate floor, it specified that no senator could serve on more than 11 committees and subcommittees. No senator could chair more than four units.

When the resolution reached the floor Feb. 3, Sen. Dick Clark (D Iowa) won an important victory by persuading the Senate to reduce the maximum number of committees and subcommittees a senator could chair to three from four. The chairman of a full committee could chair only two subcommittees rather than three as under the version of S Res 4 approved by committee. A motion to table (kill) Clark's amendment was defeated 42-47. The change was seen as a major victory for younger members over the committee chairmen, all of whom opposed it. On the vote, Republicans backed Clark 13-21 while fellow Democrats opposed him by a narrow margin, 29-26 (ND 16-23; SD 13-3).

2. **WARNKE NOMINATION.** In the first test of support for President Carter's approach to a new strategic arms limitation (SALT) treaty with the Russians, the Senate March 9 confirmed Paul C. Warnke as chief U.S. SALT negotiator. But the 58-40 vote, which resulted from strong personal lobbying by the President, was less than the two-thirds majority that would be necessary for approval of a new SALT treaty itself.

Opponents of the Warnke nomination charged that he would be too "soft" in dealing with the Russians because he underestimated the precariousness of the U.S.-Soviet military balance. They insisted that the nominee did not understand the ruthlessness of Soviet policy or the pace of Soviet weapons developments. They warned that any apparent military superiority would confer political advantages on Moscow in bargaining with the United States or its allies.

Pro-Warnke senators countered that the U.S.-Soviet nuclear balance was relatively stable because a nuclear war would so devastate the Soviet Union that the Kremlin would not risk starting one in pursuit of any of its foreign policy goals.

Supporting Warnke were 10 Republicans and 48 Democrats, while 28 Republicans and 12 Democrats opposed him (ND 37-4; SD 11-8).

3. **SENATE INCOME LIMIT.** When the Senate early in 1977 considered a new code of ethics for members, the crucial debate revolved around a proposal to limit outside earned income to 15 per cent of a senator's salary, $8,625 at the existing salary of $57,500. However, the limit did not apply to unearned income such as dividends from stocks or bonds or to income from a family farm or business. As a result, the principal effect of the proposal was to limit the ability of senators to supplement their income by accepting fees for making speeches or appearances or writing articles.

The limitation stayed in the code passed by the Senate April 1 (S Res 110), but only after an attack led by Sen. Edmund S. Muskie (D Maine) failed. Muskie first sought to apply the limit to unearned income and lost. Then he proposed deleting the 15 per cent limit entirely from the code. Only 11 Democrats voted for the deletion while 49 (ND 8-33; SD 3-16) voted against it. Republicans, on the other hand, supported Muskie 24-13, providing a final tally of 35-62 against deletion.

Proponents of the limit argued that it was necessary to help Congress regain public confidence by eliminating the appearance of conflicts of interest. They said special interest groups often gave large speaking fees to senators. Muskie argued that full disclosure of income, as required by the new code, was enough protection because voters could judge whether senators had conflicts of interest. But in the end the basic reason Muskie lost was that Congress voted itself a $12,900 pay hike only weeks before the ethics code debate. The public uproar about the 29 per cent hike left most senators convinced they had to vote for a limit on outside earnings.

4. **SENATE FRANKING PRIVILEGE.** One of the provisions of the new code of ethics the Senate adopted April 1 prohibited a senator's use of the congressional frank—that is, free mailing privileges—less than 60 days before a primary or general election. Sen. Jesse Helms (R N.C.) sponsored an amendment to increase to 90 days from 60 days the time prior to a primary election and to 180 days from 60 days the time prior to a general election during which senators could not use the frank for mass mailings.

The issue was decided by one vote when the Senate March 29 voted 47-46 to table (kill) Helms' amendment. On the vote 12 Republicans joined 35 Democrats in voting to table, while 25 Republicans and 21 Democrats were opposed (ND 24-15; SD 11-6).

The franked mail issue has been a touchy subject for Congress since the self-proclaimed "citizens' lobby" Common Cause filed a lawsuit seeking to halt what the organization claims are abuses of the privilege. Common

Cause charged that the frank unfairly discriminates against challengers to incumbents because it allows incumbents to send taxpayer-financed mail to voters. The citizens' group supported its charge with extensive figures showing that the volume of franked mail in recent years increased dramatically in the months before an election. The lawsuit had not gone to trial as of the end of 1977.

5. INCOME TAX REDUCTION. Senate Republicans moved forward with their efforts to win enactment of a permanent tax reduction after President Carter on April 14 abruptly withdrew his proposal for $50 tax rebates and cash payments to stimulate the economy.

The major permanent tax cut proposal was sponsored by Jacob K. Javits (R N.Y.) and John C. Danforth (R Mo.). It would have lowered tax rates in income brackets below $20,000 by 4 to 14 per cent, at an estimated cost of $2.2-billion in lost revenues in fiscal 1977, $10.2-billion in fiscal 1978 and $7.9-billion in fiscal 1979.

Supporters said the cut was needed to bring down unemployment and sustain economic recovery. They also argued that it was necessary to counteract the effects of inflation, which had increased the tax burden of many Americans by pushing them into higher tax brackets.

The administration, still hoping to balance the budget by 1981 and to offer several new programs before then, decried the permanent cuts as potentially inflationary and likely to "mortgage away" future revenues needed for reforms in welfare, health care and taxation.

On April 27, the Javits-Danforth amendment to the economic stimulus legislation (HR 3477—PL 95-30) was rejected, 40-59, with only five Democrats and three Republicans defecting from party ranks: R 35-3; D 5-56 (ND 5-37; SD 0-19).

6. WHEAT PRICE SUPPORTS. How much the government should spend to bail out farmers whose crops cost more to produce than they could get at market was the crucial question of the 1977 farm bill (S 275—PL 95-113). Despite President Carter's campaign promise of farm aid pegged to production costs, he fought to hold down increases in support levels in accord with a second campaign pledge, to balance the federal budget.

Congressmen, mindful of mounting farm debt and upcoming 1978 elections, pushed for higher support levels, provoking repeated veto threats. A key element was the backing of urban-bloc members for higher price supports in return for long-sought changes in the food stamp program.

Attention focused on the bill's target price for wheat because producers were reeling under price drops caused by surpluses. Wheat prices fell to a summer low of $1.65 a bushel, while farmers said it cost them between $3 and $4 a bushel to bring the grain to market. Under the target price system established in 1973, the government paid farmers the difference between a low market price and the target price.

The President started low and under pressure raised his target price proposals, but not to a level that farmers and politically sensitive members of Congress thought they could live with. The Senate Agriculture Committee set the wheat target price for the 1977 crop at $2.90, well above the administration's $2.65 figure.

Senate Budget Committee Chairman Edmund S. Muskie (D Maine) agreed with the President on the budget-busting implications of higher support levels and on May 24 asked senators to drop the 1977 crop wheat target price to $2.65. By a close 46-50 vote (R 18-20; D 28-30; ND 20-20; SD 8-10), the Senate decided to stick with the higher support prices.

7. KOREA POLICY. Signaling President Carter that it neither supported nor opposed his Korean troop withdrawal proposals, the Senate June 16 approved language to the State Department authorization bill (HR 6689—PL 95-105) stating that U.S. policy should "continue to be arrived at by joint decision of the President and Congress." The provision also said that implementation of the President's phased troop withdrawal policy should be "carried out in regular consultation with Congress."

This language was adopted by the Senate 79-15: R 21-15; D 58-0 (ND 41-0; SD 17-0). Offered by Senate Majority Leader Robert C. Byrd (D W.Va.) as a face-saving alternative to an unpopular Foreign Relations Committee recommendation affirming congressional support for Carter's withdrawal plan, the amendment was designed to forestall a direct vote on another proposal to drop the committee language. Such a vote, Byrd and others feared, might have shown embarrassingly strong opposition to the Korean plan even if it failed.

8. CUBA POLICY. The Senate Foreign Relations Committee inserted into the State Department authorization bill (HR 6689—PL 95-105) a provision that would have exempted agricultural and medical supplies from the embargo on U.S. trade with Cuba. But the amendment's sponsor, George McGovern (D S.D.), withdrew the provision on the Senate floor June 16, in order, he said, to avoid "inflammatory debate" on U.S.-Cuba relations.

Nevertheless, Robert Dole (R Kan.) offered an amendment expressing the sense of Congress that there should be no diplomatic recognition of the Castro government or even partial lifting of the trade embargo until Cuba removed its troops from Africa and compensated the United States for all the property it previously had expropriated.

Majority Leader Robert C. Byrd (D W.Va.) moved to head off a possible negotiations-chilling, up-or-down vote on the proposal by offering a substitute amendment expressing the sense of Congress that talks with Cuba be conducted on a reciprocal basis and that Cuban actions in Africa be taken into account in such talks. That amendment carried, 54-37: R 5-28; D 49-9 (ND 41-0; SD 8-9).

9. WATERWAY USER FEES. An administration-backed bill (HR 5885) to end the 200-year-old policy of making the federal government pay for the construction and maintenance of the nation's inland waterways survived a key test in the Senate June 22.

By a 44-51 vote—Republicans, 16-21; Democrats, 28-30 (ND 15-25; SD 13-5)—the Senate rejected an amendment by Adlai E. Stevenson III (D Ill.) that would have replaced the bill's barge user charges with a Transportation Department study of the need for and impact of a user charge. The bill's proposed user charges would recover 50 per cent of the building costs of new navigational aids, and 100 per cent of the cost of operating the waterways.

The decision to move away from free navigation became almost inevitable when President Carter told Congress it would have to agree to a user fee if it wanted to authorize construction of a new Locks and Dam 26 on the Mississippi River.

The project replacing the outmoded facility was particularly popular with legislators from states that relied on the Mississippi to move goods to market, and, in a classic political tradeoff, the Senate voted for the user charge in order to win approval of a new locks and dam. The final form of the user fee was not settled in 1977.

10. FINANCIAL DISCLOSURE/WATERGATE. After approving new codes of ethics early in the year, both the Senate and the House began the process of writing the standards provided in the codes into statutory law.

This was necessary in part to strengthen enforcement of the standards by allowing imposition of criminal and civil penalties and in part to apply the financial disclosure requirements to candidates for Congress. The ethics codes that were made part of each house's internal rules provided only for normal congressional disciplinary actions, such as censure, and covered only incumbents, not their challengers in elections.

Beyond these reasons was the specter of the Watergate scandal and the promises of many congressional leaders, particularly of Democrats and of President Carter, to pass tough new laws to prevent similar wrongdoing by government officials in the future.

The task wasn't completed in 1977 but progress went more than halfway. The Senate on June 27, in one of its most lopsided votes on the ethics issue all year, voted 74-5 to pass a bill (S 555) that wrote into law the Senate's ethics code as well as a number of other Watergate-spawned provisions.

In addition to requiring full financial disclosure by some 20,000 top-level federal employees (including members of Congress, the President and Vice President and federal judges) in all three branches of government and by candidates for federal office, the bill provided for appointment of a temporary special prosecutor to investigate wrongdoing by the President and other key officials. The bill also established an Office of Government Crimes in the Justice Department and an Office of Congressional Legal Counsel. And it limited the freedom of important government officials to take jobs after leaving government with private firms with which their agency had dealings.

The Senate vote of 74-5 was indicative of the momentum that the "clean government" movement had acquired by mid-1977. All five voting against S 555 were Republicans: Curtis (Neb.); Schmitt (N.M.); Hayakawa (Calif.); Scott (Va.); Hansen (Wyo.). Fifty-one Democrats (ND 36-0; SD 15-0) voted in favor.

In the House, several companion bills were reported by the end of 1977 but none had come to the floor for action.

11. BREEDER REACTOR. President Carter's crusade to restrict the worldwide availability of plutonium—a byproduct of nuclear fission capable of being made into nuclear weapons—was dealt a severe blow July 11 when the Senate refused, 38-49, to scrap the Clinch River nuclear breeder reactor.

The Clinch River plant became a symbol of the struggle over the future of nuclear power in America. Carter April 7 announced a new policy aimed at curbing the availability of plutonium. The Clinch River plant, hailed by its defenders as the next generation of nuclear power plants, would use plutonium for fuel and would generate more of the poisonous substance than it used.

Carter asked Congress to authorize only $33-million for the Clinch River plant, just enough to shut it down. The Senate Committee on Energy and Natural Resources voted to include $75-million for the plant in a funding authorization bill (S 1811) for the Energy Research and Development Administration (ERDA).

An amendment by Sen. Dale Bumpers (D Ark.) to reduce Clinch River's funding to Carter's preferred amount of $33-million was the watershed Senate vote on the issue. Bumpers' amendment was rejected, 38-49: R 6-27; D 32-22 (ND 27-11; SD 5-11).

The Senate subsequently approved the bill with the $75-million funding authorization level for Clinch River and President Carter vetoed the bill Nov. 4. The ultimate fate of the Clinch River plant was left hanging at the close of Congress' first session because actual funding for the project was included in a supplemental appropriations bill (HR 9375) that had not been sent to Carter.

12. NEUTRON BOMB PRODUCTION. Senate concern over the Soviet military buildup in Europe was evident in the 38-58 vote by which the Senate July 13 refused to block production of a new nuclear weapon. The "enhanced radiation" warheads (which opponents labeled "neutron bombs") were designed to counter the large Soviet tank force by killing tank crews without causing widespread damage to the surrounding area.

Opponents of the new weapons warned that the new warheads for short-range missiles and artillery would foster the illusion that a nuclear war could be fought within limited, acceptable bounds. This belief would increase the risk that a nuclear war might break out, they said, and would inevitably escalate to a global scale.

Supporters of the radiation warheads insisted that because their use was more plausible, they would more likely deter any Russian attack in Europe. If Moscow concluded that the only U.S. nuclear weapons in NATO were so destructive that the alliance would shun their use for fear of the side-effects, they warned, Soviet probes would be more likely.

The 38-58 vote came on an amendment by Mark O. Hatfield (R Ore.) to the bill (HR 7553—PL 95-96) appropriating funds for the Energy Research and Development Administration (ERDA), which conducts research on nuclear weapons for the Pentagon: R 10-28; D 28-30 (ND 27-14; SD 1-16).

13. PUBLIC FINANCING OF CONGRESSIONAL RACES. A coalition of Republicans and southern Democrats combined to sustain a Senate filibuster and effectively kill President Carter's plan to finance congressional elections with public money. Failing three times to muster the needed support to invoke cloture, the bill's Senate sponsors gave up Aug. 2.

The bill (S 926) would have established spending ceilings in Senate general election contests while providing a combination of outright subsidies and matching grants to candidates.

Supporters claimed that public financing would curb the influence of special interests and give challengers, who are usually outspent by incumbents, a large financial base.

Opponents argued that it would have the opposite effect, with the spending ceilings protecting incumbents against effective challenges. The result, Republican leaders contended, would be permanent Democratic majorities in Congress.

After a week of debate the Senate began taking cloture votes July 29. On the first two votes, the bill's backers could come no closer than 11 votes of the required three-fifths majority (60 votes). On the third vote Aug. 2 they had hoped to come closer, but when the roll call showed them eight votes short, 52-46 (R 4-33; D 48-13), the Democratic leadership dropped the fight. A majority of southern Democrats (ND 42-1; SD 6-12) joined Republicans in blocking cloture.

14. NATURAL GAS DEREGULATION. Rejecting President Carter's position, the Senate Oct. 4 ended 14 days of highly dramatic fighting over natural gas pricing by voting 50-46 to end federal regulation over sales of new gas.

The vote on an amendment to S 2104 by Lloyd Bentsen (D Texas) and James B. Pearson (R Kan.) came the day after Majority Leader Robert C. Byrd (D W.Va.) teamed up with Vice President Walter F. Mondale to break a nine-day filibuster waged primarily by Howard M. Metzenbaum (D Ohio) and James Abourezk (D S.D.).

Natural gas pricing had been an energy policy battleground for 23 years. In 1975, the Senate had voted 50-41 to end federal regulation over natural gas.

A central portion of President Carter's proposed energy program called for continued federal price controls over natural gas, although at higher ceiling prices than before. Carter also sought to extend federal price regulation for the first time to cover new gas sales within states where gas is produced.

The Senate voted instead to back the Bentsen-Pearson proposal, which would end immediately federal regulation over new gas found onshore, subject to a two-year ceiling price of $2.48 per thousand cubic feet, and would end regulation of new gas found offshore after 1982.

The vote on the Bentsen-Pearson amendment was 50-46: R 34-3; D 16-43 (ND 5-35; SD 11-8).

15. ABORTION. The Senate voted Nov. 3 to sharply restrict its position on the use of federal funds for abortion, hoping to break a bitter deadlock over the issue and unsnarl appropriations for two major government departments. Though unsuccessful then, the action paved the way for a compromise with the House in December (H J Res 662—PL 95-205).

By a vote of 62-27, the Senate offered to permit federal funding of abortions only in cases of danger to the life of the mother, rape, incest and where pregnancy would cause a woman "severe and long-lasting physical health damage." Previously, the Senate had sought broader medical exceptions, making abortions available to mentally ill women, for example, and in cases of potential genetic damage. Most of the votes were by a margin of about 2 to 1. On the November vote, Democrats favored the modifications by a margin of 45-12 (ND 34-6; SD 11-6), while Republicans split 17-15.

After defeating other attempts at compromise, the House finally managed to rework the Nov. 3 proposal, requiring rape and incest victims to have promptly reported such offenses and demanding that at least two doctors certify cases of severe physical illness. At that point the Senate, with no hope of getting a more lenient provision, agreed.

16. SOCIAL SECURITY FINANCING. As it debated ways to rescue the financially troubled Social Security system, Congress in 1977 faced the task of choosing between various proposals for tax increases. Reflecting the effects of inflation, recession and sharp legislated increases in benefits, Social Security payments had outstripped revenues each year since 1975. Additional funding was sought to wipe out such shortfalls and help the program weather anticipated future strains.

With both houses determined to avoid proposals that financed Social Security even partly through income tax revenues, higher payroll taxes became the main alternative. There were still some choices left, however, and the Senate in November defeated a Republican move to rely largely on increases in payroll tax rates.

Sponsored by Carl T. Curtis (R Neb.), the amendment was a substitute for a Finance Committee plan that featured higher payroll taxes for employers than for employees—a controversial departure from the program's central principle of equal contributions by both.

When a move to table the amendment produced a tie Nov. 4, Vice President Mondale cast the deciding vote to kill the Curtis proposal 42-41: R 2-29; D 39-12 (ND 35-3; SD 4-9). It was the first time a Vice President had cast a tie-breaking vote since 1973.

The Senate plan for heavier employer taxes did not survive in conference however. The final Social Security bill (HR 9346—PL 95-216), approved in December, increased payroll taxes $227-billion over the next 10 years.

House Key Votes

1. HOUSE OFFICE ALLOWANCE BAN. The House early in 1977 passed a tough new ethics code, but only after much grumbling by members and a stiff lobbying effort by Speaker Thomas P. O'Neill Jr. (D Mass.), who made approval of the code the first and one of his most important commitments as new House Speaker.

The closest vote on the ethics package (H Res 287) came on a section that ended a long-established practice of unofficial office accounts. Office accounts, a sort of private bank account, were maintained by an estimated 140 House members, purportedly to help defray expenses not fully covered by official House allowances. But the accounts were not subject to any regulations. Members were not required to reveal the source or amounts of contributions. Money in the accounts could be used for any purpose.

The accounts became an issue in late 1976 when then-House Majority Whip John J. McFall (D Calif.) admitted having received a $4,000 secret contribution to his office account from a South Korean businessman who was the subject of a Justice Department investigation into allegations of influence peddling on Capitol Hill.

In addition to ending office accounts, the new ethics code also provided a $5,000 increase in official allowances for members, ostensibly to compensate for the loss of the accounts. Republicans charged that the increase was nothing more than a payoff to members to win support for ending the unofficial accounts. Democrats conceded as much.

The key vote on the issue came March 2 during debate on the ethics code when Rep. Bill Frenzel (R Minn.) moved to delete the section ending unofficial accounts and hiking official allowances by $5,000.

Frenzel favored ending the accounts but because of the parliamentary situation at the time had to seek to kill the entire section in order to block the $5,000 allowance increase. He lost 187-235. He was supported overwhelmingly by fellow Republicans, 126-15, but was simply out gunned by the huge Democratic majority in the House, 61-220 (ND 30-165; SD 31-55).

2. TAX REBATES. Worried by signs of a possible economic downturn and by persisting high unemployment, the new Carter administration made economic stimulus one of its first priorities in 1977.

The centerpiece of its stimulus plan was a proposal to provide $50 tax rebates or cash payments to most Americans, at a cost of $11.7-billion. Carter said rebates would provide the most "immediate" boost to the economy. He objected to permanent tax cuts on the grounds that they would take away his flexibility in pursuing the twin goals of balancing the budget by 1981 and proposing major new programs in areas such as welfare, tax reform and health care. Carter later dropped the tax rebate proposal.

The House Ways and Means Committee approved the Carter proposal, although it voted to limit rebates to families with incomes below $30,000. House Republicans, though, argued aggressively for a permanent tax reduction. Rep. Barber B. Conable Jr. (R N.Y.) said the rebate scheme "offers neither a sharp stimulative impact nor a permanent reduction upon which consumers can base long-term spending plans."

The key vote came when Conable proposed that the rebate bill (HR 3477—PL 95-30) be sent back to the committee with instructions that the individual rebates and payments be dropped in favor of tax reductions for the seven lowest tax brackets. That motion was defeated 194-219: R 140-1; D 54-218 (ND 15-171; SD 39-47). The narrow margin of House support was viewed as a key factor in Carter's subsequent decision to abandon the rebate plan.

3. COMMON-SITE PICKETING. On its first test of strength in the 95th Congress, organized labor suffered a stunning loss when the House in March narrowly defeated legislation (HR 4250) to legalize common-site picketing in the construction industry.

Sought by labor for more than 25 years, the controversial picketing rights would allow unions to protest the actions of a single contractor by setting a picket line around an entire building site, in hopes of shutting it down. The Supreme Court had ruled such practices illegal in 1951.

The March 23 vote to kill the bill threw labor's legislative plans into temporary disarray. While, as expected, Republicans and southerners provided the main source of opposition, presumed allies—especially among newly elected Democrats—deserted labor as well. Unions readily conceded they had done a poor job of selling the bill, especially compared with the concerted efforts of contractor and business groups in opposition. The bill was defeated by a 205-217 key vote: R 14-129; D 191-88 (ND 171-23; SD 20-65).

The common-site picketing defeat did not seriously jeopardize other labor priorities, however. After shaping up their lobbying operations, unions pushed effectively for jobs programs and higher minimum wages, and they overpowered business opponents in preliminary fights over wide-ranging revisions of collective bargaining laws.

4. DEFENSE SPENDING. Opponents of major cutbacks in defense spending appeared to maintain the political momentum they showed in the 94th Congress.

During his presidential campaign, President Carter had promised "savings" of $5-billion to $7-billion in the Pentagon budget. But after the election, he emphasized that the savings would be realized gradually from reductions in the rate at which annual defense spending would increase. Carter's $120.3-billion defense request was $2.8-billion lower than President Ford's, but more than $10-billion above the fiscal 1977 budget.

Congressional critics of the Pentagon had been on the defensive since the collapse of South Vietnam in 1975 because of mounting evidence of a Soviet military buildup. But the liberal majority of the House Budget Committee recommended allowing only $116.2-billion for defense in the first budget resolution (H Con Res 195). They argued that this would be consistent with the panel's general policy of limiting the amount by which any part of the budget could increase over the previous year's level.

Defense hard-liners concluded that it would be politically impossible to increase military programs above the level sought by Carter. But they rounded up a solid majority April 27 for an amendment by Omar Burleson (D Texas) to H Con Res 195 that restored the defense ceiling to the $120.3-billion Carter request.

The Burleson amendment was adopted 225-184: R 119-20; D 106-164 (ND 35-149; SD 71-15).

5. COMMUNITY DEVELOPMENT. One of the most divisive House floor fights in 1977 was a regional one over the formula to be used to allocate $3.5-billion to cities under the Community Development Block Grant program.

Under existing law, the money was doled out according to a needs formula based on population, amount of overcrowded housing and extent of poverty—factors that tended to favor growing cities in the South and West.

But in an effort to send funds to the nation's most ailing cities, most of them located in the Northeast and industrial Midwest, a new formula was devised (HR 6655—PL 95-128).

It was based on the amount of a city's housing built before 1940, the extent of poverty and growth lag—the extent to which a city's population had failed to grow at the average rate for all metropolitan cities since 1960. Those factors were more likely to reflect sick city problems such as deteriorating housing and a declining tax base. Cities could use whichever method gave them the most money.

But angry representatives from the Sunbelt denounced the new formula saying it would force their citizens to pay for the revitalization of cities such as Newark and Detroit.

On May 10 during House debate on the question, two California congressmen tried to remove the second formula and retain the existing distribution method. Their effort failed 149-261: R 45-89; D 104-172 (ND 32-156; SD 72-16).

But the vote broke down more on regional than on party lines. All but eight of the voting northeastern and midwestern members opted to retain the two formulas in the bill. But only 28 voting members from the West and South favored the two formulas.

6. AUTO EMISSIONS. Despite lobbying from the Carter administration that included personal calls from the President, the House May 26 voted 255-139 in favor of an amendment sought by the automobile industry that delayed reduction of automobile exhaust pollutants (HR 6161—PL 95-95). The amendment was cosponsored by John D. Dingell (D Mich.) and James T. Broyhill (R N.C.).

Most Republicans voted for the amendment (105-21), but Democrats were split fairly evenly, 150-118 (ND 81-104; SD 69-14).

Though the key vote for the Dingell-Broyhill amendment appeared to indicate a resounding defeat for Carter and environmentalists, a compromise supported by the administration had lost earlier by just 12 votes, 190-202.

The auto emissions amendment extended current standards to 1980, a year longer than had the House Commerce Committee, and also reduced the cleanup level required for CO and NOx, dropping the standards set in the 1970 Clean Air Act.

The Senate avoided a similar floor fight by adopting a compromise that extended HC standards through 1980, but retained for the 1980s the original law's goals for CO and NOx.

After much haggling, the House and Senate conferees kept for the 1980s the original CO and NOx goals, just what the Dingell-Broyhill amendment had sought to prevent.

7. LEGAL SERVICES. The House turned back an effort to impose more stringent limitations on the outside political activities of Legal Services Corporation attorneys than applied to state and federal employees under the Hatch Act. The Hatch Act prohibitions against participation in partisan political activities were contained in the original Legal Services Corporation Act of 1974.

The controversial Legal Services Corporation had been plagued since its creation with charges that it was used by "activist" attorneys as a base for partisan political activities, radical organizing and lobbying rather than serving the day-to-day needs of individual poor people. Conservatives sought to extend the prohibitions on corporation staff attorneys' partisan political activities to nonpartisan political activities—such as running for school and library board positions—as well as to participate in fund raising for political candidates.

The key vote on these new limitations came June 9 on an amendment to the Legal Services authorization bill (HR 6666—PL 95-222) offered by Rep. M. Caldwell Butler (R Va.). It was defeated 178-198: R 106-16; D 72-182 (ND 26-149; SD 46-33).

Opponents of the amendment argued successfully that corporation attorneys should be entitled to the same political rights as other government workers. The final version of the bill, extending the corporation for three years, maintained the Hatch Act restrictions.

8. WATER PROJECTS FUNDING. President Carter touched a sensitive nerve in Congress when he recommended April 18 that funding for 18 water projects be cut or reduced because they were wasteful, unsafe or environmentally unsound.

When the House failed by only 24 votes to approve an administration amendment to curb some of the projects, supporters of the cutback considered it a victory.

The key 194-218 vote against modifying 17 projects meant that the House would have trouble overriding a Carter veto, which would require a two-thirds majority.

The strongest opposition to the amendment, which was offered by Reps. Silvio O. Conte (R Mass.) and Butler Derrick (D S.C.), came from representatives of the Southwest, Southeast and West. Republicans split 65-74, as did Democrats, 129-144 (ND 111-78; SD 18-66).

The feeling of victory was short lived, however, because Carter eventually decided to accept a Senate compromise that reduced funding for only nine of the criticized projects (HR 7553—PL 95-96). House members who had supported the President said they felt betrayed by his compromise.

The administration then began a review of overall water resource policy, expected to be completed in February 1978, which would provide objective guidelines for the next round of project cutbacks.

9. ABORTION. By a margin of 201-155, the House June 17 voted to outlaw the use of federal funds to pay for abortions, beginning a painful fight that tied up fiscal 1978 appropriations for the Departments of Labor and Health, Education and Welfare (HEW) until December (HR 7555).

Sponsored by Henry J. Hyde (R Ill.), champion of the anti-abortion forces in Congress, the abortion rider contained no exceptions—even for women who might otherwise die in childbirth. More moderate language—exempting women whose lives were endangered—was enacted after much feuding in 1976, as part of the fiscal 1977 Labor-HEW bill. The restrictions aimed to curb abortions under the Medicaid program, which pays the health bills of the poor.

The June key vote, the first of several dozen votes taken on the abortion issue by both chambers in 1977, showed a majority of the House in favor of the hardest line possible. Republicans stood solidly with Hyde, voting 98-21 for the stringent position, while Democrats divided 103-134 against it (ND 65-97; SD 38-37).

The vote thus foreshadowed an uncompromising stance by the House, which forced the Senate—despite strong preferences for liberal exceptions for women with medical reasons for seeking abortions—to gradually give way and eventually agree to a bill more restrictive than it preferred.

10. NATURAL GAS PRICES. With Speaker Thomas P. O'Neill Jr. (D Mass.) leading the way, the House turned back the most vigorous challenge to President Carter's energy program Aug. 3 when it rejected, 199-227, a proposal to end federal regulation over sales of newly discovered natural gas.

Natural gas pricing, a policy battleground for 23 years, was the most hotly contested feature of Carter's omnibus energy program in 1977.

Carter proposed extending federal regulation to cover for the first time sales of new gas within states where it was produced. He also proposed changing the formula by which federal gas price ceilings were set. Instead of basing price ceilings on the costs of production plus a return on investment, Carter proposed tying gas prices to oil prices on a British thermal unit (Btu) equivalency basis. Under that scheme, the initial ceiling price for new gas would start at $1.75 per thousand cubic feet (mcf), up from the then current level of $1.46 per mcf. That new ceiling price would rise as oil prices rose.

The Carter plan was included in the omnibus bill (HR 8444) passed by the House Aug. 5, 244-177.

But the key vote on natural gas pricing came on an amendment to the bill sponsored by Clarence J. Brown (R Ohio), Robert (Bob) Krueger (D Texas) and Timothy E. Wirth (D Colo.). Their amendment would have ended federal price regulation over new natural gas found onshore, retroactive to April 20, 1977, and over new gas found offshore by April 20, 1982.

The House rejected the amendment, 199-227: R 127-17; D 72-210 (ND 25-169; SD 47-41).

11. CRUDE OIL TAX. A last-minute surprise Republican attempt to kill what the administration termed the "centerpiece" of President Carter's national energy plan was narrowly beaten Aug. 5 by a key vote of 203 to 219.

The main thrust of Carter's energy plan was to encourage Americans to conserve energy. A primary goal was to reduce imports of foreign oil. To serve both those interests, Carter's program aimed to induce Americans to conserve oil by driving up its cost to its real price on world markets instead of keeping prices artificially low through government price controls.

Rather than lift the controls, however, Carter proposed imposing a stiff tax on domestically produced oil which, over three years, would drive the market price of domestic oil to world levels. Under Carter's plan, the $39-billion that the tax was estimated to rake in by the end of fiscal 1982 would have been rebated to the public.

The crude oil tax was not allowed to be the subject of a straight up-or-down vote under the closed rule that the House leadership laid down to cover debate on the omnibus bill.

However, just before passage, Rep. William A. Steiger (R Wis.) moved to recommit the bill (HR 8444) to committee with instructions that it delete the crude oil tax.

The Steiger motion was defeated 203-219: R 137-3; D 66-216 (ND 16-178; SD 50-38).

12. B-1 BOMBER. After energetic lobbying by the House Democratic leadership, the House Sept. 8 backed President Carter's decision to cancel production of the B-1 bomber by a three-vote margin.

The Air Force had planned to buy a fleet of 244 B-1s at a cost of more than $100-million a copy. During his campaign, Carter had opposed the plane as wasteful and unnecessary, but after the election he became noncommittal about the project's future.

On June 30 he called for cancellation of the B-1, saying that its mission could more effectively be performed by the cruise missile. The House already had voted against cancellation of the $1.4-billion appropriation for B-1 production in the fiscal 1978 defense appropriations bill (HR 7933—PL 95-111). Soviet intransigence in U.S.-Soviet arms limitation talks fueled congressional skepticism about the Carter move.

But on Sept. 8 the House reversed its earlier position by a 202-199 key vote: R 33-103; D 169-96 (ND 145-32; SD 24-64).

13. YOUTH DIFFERENTIAL FOR MINIMUM WAGE. By a dramatic one-vote margin, the House Sept. 15 rejected a proposal to create a lower minimum wage for young workers. Though denounced by unions as unjust and exploitative, the idea of a youth "subminimum" had been gaining momentum, appealing to members of both parties as a possible answer to the staggering unemployment problems of teenagers. Otherwise, proponents argued, pending legislation to increase the minimum wage would increasingly price young people out of the job market.

In contrast to past fights on the issue, northern moderates headed the push for a youth subminimum on the House floor. During debate on the minimum wage bill (HR 3744—PL 95-151), Robert J. Cornell (D Wis.) offered an amendment to permit employers to pay workers aged 18 and younger 85 per cent of the minimum wage for the first six months on the job. With traditionally liberal members joining Republicans and southern conservatives on the issue, labor feared the Cornell amendment would prove unbeatable, but it wasn't.

Though the proposal would have failed on a tie vote as well, House Speaker Thomas P. O'Neill Jr. (D Mass.) cast the final vote against the amendment, for a total key vote of 210-211: R 130-12; D 80-199 (ND 33-156; SD 47-43).

14. HUMAN RIGHTS. In a compromise between the Carter administration and Congress, the fiscal 1978 foreign aid appropriations bill (HR 7797—PL 95-148) contained language directing U.S. officials at international banks to "oppose and vote against" loans for Vietnam and six other nations with poor human rights records.

The House had voted June 23 to prohibit the World Bank and other lending facilities to use U.S. funds for assisting Cuba, Laos, Mozambique, Cambodia, Angola and Uganda in addition to Vietnam. But the Senate and President Carter refused to accept this restriction after the banks warned that they could not accept contributions with political strings attached. The conference report on the appropriations bill then was sent to the floor of each chamber with the provision left in disagreement.

Following compromise negotiations between the President and congressional leaders, where it was agreed that the U.S. representatives must "oppose and vote against" loans to the seven countries, the House Oct. 12, by a 273-126 key vote, recommitted the conference report for stitching in the new language. The recommittal action split Republicans, 48-89, but was supported by most Democrats, 225-37 (ND 166-13; SD 59-24).

15. HOUSE OBEY REFORMS. The House in 1977 won considerable praise from longtime reform advocates for passage of a tough new ethics code, but late in the year it choked on a new package of reforms (H Res 766) drawn up by the Commission on Administrative Review headed by Rep. David R. Obey (D Wis.). The package never got to a formal vote when the House Oct. 12 rejected a modified closed rule for floor action on H Res 766. Without a rule setting forth parliamentary ground rules for debate the proposals could not be brought up for floor action.

Democrats, disgruntled either with portions of the package or the limited number of amendments allowed, joined a unanimous Republican bloc to defeat the rule 160-252: R 0-139; D 160-113 (ND 131-54; SD 29-59).

Democratic leaders conceded they had lost by pushing a package that had enough controversial proposals to alienate a huge majority in the House. One part called for appointment of a committee to suggest committee reforms, an idea that could threaten jurisdictions of powerful committee chairmen. Another provided for a grievance panel to hear discrimination complaints from House employees. Other parts called for naming a professional administrator to handle housekeeping duties and an auditor to check the books, and a new $12,000 allowance for each member for computer services.

Anticipating controversy on the package, Obey sought and got a rule allowing only a handful of amendments. Republicans, critical of the computer allowance cost, the lack of total independence for the auditor and other provisions, called it a "gag rule" that would prevent them from offering "true reform" amendments.

16. OIL CARGO PREFERENCE. A decade-long effort by maritime interests to win enactment of legislation giving U.S. built and operated tankers a certain percentage of all oil imported into the United States was rejected by a surprisingly wide margin Oct. 19.

The bill's backers—maritime unions and shipping interests—conducted an expensive lobbying campaign, including a $1-million newspaper and television promotion effort. Opposing them were the U.S. Chamber of Commerce, Ralph Nader's Congress Watch, several oil companies, environmental and farm groups and Common Cause.

Also contributing to the 165-257 defeat of the bill (HR 1037) was a split within the Carter administration, charges by Republicans that the bill represented a political payoff for contributions by maritime unions and shipping interests to Carter's campaign in 1976 and reluctance by first- and second-term members to support the bill because of the negative publicity it received. Only 17 Republicans voted for the bill, while a large number of liberal Democrats opposed it: R 17-125; D 148-132 (ND 105-86; SD 43-46).

	1 2 3 4 5 6 7 8 9 10 11 12 13 14 15 16
KANSAS Dole (R)	N N Y N Y N N N N Y N N N Y N N
MASSACHUSETTS Kennedy (D)	N Y N Y N N Y Y N Y Y Y Y N Y Y
TENNESSEE Baker (R)	N N N N Y N Y ? N Y N N N Y Y N

Y - Yea
N - Nay
? - Did not vote or otherwise make a position known.

1. S Res 4. Senate Reorganization. Stevenson, D-Ill., motion to table (kill) the Clark, D-Iowa, amendment to provide 1) that a chairman of a major committee may serve as chairman of only one subcommittee on his major committees and as the chairman of one minor committee subcommittee and 2) that a chairman of a minor committee may not serve as a subcommittee chairman on his minor committee and may serve as a chairman of one subcommittee on each of his two major committees, and 3) to allow any other senator to serve as chairman of only one subcommittee on each of the three committees on which he serves. All limitations were to become effective with the 96th Congress. Tabling motion rejected 42-47: R 13-21; D 29-26 (ND 16-23; SD 13-3), Feb. 3, 1977. (Clark amendment subsequently was adopted by voice vote.)

2. Warnke SALT Nomination. Confirmation of President Carter's nomination of Paul C. Warnke of the District of Columbia to head the U.S. delegation to the Strategic Arms Limitation (SALT) talks with the Soviet Union. Confirmed 58-40: R 10-28; D 48-12 (ND 37-4; SD 11-8), March 9, 1977. A "yea" was a vote supporting the president's position.

3. S Res 110. Senate Ethics Code. Muskie, D-Maine, amendment to delete from the bill a provision placing a limit on outside earned income equal to 15 percent of a senator's annual salary, and to retain the existing limit of $25,000 on the amount of honoraria a senator could earn in a year. Rejected 35-62: R 24-13; D 11-49 (ND 8-33; SD 3-16), March 22, 1977.

4. S Res 110. Senate Ethics Code. Nelson, D-Wis., motion to table, and thus kill, the Helms, R-N.C., amendment to increase to 90 days, from 60 days, the amount of time prior to a primary election and to 180 days, from 60 days, the amount of time prior to a general election during which senators could not use the frank for mass mailings. Motion to table agreed to 47-46: R 12-25; D 35-21 (ND 24-15; SD 11-6), March 29, 1977.

5. HR 3477. Economic Stimulus Tax Cuts. Danforth, R-Mo., and Javits, R-N.Y., amendment to permanently reduce income tax rates in the income brackets below $20,000 by 4 to 14 percent. Rejected 40-59: R 35-3; D 5-56 (ND 5-37; SD 0-19), April 27, 1977. A "nay" was a vote supporting the president's position.

6. S 275. 1977 Farm-Food Bill. Muskie, D-Maine, amendment to reduce the target price for the 1977 wheat crop to $2.65 a bushel from the $2.90 in the bill. Rejected 46-50: R 18-20; D 28-30 (ND 20-20; SD 8-10), May 24, 1977. A "yea" was a vote supporting the president's position.

7. HR 6689. State Department Authorization. Byrd, D-W.Va., amendment to state that U.S. policy toward South Korea should be arrived at by joint decision of the president and Congress. Adopted 79-15: R 21-15; D 58-0 (ND 41-0; SD 17-0), June 16, 1977.

8. HR 6689. State Department Authorization. Byrd, D-W.Va., substitute amendment, to the Dole amendment, expressing the sense of Congress that negotiations with Cuba be carried out on a reciprocal basis, that the vital concerns of the United States concerning the basic rights and interests of U.S. citizens be protected and that the use of Cuban military forces outside Cuba be taken into account in any such negotiations. Adopted 54-37: R 5-28; D 49-9 (ND 41-0; SD 8-9), June 16, 1977.

9. HR 5885. Water Resources, User Fees. Stevenson, D-Ill., substitute amendment, to the Domenici, R-N.M., amendment, to authorize construction of replacement for the old Locks and Dam 26 at Alton, Ill., by the Army Corps of Engineers and to order an 18-month Transportation Department study of waterway user charges. Rejected 44-51: R 16-21; D 28-30 (ND 15-25; SD 13-5), June 22, 1977.

10. S 555. Public Officials' Integrity Act. Passage of the bill to establish a formal mechanism for appointment of a special prosecutor to investigate alleged crimes by high-level federal officials, to provide for full financial disclosure by high-level federal officials and to set up an Office of Government Crimes in the Justice Department to investigate crimes by public employees at all levels. Passed 74-5: R 23-5; D 51-0 (ND 36-0; SD 15-0), June 27, 1977.

11. S 1811. ERDA Authorization — Civilian Nuclear Energy Applications. Bumpers, D-Ark., substitute amendment, to the Church, D-Idaho, amendment, to limit spending on the Clinch River breeder reactor project to $33 million in fiscal year 1978 for the purpose of terminating the project. Rejected 38-49: R 6-27; D 32-22 (ND 27-11; SD 5-11), July 11, 1977. A "yea" was a vote supporting the president's position. (The Church amendment to reduce the Clinch River authorization to $75 million from the $150 million authorized in the bill was subsequently adopted by voice vote.)

12. HR 7553. Public Works-ERDA Appropriations, Fiscal 1978. Hatfield, R-Ore., amendment to prohibit production of any enhanced radiation weapon (neutron bomb). Rejected 38-58: R 10-28; D 28-30 (ND 27-14; SD 1-16), July 13, 1977.

13. S 926. Campaign Financing. Byrd, D-W.Va., motion to invoke cloture and end debate on the bill to permit use of federal tax revenues to help pay for Senate general election campaigns. Motion rejected 52-46: R 4-33; D 48-13 (ND 42-1; SD 6-12), Aug. 2, 1977. A three-fifths majority vote of the total Senate membership (60) is necessary to invoke cloture. A "yea" was a vote supporting the president's position.

14. S 2104. Natural Gas Pricing. Adoption of the Pearson, R-Kan./Bentsen, D-Texas, amendment to end federal price controls for natural gas found onshore, retroactive to Jan. 1, 1977, and cease regulation of new offshore gas after Dec. 31, 1982, but to impose a price limit equal to the price of imported No. 2 heating oil for two years and impose an incremental pricing provision to protect homeowners, schools and hospitals by allocating lower-cost old gas for their use. Adopted 50-46: R 34-3; D 16-43 (ND 5-35; SD 11-8), Oct. 4, 1977. A "nay" was a vote supporting the president's position.

15. HR 7555. Labor-HEW Appropriations, Fiscal 1978. Brooke, R-Mass., motion to concur in a House amendment relating to abortion with an amendment that modified the previously adopted Senate position to require "severe 'and' long-lasting physical health damage" as a condition for qualifying for a federally funded abortion. Motion agreed to 62-27: R 17-15; D 45-12 (ND 34-6; SD 11-6), Nov. 3, 1977.

16. HR 9346. Social Security Financing. Nelson, D-Wis., motion to table, and thus kill, the Curtis, R-Neb., amendment to raise the Social Security tax rate above the levels recommended by the Senate Finance Committee and to increase the wage base equally for employers and employees at the levels recommended by the committee for employees (the committee proposal raised the wage base for employers to $75,000 as of 1985 and for employees to $33,900 as of 1987). Motion to table agreed to 42-41: R 2-29; D 39-12 (ND 35-3; SD 4-9), Nov. 4, 1977 (with Vice President Mondale casting a "yea" vote to break the 41-41 tie).

1977 Key Votes - 10

	1 2 3 4 5 6 7 8 9 10 11 12 13 14 15 16
ILLINOIS	
12 Crane (R)	Y Y N Y N Y✔ N Y Y Y N Y N N N
16 Anderson (R)	Y Y N N N Y N Y X Y Y Y Y Y N N

Y - Yea
N - Nay
X - Paired against
✔ - Paired for
? - Did not vote or otherwise make a position known.

1. H Res 287. House Ethics Code. Frenzel, R-Minn., amendment to delete from the resolution the section banning members from maintaining private unofficial office accounts and to increase by $5,000 the amount available to each member for official expenses. Rejected 187-235: R 126-15; D 61-220 (ND 30-165; SD 31-55), March 2, 1977.

2. HR 3477. Stimulus Tax Cuts. Conable, R-N.Y., motion to recommit the bill to the Ways and Means Committee with instructions to report it back with a substitute amendment reducing the tax rates in the lowest seven tax brackets rather than providing a $50 tax rebate and $50 payments to federal assistance recipients. Rejected 194-219: R 140-1; D 54-218 (ND 15-171; SD 39-47), March 8, 1977.

3. HR 4250. Common-Site Picketing. Passage of the bill to permit a labor union with a grievance with one contractor to picket all contractors on the same construction site and to establish a construction industry collective bargaining committee. Rejected 205-217: R 14-129; D 191-88 (ND 171-23; SD 20-65), March 23, 1977.

4. H Con Res 195. Fiscal 1978 Budget Targets. Burleson, D-Texas, substitute amendment to the Pike, D-N.Y., amendment to increase fiscal 1978 budget authority by $4.1 billion and outlays by $2.3 billion to bring spending for national defense to the levels requested by the president. Adopted 225-184: R 119-20; D 106-164 (ND 35-149; SD 71-15), April 27, 1977. A "yea" was a vote supporting the President's position.

5. HR 6655. Housing and Community Development Programs. Hannaford, D-Calif., amendment to delete from the bill a new alternative formula for allocation of community development block grant funds. Rejected 149-261: R 45-89; D 104-172 (ND 32-156; SD 72-16), May 10, 1977.

6. HR 6161. Clean Air Amendments. Dingell, D-Mich., substitute for Title II to delay and relax automobile emissions standards, to reduce the warranties for emissions control devices, and make other changes in existing law regarding mobile sources of air pollution. Adopted 255-139: R 105-21; D 150-118 (ND 81-104; SD 69-14), May 26, 1977.

7. HR 6666. Legal Services Corporation. Butler, R-Va., amendment to prohibit legal services attorneys from taking active part in either partisan or non-partisan political activities. Rejected 178-198: R 106-16; D 72-182 (ND 26-149; SD 46-33), June 9, 1977.

8. HR 7553. Public Works-ERDA Appropriations, Fiscal 1978. Conte, R-Mass./Derrick, D-S.C., amendment to delete funding for 16 water projects and reduce funding for one more project, but to retain the total appropriations amount in the bill. Rejected 194-218: R 65-74; D 129-144 (ND 111-78; SD 18-66), June 14, 1977. A "yea" was a vote supporting the president's position.

9. HR 7555. Labor-HEW Appropriations, Fiscal 1978. Hyde, R-Ill., amendment to prohibit the use of federal funds to finance or encourage abortions. Adopted 201-155: R 98-21; D 103-134 (ND 65-97; SD 38-37), June 17, 1977.

10. HR 8444. National Energy Policy. Brown, R-Ohio, amendment to end federal controls on the price of new onshore natural gas retroactive to April 20, 1977, and on new offshore natural gas beginning April 20, 1982, and to extend the Emergency Natural Gas Act of 1977 for three years. Rejected 199-227: R 127-17; D 72-210 (ND 25-169; SD 47-41), Aug. 3, 1977. A "nay" was a vote supporting the president's position.

11. HR 8444. National Energy Policy. Steiger, R-Wis., motion to recommit the bill to the ad hoc committee on energy with instructions to report it with an amendment deleting the proposed crude oil equalization tax. Motion to recommit rejected 203-219: R 137-3; D 66-216 (ND 16-178; SD 50-38), Aug. 5, 1977. A "nay" was a vote supporting the president's position.

12. HR 7933. Defense Department Appropriations, Fiscal 1978. Addabbo, D-N.Y., amendment, to the Mahon, D-Texas, motion, to recede and concur with the Senate amendment to delete $1.4 billion for the production of five B-1 bombers. (The Mahon motion would have insisted on the original House position appropriating the B-1 funds.) Adopted 202-199: R 33-103; D 169-96 (ND 145-32: SD 24-64), Sept. 8, 1977. A "yea" was a vote supporting the president's position.

13. HR 3744. Minimum Wage. Cornell, D-Wis., amendment to permit employers to pay only 85 percent of the minimum wage to young workers under age 18 during their first six months on a job. Rejected 210-211: R 130-12; D 80-199 (ND 33-156; SD 47-43), Sept. 15, 1977. A "nay" was a vote supporting the president's position.

14. HR 7797. Foreign Aid Appropriations, Fiscal 1978. Cederberg, R-Mich., motion to recommit to House-Senate conferees the conference report on the bill appropriating $6.8 billion for foreign aid programs for fiscal 1978. Motion agreed to 273-126: R 48-89; D 225-37 (ND 166-13; SD 59-24), Oct. 12, 1977.

15. H Res 766. Obey Commission House Reforms. Adoption of the rule (H Res 819) providing for House floor consideration of H Res 766, proposing numerous changes in House rules and procedures dealing with employee discrimination in Congress, committee reform, congressional travel and perquisites and House administration. Rejected 160-252: R 0-139; D 160-113 (ND 131-54; SD 29-59), Oct. 12, 1977. (Rejection of the rule prevented the House from debating the reforms on their merits.)

16. HR 1037. Cargo Preference. Passage of the bill to guarantee U.S. flag ships a 9.5 percent share of the country's oil imports. Rejected 165-257: R 17-125; D 148-132 (ND 105-86; SD 43-46), Oct. 19, 1977.

1978 Key Votes

Foreign Policy, Economics, Defense Top 1978 Key Votes

Foreign policy, defense and economic issues dominated key congressional votes during the 1978 session.

Domestic social issues played a small part in the key votes selected by Congressional Quarterly. This reflected the nature of the session, and of the entire 95th Congress.

Limited by a shortage of funds and restrained by a public more concerned about inflation than new government initiatives, Congress and President Carter made little effort to enact broad new social programs.

President Carter, like presidents before him beset by lack of a strong domestic base and lagging in popular acclaim, put much emphasis on foreign policy issues, and that produced a number of key votes.

Economy and Labor

In an election year dominated by controversy over government spending, several key votes involved fiscal policy issues.

In May, House Democrats narrowly defeated a Republican substitute for the first fiscal 1979 budget resolution that called for curbs on federal spending and a larger tax cut than the Carter administration and the Democratic majority had proposed.

A month later, shortly after California voters approved a state constitutional amendment slashing property taxes, the House voted the first of a series of across-the-board cuts in federal spending by approving a 2 percent cut in the appropriations bill for the Labor and Health, Education and Welfare departments. Similar cuts were offered to several other appropriations bills, but most were dropped in conference.

Riding the crest of a middle-class taxpayers' revolt, Congress enacted a tax bill that differed sharply from those of recent years by skewing the tax cuts much more toward the upper end of the income scale. An eleventh-hour liberal effort to provide larger tax cuts for persons earning less than $50,000 failed in the House. Although the Senate approved a proposal to tilt the tax cuts toward persons earning between $10,000 and $30,000, most of the extra cuts were dropped in conference.

On issues of particular interest to organized labor, the House in March narrowly rejected an effort to attach a specific anti-inflation goal to the Humphrey-Hawkins full employment bill, but an inflation target was later added to the measure in the Senate. In a bitter defeat for labor, the Senate failed by two votes to halt a filibuster against the labor law "reform" bill, thus dooming organized labor's No. 1 legislative priority.

Defense

The 1978 session of Congress appeared to be more content than many in recent years with the administration's defense budget. All attempts during the year to significantly alter — either up or down — the spending level for defense recommended by the White House were rejected handily.

Attempts in the Senate to make changes in the defense category of the annual congressional budget resolution were turned back in April, and the fiscal 1979 defense procurement and appropriations bills remained immune to the budget-cutting fever that swept Congress.

Amendments to make across-the-board cuts in defense as well as to cancel some expensive weapons systems sought by the Pentagon failed in both houses.

Carter also succeeded in making his own imprint on defense policy. Congress backed him in his refusal to continue the B-1 bomber project or add another $2 billion nuclear aircraft carrier to the Navy fleet. On the latter issue, Carter had to veto the defense authorization bill to back up his intention to set his own priorities for national security.

Foreign Affairs

President Carter had remarkably good success in Congress with foreign policy issues in 1978. He won the bulk of what he wanted.

The tone was set early in the year when the Senate consented to the ratification of the two Panama Canal treaties that will end U.S. control of the canal by the end of the century. Then Carter persuaded Congress to let him sell sophisticated jet fighter planes to Saudi Arabia, against the vigorous opposition of the politically potent coalition of groups supporting Israel.

Carter also got Congress to lift the arms sale embargo on Turkey — an embargo the administration argued was hurting relations with a key NATO ally.

Another victory, not entirely of the administration's doing, was won when Congress refused to lift economic sanctions against Rhodesia immediately. There was considerable sentiment, particularly among congressional conser-

---

How Votes Were Selected

Congressional Quarterly each year selects a series of key votes on major issues.

Selection of Issues. An issue is judged by the extent it represents one or more of the following:
- A matter of major controversy.
- A test of presidential or political power.
- A decision of potentially great impact on the nation and lives of Americans.

Selection of Votes. For each series of related votes on an issue, only one key vote is ordinarily chosen. This vote is the Senate roll call, or House recorded vote, that in the opinion of Congressional Quarterly was important in determining the outcome.

In the descriptions of the key votes, the designation ND denotes northern Democrats and SD denotes southern Democrats.

vatives, to lift the ban quickly to aid the troubled white minority government of Rhodesia. This was prevented when a more middle-of-the-road provision on sanctions was approved.

Senate Key Votes

1. NATURAL GAS PRICING. Months after House and Senate conferees took up two vastly different versions of natural gas pricing legislation, they narrowly approved a complicated compromise (HR 5289). The stalemate, broken in May 1978, had held up passage of other sections of President Carter's energy program.

But by August, just as final signatures were being placed on the conference report, a coalition of 24 senators announced their opposition to the compromise.

The bipartisan group of opponents included Democrats who were staunch supporters of price regulation and Republicans who wanted price controls lifted. Neither side liked the complicated scheme to raise prices gradually until 1985, when price controls on newly discovered gas would be lifted. The compromise established more than 18 categories of gas based on where the gas was found and who was using it.

Rather than trying to defeat the conference report, the coalition sought to recommit it with instructions that the disputed sections on gas pricing be removed and that other sections giving the president authority to allocate gas in emergencies be retained.

Determined to prevent what would have been a fatal blow for the energy bill, the administration launched a sophisticated lobbying campaign for the compromise, enlisting special support from Vice President Walter F. Mondale.

When, on Sept. 19, Sen. Howard M. Metzenbaum, D-Ohio, offered the motion to recommit, it failed, 39-59: R 21-15; D 18-44 (ND 13-30; SD 5-14).

On Sept. 27, President Carter won a major victory when the Senate approved the conference report, 57-42.

2. PANAMA CANAL TREATIES. No other single foreign policy issue of 1978 attracted as much attention, aroused as many emotions and consumed as much time and effort of the administration, the Senate and outside lobbying groups as did approval of two Panama Canal treaties. In the end, President Carter won a major victory when the Senate consented to ratification of the two pacts by identical 68-32 votes (R 16-22; D 52-10; ND 39-4; SD 13-6). The votes were just one over the constitutionally required two-thirds majority.

The treaties were the product of negotiations that formally began in 1964 but had in fact gone on intermittently ever since the original pact was signed in 1903. The basic treaty would turn over the U.S.-constructed, owned and operated Panama Canal to Panama by the year 2000. A second treaty — the neutrality treaty — would guarantee the United States and Panama the right to defend the canal after Dec. 31, 1999. The neutrality treaty was approved March 16, the transfer treaty on April 18.

The victory was especially significant for President Carter because opponents of the treaties had mounted a major nationwide grassroots lobbying campaign to defeat the pacts. Carter also had staked his administration's ability to conduct foreign policy on their ratification.

3. MIDEAST JET SALES. Given its first major role in shaping events in the Middle East, the Senate May 15 went along with the Carter administration's controversial plan to sell $4.8 billion worth of jet fighters to Saudi Arabia, Israel and Egypt.

The Senate's 44-54 vote (R 11-26; D 33-28; ND 26-17; SD 7-11) to turn down a resolution to block the sales was a victory for the Carter administration but a bitter defeat for Israel and U.S. Jewish organizations strongly opposed to the weapons package.

The package contained 60 F-15 fighters for Saudi Arabia, 50 F-5Es for Egypt and 15 F-15s and 75 F-16s for Israel. The major issue was the sale of the F-15s — America's most sophisticated fighter — to Saudi Arabia because of Israel's fears over its security.

Under arms sales procedures, House action was not required because the contracts automatically go through in 30 days unless rejected by both chambers.

Supporters of the sale argued the administration must be "evenhanded" in its relations with Israel and the Arab states because of the complex weave of U.S. economic and strategic interests in the Middle East.

4. RHODESIAN POLICY. In the fiscal 1979 military aid authorization bill (S 3075) Congress permitted the president to drop economic sanctions against Rhodesia after Dec. 31, 1978, if he determined that the Salisbury government had demonstrated a willingness to negotiate in good faith at an all-parties peace conference that included guerrilla factions, and a new government had been installed after being chosen in free elections under international supervision.

This final provision was close to a proposal adopted in the Senate that was sponsored by two Republicans: Sens. Clifford P. Case, N.J., and Jacob K. Javits, N.Y. That proposal was approved July 26 by a 59-36 vote. But prior to that in the key vote that set the stage for approval, the Senate refused by a 39-57 vote (R 27-11; D 12-46; ND 2-38; SD 10-8) to table and thereby kill the Case-Javits plan.

Unlike most other important foreign policy issues, the Carter administration's position on the Rhodesia moves was never publicly made clear. Many members of Congress had strongly criticized the administration for what they felt was too favorable U.S. treatment toward the black guerrillas fighting the coalition of moderate blacks and the minority white government.

But Senate sources said Carter lobbyists passed the word that the Case-Javits plan was acceptable when it became clear that nothing better could be obtained. Moreover, these sources told reporters, it was evident to participants in the debate that had the Case-Javits plan not prevailed, some other proposal to lift sanctions completely stood a good chance of winning Senate approval.

The importance of the administration's willingness to go along with Case-Javits was seen when the House later approved an amendment to the same bill that would have dramatically changed U.S. policy toward Rhodesia in a manner much more favorable to the minority white government. Conferees acceptance of the Senate approach put Congress on record favoring a more middle-of-the-road policy toward Rhodesia.

5, 6. DEFENSE SPENDING. In the face of conflicting concerns about a Soviet military buildup in Eastern

Europe, on the one hand, and the ever expanding federal budget and its impact on inflation, on the other, the Senate decided to approve basically the amount recommended by President Carter for national defense in fiscal 1979.

In the first concurrent resolution on the budget (S Con Res 80), the Senate Budget Committee recommended a national defense spending level of $129.8 billion, which was only slightly higher than the $128.4 billion requested by the administration.

By nearly identical votes, the Senate rejected an amendment that would have increased the defense spending level and another that would have decreased it.

A $1.6 billion increase proposed by John G. Tower, R-Texas, was rejected April 26 by a vote of 21-74: R 17-17; D 4-57 (ND 0-42; SD 4-15).

On April 25 Thomas F. Eagleton, D-Mo., had recommended a $1.4 billion reduction in the defense level, but his proposal was rejected 21-70: R 4-31; D 17-39 (ND 17-20; SD 0-19).

7. AIRLINE DEREGULATION. During Senate consideration of legislation — actively promoted by the Carter administration — to increase competition in the commercial passenger airline industry, Edward M. Kennedy, D-Mass., offered an amendment to strengthen the bill.

In 1977, the Senate Commerce Committee had voted to weaken Carter's plan by requiring any airline company seeking to offer a new service to prove to the Civil Aeronautics Board (CAB) that the service was "consistent with the public convenience and necessity."

Under Kennedy's amendment, the CAB was ordered to presume a new service to be in the public interest unless an opponent of the new service could convince the board that it was not.

Supporters of the amendment argued that it would increase competition by giving a company's applications an important procedural advantage. But its opponents argued that the Kennedy amendment went too far in deregulating the industry and predicted it would harm the airline companies' financial stability and, ultimately, the level of service they offered the nation.

The Kennedy amendment prevailed on a vote of 69-23: R 28-6; D 41-17 (ND 30-9; SD 11-8), and it subsequently was incorporated in the enacted version of the bill.

8. WATERWAY USER FEES. A controversial measure to impose fees on the users of the nation's inland waterways for the first time had been before Congress for 38 years and once again was endangered by Senate inaction. The legislation had been considered throughout the 95th Congress, and in May Sens. Pete V. Domenici, R-N.M., and Adlai E. Stevenson III, D-Ill., proposed a compromise that had the administration's backing. Their proposal called for an authorization for construction of a new lock and dam on the Mississippi River at Alton, Ill., with a phased-in tax on barge fuel plus a user charge sufficient to recover 10 percent of the capital costs of any newly constructed waterway within the first 10 years of the waterway's operation. In the administration's opinion, Transportation Secretary Brock Adams informed the Senate, the scheme offered "the minimum acceptable basis from which to develop an adequate House-Senate conference bill." Anything less, and Carter would veto the bill, Adams said.

Finance Committee Chairman Russell B. Long, D-La., however, was not happy with the plan. He proposed a substitute bill delaying the tax's imposition — in order to ensure that construction of the Alton lock and dam would be under way before the tax was collected — and eliminating the provision that new waterway projects be required to recover a portion of their construction costs through a user charge.

In a direct challenge to Adams' and President Carter's credibility, the Senate rejected the Domenici-Stevenson version of the bill — which would have been much more expensive for the barge industry — and opted for Long's alternative. The vote May 3 rejecting the Domenici-Stevenson version was 43-47: R 16-19; D 27-28 (ND 22-15; SD 5-13).

9. D.C. VOTING RIGHTS. Supporters of the long struggle for voting rights in the District of Columbia achieved a milestone Aug. 22 when the Senate passed a constitutional amendment giving added voting rights and full representation in Congress to D.C. residents.

A coalition of reform groups led by Majority Leader Robert C. Byrd, D-W. Va., and Sen. Edward M. Kennedy, D-Mass., led the fight for the amendment (H J Res 554) which passed by a vote of 67-32. This was just one over the required two-thirds majority for constitutional amendments.

The House passed the amendment March 2 by a 289-127 but the significant battle came in the Senate. There was relatively little opposition to allowing the District additional voting rights in the House based on population. The District already had a non-voting delegate in that chamber.

But opponents of the amendment contended that the Senate was based on states and the District wasn't the same as a state and never would be.

The vote in the Senate was considered a symbolic milestone for both the Republican Party and black voters. Though the District's predominantly black population was expected to elect Democrats for the foreseeable future, the Republican leadership actively lobbied for the amendments as part of its effort to win the support of black voters.

The amendment must be ratified by 38 states within seven years before it becomes part of the Constitution.

10. EQUAL RIGHTS AMENDMENT. The Senate gave final approval to a resolution (H J Res 638) granting states 39 additional months to ratify the proposed Equal Rights Amendment to the Constitution.

Passage of the resolution Oct. 6 by a 60-36 vote capped a year-long lobbying effort by backers of the ERA and marked the first time Congress had extended the ratification period for a constitutional amendment since it began setting time limits in 1917.

The key vote, however, was not the passage. The crucial vote came two days earlier when the Senate rejected a proposal which, had it succeeded, would have forced the extension's supporters to pull the resolution off the floor and probably would have ended any hope of extending the deadline. That proposal, sponsored by Sen. Jake Garn, R-Utah, would have allowed states that already ratified ERA to rescind their actions during the extension period. Garn's rescission amendments was rejected 44-54 (R 24-13; D 20-41; ND 5-37; SD 15-4).

Supporters of the rescission argued that it would be unfair to give state legislatures that have rejected ERA additional time to ratify without at the same time giving those that had ratified the choice of reconsidering their votes. Opponents said rescission would be unconstitutional and that states would not take ratification seriously if they could rescind their decision later.

The extension resolution was approved by the House Aug. 15. It did not require the president's signature and took effect upon Senate approval.

11. HOSPITAL COST CONTROL. The Senate Oct. 12 handed President Carter a surprise victory on hospital cost containment, but the bill (HR 5285) that passed was far weaker than the president's 1977 request to cap all hospital revenue increases at 9 percent annually.

Opposed by the medical and hospital establishment and by organized labor, the bill had languished in three of four congressional health committees in 1977, as administration negotiators stiffly resisted compromise.

By fall 1978, most observers had written off the legislation as dead. One Senate committee favored a different, industry-backed bill and a House committee had gutted a bill that included significant compromises, reluctantly accepted by the administration. The compromises included a wage "pass-through" to protect blue-collar hospital workers, and a built-in delay for the revenue controls, intended to let hospitals themselves try to cut costs.

The wage provision brought labor on board but hospitals still complained that a "meat ax" revenue control — even on a standby basis — would destroy an industry with widely varying and unpredictable costs. Instead they endorsed a Senate committee proposal to revise Medicare and Medicaid reimbursement procedures by providing for fixed reimbursement rates, tailored to different hospital types.

Days before adjournment, administration allies forced a dramatic floor fight, compelling senators to choose between the narrower Medicare-Medicaid bill and an administration hybrid that combined the federal reimbursement reforms, standby revenue controls for all hospitals, and numerous exemptions. Opponents charged that the administration had shot its bill full of exemptions to buy votes, but backers argued that support for the bill would be a meaningful anti-inflation vote. Timing may also have brought some senators on board because few expected the House to act on the measure in the last crowded days of the session.

In a key vote the Senate by a 42-47 vote (R 25-6; D 17-41 (ND 4-35; SD 13-6) refused to table (kill) the hybrid administration substitute for the narrower Medicare-Medicaid proposal.

12. COURT-ORDERED BUSING. By only a two-vote margin, the Senate Aug. 23 rejected an amendment to restrict the authority of the courts to order busing of school children as a remedy in desegregation cases.

Leading busing opponent Joe Biden, D-Del., said the closeness of the vote signaled the "death knell" of the pro-busing position in the Senate. The amendment, to the Elementary and Secondary Education Act (ESEA) extension bill (S 1753), was rejected only after Majority Leader Robert C. Byrd, D-W.Va., urged his colleagues not to plunge the Senate into an extremely controversial issue near the end of the session.

The amendment, offered by Biden and William V. Roth Jr., R-Del., was tabled by a 49-47 vote: R 12-26; D 37-21 (ND 34-8; SD 3-13).

Incorporating the substance of S 1651, the first bill ever reported by a congressional committee that sought to restrict court busing authority, the amendment would have barred any court from ordering busing without first determining that a "discriminatory purpose in education was a principal motivating factor" for the violation the busing was designed to correct.

All previous congressional attempts to limit busing had restricted only the authority of the Department of Health, Education and Welfare to require busing.

13. EMERGENCY FARM AID. Stampeded by three months of angry and unrelenting pressure from a militant new farm group, the Senate March 21 passed a multi-part farm bill that one opponent called a "three-headed monster."

The bill (HR 6782) combined three strategies for raising farm income — paid land diversion, boosts in price supports for corn, wheat and cotton, and a controversial "flexible parity" plan that permitted a farmer to set his own price support level by deciding how much land to take out of production.

Farmers of the ad hoc American Agriculture Movement (AAM) had camped out on Capitol Hill since January, demanding relief from financial problems caused by record grain surpluses, high production costs, widespread drought and heavy borrowing.

Opponents warned that the unwieldy Senate package combined contradictory methods of hiking farm income and that even if the Agriculture Department could figure out how to administer it, the various components would cancel each other out. Land diversion is intended to raise market prices by shrinking surplus production, while price supports tend to encourage production while supplementing farm income.

There were also heated warnings from Senate Budget Committee Chairman Edmund S. Muskie, D-Maine, that the bill was far too expensive — both in terms of federal payments to farmers and the overall impact on inflation. No cost estimates for the total package had been prepared because no one had anticipated that the Senate would adopt all options.

As senators voted 67-26 (R 26-11; D 41-15; ND 23-14; SD 18-1) to pass the the multi-part bill, farmer-lobbyists watched from crowded galleries. Members later said privately that some of their colleagues were exasperated with the farmers and apparently expected the urban-dominated House, or conferees, to extract a workable farm program from the flawed bill.

14. SENATE TAX BILL. When the tax bill reached the Senate floor, the Senate Finance Committee had already changed it to be more generous to people earning less than $11,000 (as well as providing additional tax breaks for the generally wealthy people who claim capital gains). But liberals, led by Dale Bumpers, D-Ark., and Edward M. Kennedy, D-Mass., argued that the bill still provided insufficient help to people earning between $10,000 and $30,000.

Bumpers and Kennedy thus proposed pumping $4.5 billion more into the bill (the Finance Committee had already added $6.3 billion), earmarking the extra funds for people in those middle income ranges. An aggressive effort paid off, as the Bumpers-Kennedy amendment was approved, 52-43 on Oct. 6: R 13-23; D 39-20 (ND 32-9; SD 7-11).

That success was short-lived, however. Most of the extra tax cuts provided by the amendment were removed from the bill in conference committee in an effort to meet budgetary standards imposed by the Carter administration.

15. LABOR LAW REFORM. Organized labor's legislative high-water mark in 1978 came June 14, when it struggled to within two Senate votes of the 60 needed to end a conservative filibuster against legislation (HR 8410) revising federal labor law.

The 58-41 defeat of a cloture motion offered by Majority Leader Robert C. Byrd, D-W.Va., represented the fourth in a series of six attempts to cut off a five-week filibuster against the bill, which was labor's overriding legislative goal for the year.

The cloture motion picked up substantial support from Republicans, who opposed it by a 14-24 margin. But labor lobbyists could make scarcely a dent in opposition among southern Democrats, whose 3-15 vote against the motion was in sharp contrast to the near-unanimous 41-2 vote among northern Democrats.

After two more unsuccessful cloture tries, bill sponsors were finally forced to recommit the bill to the Human Resources Committee, in hopes of coming up with a new version that could overcome a renewed filibuster. But a final "bare-bones" version of the bill, stripped of most of the controversial provisions of HR 8410, died when it became clear that opponents were prepared to resist the bill in any form.

The target of one of the most intense grassroots lobbying campaigns in history, HR 8410 would have amended the 1935 National Labor Relations Act by increasing the penalties for labor law violations, speeding up the process of settling unfair labor practice cases, and strengthening union rights during organizing campaigns.

House Key Votes

1. WATER POLICY. Despite opposition from the Democratic leadership in both the House and Senate, President Carter successfully vetoed a bill (HR 12928) funding several dams and other water projects he opposed.

The confrontation was a rehash of a 1977 battle over a similar public works appropriations bill, but this time Carter carried through his veto threat. The House Oct. 5 refused to override the veto. The vote was 223-190, 53 votes short of the two-thirds needed for an override. Carter's characterization of the expenditures as wasteful won important support from Republicans, who split on the issue, 73-62. A majority of Democrats also voted against Carter, 150-128 (ND 92-99; SD 58-29).

Later, Carter signed a version of the bill modified to meet his objections (H J Res 1139). But congressional leaders made it clear that the compromise was for fiscal 1979 appropriations only. The same conflict promised to resurface in the 96th Congress.

The dispute was part of a continuing battle between Carter and Congress over national water policy. Carter wanted to base funding on strict economic and environmental criteria, while Congress preferred to consider politics and other so-called "pork barrel" factors.

At issue in the public works bill were six projects from Carter's 1977 "hit list" that had been deleted in fiscal 1978 funding but restored by Congress for fiscal 1979. The president complained that taxpayers would pay about $1.8 billion over the next several years to complete those six projects and 26 other new ones added by Congress. He also opposed provisions mandating the hiring of 2,300 new government employees by the water development agencies and deleting funds for the Water Resources Council.

2. NATIONAL ENERGY BILL. From the earliest stages of congressional action on President Carter's energy program, the strategy of House Speaker Thomas P. O'Neill Jr. had been to keep the five-part package intact. He wanted to give members only one vote on energy so they would be forced to swallow the bill whole and would be unable to pick off, and possibly to defeat, individual pieces.

By the end of the session, Carter's original bill had survived the House, had been gutted by the Senate and had been rewritten in conference. As a result, O'Neill's strategy appeared all the wiser. The most controversial section, on natural gas pricing (HR 5289), would be sheltered by the more popular provisions, such as one giving homeowners tax credits for insulation (HR 5263).

Opponents of the natural gas bill realized their best chance at defeating it was to split the package and force a separate vote on the gas pricing section.

The odd coalition of opponents included members who preferred tough price controls to protect consumers and those who wanted an immediate end to price controls, instead of the gradual decontrol the bill provided.

The crucial vote was on a parliamentary maneuver leading to adoption of the rule (H Res 1434), which called for a single vote on the five-part package. The House floor was jammed Oct. 13 for what all knew would be a close vote. When time ran out, the tally was 200-200. But last minute votes by several members and switches by others gave the administration and the Democratic leadership the 207-206 victory: R 8-127; D 199-79 (ND 136-55; SD 63-24). The rule itself was adopted by voice vote.

Two days later, after an all-night session, the House voted 231-168 for the package, sending the measure to the president.

3. EMERGENCY FARM AID. The stunning lobbying success of the militant American Agriculture Movement (AAM) came to a grinding halt April 12 when the House emphatically rejected the conference report on a "flexible parity" farm bill (HR 6782) that would have allowed a farmer to idle up to half his land in return for sharply boosted support payments.

The margin of defeat (150-268) surprised observers almost as much as the longevity of the flexible parity concept, which had survived House, Senate and conference scrutiny despite veto threats from the president and repudiation by farm economists. (Conferees had discarded more modest price supports and land diversions from a grab-bag Senate bill, retaining only the flexible parity program.)

By shrinking production, the program would push food prices to intolerable heights, while payments to farmers would deplete the U.S. Treasury, critics warned.

But AAM farmer-lobbyists insisted that the expensive program was all that stood between them and bankruptcy. Soaring production costs, price-depressing surpluses, drought losses and meager support from the Carter administration had pushed them to the wall, producers said. Hardest hit were younger grain producers, whose high land and equipment costs had pushed them deeply into debt.

Established farm groups had failed to wring adequate support from Congress in 1977, so AAM members had left their farms to press their needs in Washington, they said. But the four months of unrelenting pressure from the gloomy farmers built countervailing pressures that finally showed in the House vote on the conference agreement.

Urban members, more concerned with inflated food prices than farm economics, apparently heeded administration warnings that the scheme was highly inflationary. Republican spokesmen characterized the vote as "anti-inflation."

Probably the most important element in the defeat was the fact that the flexible parity scheme benefited one segment of agriculture at the expense of another. Livestock and dairy producers feared sharply higher feed grain prices, and let their representatives know it. With the farm community divided, rural members themselves divided their votes and reportedly did little to recruit urban support for the measure. With majorities of both Republicans and Democrats voting no, the House by a 150-268 vote (R 70-75; D 80-193; ND 26-160; SD 54-33) defeated the bill. Congress later passed a pared-down version of HR 6782 that gave the president authority to raise grain and cotton target prices.

4. PUBLIC FINANCING OF ELECTIONS. Twice in 1978 a coalition of Republicans and southern Democrats succeeded in blocking House floor consideration of a proposal to extend public financing to congressional elections.

The clearest vote on the issue came in July on an attempt to open the fiscal 1979 Federal Election Commission (FEC) authorization bill (HR 11983) to a public financing amendment. An earlier effort was scuttled in March when the House refused to consider a controversial campaign financing bill (HR 11315) that was to have served as a vehicle for a public financing amendment. The Democratic leadership promoted the bill, which included controversial limits on party and political action committee (PAC) spending.

The extent of the public financing proposal was limited — applying only to House general elections and providing funds to candidates on a matching basis without any direct subsidies. Participation by candidates would have been voluntary.

Newer House members along with Common Cause and the Democratic Study Group led the major thrust for public financing in July. Without a majority on the Rules Committee, they were forced to try a complex set of parliamentary maneuvers to even bring their proposal to a floor vote. They failed, as the House voted 213-196 on July 19 not to allow a public financing amendment to the $8.6 million FEC authorization bill. A large majority of Republicans (106-30) and southern Democrats (62-22) joined to block consideration of the amendment.

5. TURKISH ARMS EMBARGO. By a three-vote margin, the House gave President Carter one of several significant foreign policy victories by permitting the president to drop the U.S. arms embargo against Turkey.

The issue had been troublesome since Congress in 1974 approved a total ban on military aid and arms shipments to Turkey in reaction to that country's invasion of Greek-populated sections of Cyprus in which U.S.-supplied armaments, intended for the defense of Turkey, were employed in violation of U.S. foreign aid laws. The ban took effect in 1975 and was somewhat modified later after a tough fight in the House.

The Carter administration's decision to ask the 95th Congress to repeal the embargo was prompted by fears that Turkey, a U.S. ally, would reduce its commitment to NATO, thus threatening the alliance's southeastern line of defense.

In the Senate, Carter's request passed with less trouble —57-42. But in the House, the margin on the vote July 26 was only 208-205: R 78-64; D 130-141 (ND 64-123; SD 66-18).

Paving the way for Carter's victory were at least three factors: an intense, two-month lobbying campaign by the White House and the State and Defense Departments; a last-minute compromise proposal on which the vote came; and the willingness of two members — Butler Derrick, D-S.C., and Richard T. Schulze, R-Pa. — to switch their votes when they were desperately needed by the administration. But the key element in the victory for Carter was the Republican Party. A majority of the GOP backed the repeal, while a majority of Carter's own party members went against the president.

6. FOREIGN AID CUTS. The House, in a significant and surprising turnaround from 1977, refused to make deep cuts in foreign aid appropriations. The U.S. foreign aid program — which almost always is in some sort of trouble in Congress — was thought particularly vulnerable in 1978 to the budget-cutting fever that swept through the House in mid-year. However, an effective lobbying campaign by the Carter administration and a coalition of House members, plus some outside groups devoted to foreign aid, prevented major cuts in the aid funding bill.

The key action came on a proposal by Rep. Clarence E. Miller, R-Ohio, to cut the appropriations bill (HR 12931) by 8 percent across-the-board except for funds for Israel and Egypt. The House rejected this by a 15-vote margin, 184-199. In 1977, the House approved a Miller 5-percent cut, 214-168. On this issue, there was a turnaround of 44 members who supported Miller in 1977 and opposed him in 1978: 25 Republicans and 19 Democrats. On the 1978 vote the breakdown was R 88-43; D 96-156 (ND 42-133; SD 54-23).

The House did accept a smaller cut in the aid funding: 2 percent except for allocations for Israel, Egypt, Jordan and Syria. However, conferees on the bill deleted these cuts.

7. BANK CURBS. Another dramatic House turnaround on foreign aid *(see previous item)* came on efforts to tell international lending institutions, such as the World Bank, how they could use U.S. contributions. In 1977 an amendment by Rep. C. W. Bill Young, R-Fla., to prohibit funds in the appropriations bill from being used by the banks in Uganda, Cambodia, Laos or Vietnam was approved overwhelmingly, 295-115. In 1978, the same Young amendment to the appropriations bill (HR 12931) was rejected 198-203: R 101-35; D 97-168 (ND 52-134; SD 45-34).

Eighty-eight members switched their position from support of Young in 1977 to opposition in 1978. Those switches, plus the addition of some members who didn't vote in 1978, were enough to give the administration a major victory. Of the total, 63 members were Democrats and 25 Republicans.

Opponents of the Young amendment argued that the restriction would play havoc with international lending programs and probably would destroy the banks. They argued that the charters of the multinational lending institutions did not permit the banks to accept funds with conditions. Consequently, the banks would have to refuse American funding, probably crippling their operations.

The Carter administration strongly opposed the Young amendment as it had in 1977.

8. B-1 BOMBER. Prodded by lobbying of rare intensity by the Carter administration, the House Feb. 22 finally acceded to the president's decision to cancel the controversial B-1 bomber project.

Carter had announced in June 1977 that he was canceling the $23 billion program to produce 244 planes, and Congress subsequently canceled all new funding for the program. But on Dec. 6 of that year the House voted 166-191 against a Carter request to also rescind $462 million that had been previously appropriated to build the first two production versions of the bomber.

House opponents of the rescission argued that production of the two planes would preserve for a time the option of reversing Carter's decision, should the Soviet military buildup continue.

But the White House was adamantly opposed to going forward with the program, and the administration gradually won more and more Democrats to the president's side of the argument. On Feb. 22 the rescission was approved on a 234-182 vote: R 30-106; D 204-76 (ND 155-38; SD 49-38).

9. AIRCRAFT CARRIER VETO. In a major victory for the administration on defense policy, the House Sept. 7 by a surprisingly wide margin rejected an attempt to override President Carter's Aug. 17 veto of the fiscal 1979 weapons procurement bill (HR 10929) that contained a $2 billion authorization for another nuclear aircraft carrier for the Navy. Carter insisted on setting his own defense priorities and argued that another giant, 1,000-foot-long carrier was wasteful and unnecessary. And he maintained the money for the ship would have diverted funds from important defense programs that he preferred.

Only 31 days earlier, on Aug. 7, the House had voted 156-218 against an amendment that would have deleted the appropriation for the carrier from the Pentagon's annual funding bill. But in September, carrier supporters could not even muster a majority of the House in favor of overriding the veto (a two-thirds vote would have been needed to override). The vote was 191-206: R 107-23; D 84-183 (ND 34-150; SD 50-33).

Subsequently, Congress, in a revised arms procurement measure for fiscal 1979, agreed to drop the carrier authorization.

10. CONSUMER PROTECTION AGENCY. Legislation to establish an agency within the federal government to represent the interests of the consumer had been actively sought by consumer groups since 1961, but the bill had died at the end of four successive Congresses. The Senate had approved a bill establishing such an agency in 1970. The House approved similar legislation in 1971 and 1974. Both houses approved a bill in 1975, but the bill was never sent to the White House because President Ford threatened to veto it.

In the 95th Congress, however, President Carter made establishment of a consumer agency his top consumer priority. When the bill (HR 6805) became stalled in the House in 1977, consumer groups showered potential swing votes with nickels — five cents representing what supporters of the idea said would be the cost per capita of the proposed agency. A compromise proposal, establishing a scaled-down Office of Consumer Representation, was unveiled in October 1977. But it barely squeaked through the House Rules Committee as consumer activists found their intense lobbying efforts surpassed by a coalition of business interests.

On Nov. 1, 1977, House Speaker Thomas P. O'Neill Jr., D-Mass., pulled the bill from the House calendar when his vote count indicated the legislation probably would lose.

Early in 1978, Carter reiterated his support for the bill and it was once again scheduled for House floor action.

On Feb. 8 the House finally voted on the measure, but it lost on a 189-227 vote: R 17-126; D 172-101 (ND 147-40; SD 25-61), ending consumers' hopes of enacting the bill in the 95th Congress. "I have been around here for 25 years," O'Neill remarked. "I have never seen such extensive lobbying."

11. LOBBY DISCLOSURE. Critics of existing lobby disclosure laws won a battle in 1978 but eventually lost the war. Legislation to impose strict new registration requirements on groups that lobby Congress was approved by the House in April by a 259-140 vote (R 75-67; D 184-73; ND 143-39; SD 41-34). But that was as far as supporters could go. When the bill (HR 8494) got to the Senate, the Governmental Affairs Committee was not able to resolve differences between different versions.

The bill passed by the House was far stronger than the version sent to the floor by the Judiciary Committee. The final bill required disclosure of grassroots lobbying activities such as computerized mass mailings and disclosure of the names of organizations contributing $3,000 or more to a lobby group.

The major debates on the issue during the 95th Congress focused on whether to require disclosure of grassroots lobbying efforts such as organized letter-writing campaigns, and disclosure of the names of major organizations contributing to registered lobby groups.

12. FISCAL POLICY. In an election year dominated by the issue of government spending, Republicans in the House mounted a united — and nearly successful — assault on the fiscal policy proposals of the president and the Democratic Congress.

The Republican critique hit not only at the specific spending and tax proposals of the administration and the Democratic majority, but it was directed also at the approach to budget-writing followed by the House Budget Committee.

Specifically, GOP leaders in the House complained that the majority party had failed to use the four-year-old congressional budget process as originally intended. They said that the Democrats, rather than making overall fiscal policy decisions first and only then setting specific spending and tax policies to fit the macroeconomic pie, merely used the budget process to add up a series of smaller decisions made without reference to the big picture.

The result, they said, was that the Democrats had failed to control the growth of federal spending. That, in turn, according to the Republican view, kept the federal deficit at unacceptably high levels and prevented the Democrats from proposing a tax cut as large as the GOP would like.

As an alternative, House Republicans rallied behind a proposal by Marjorie S. Holt, R-Md., to set overall spending goals that would allow all federal programs to grow only enough to keep pace with inflation — about 8 percent, compared to the 11 percent growth rate provided by the committee recommendation. Republicans said the Holt proposal, offered as a substitute to the House Budget Committee's proposed first fiscal 1979 budget resolution (H Con Res 559), would be the first step in a Republican plan to balance the federal budget in five years.

Democrats scoffed at the proposal, questioning whether it was economically realistic and suggesting that it failed to make the difficult decisions about where to limit federal spending.

The key test of the Republican approach came May 3, when the Holt amendment, supported by all House Republicans but one and by 58 Democratic defectors, fell only six votes short of winning, 197-203: R 139-1; D 58-202 (ND 24-155; SD 34-47).

13. SPENDING CUTS. One week after California voters approved their tax-cutting Proposition 13, the House adopted the first of a series of across-the-board cuts in federal spending.

The annually unsuccessful efforts of Clarence E. Miller, R-Ohio, to propose across-the-board cuts in controllable spending in appropriations bills were finally rewarded June 13, when the House adopted his amendment to reduce controllable spending in the fiscal 1979 Labor-Health, Education and Welfare (HEW) bill (HR 12929) by a total of 2 percent. The amendment limited reductions in individual programs to no more than 5 percent.

The amendment, which would have cut spending in the $56.6 billion bill by an estimated $380 million, was adopted on a 220-181 vote: R 122-18; D 98-163 (ND 47-133; SD 51-30).

Inspired by a report of the HEW Inspector General that up to $7 billion a year was lost by the department to waste, fraud and abuse, the House also approved a Robert H. Michel, R-Ill., amendment to cut HEW spending by $1 billion, with the reductions to come out of the programs identified as having serious losses.

But while it embraced the overall cuts, the House solidly rejected requests from the Carter administration to make specific reductions in Appropriations Committee-approved totals for health and education programs.

The Miller amendment was quietly dropped in conference with the Senate, but the $1 billion waste, fraud and abuse cut was enacted.

Across-the-board cut amendments were introduced on several other appropriations bills, but most of them did not survive in the final versions.

14. TUITION TAX CREDITS. The chances for enactment of separate legislation providing federal tax breaks for education expenses ended Oct. 12, when the House refused to accept a tuition tax credit bill (HR 12050) that included credits for college, but not private elementary and secondary school, tuition.

The surprise adoption of a Bill Gradison, R-Ohio, motion to recommit the conference report on HR 12050 with instructions to restore the House-passed elementary and secondary credits effectively killed the bill, since Senate opposition to credits below the college level was insurmountable. The motion was agreed to 207-185: R 100-23; D 107-152 (ND 91-86; SD 16-66).

The key factor in the approval of the Gradison motion, and the resulting death of the bill, was the presence of a large block of House members who were more interested in parochial school tuition credits than in the college aid. Feeling that they would have a better chance of overcoming the serious constitutional obstacles to the parochial credits if they were coupled with the college credits, supporters decided that they would be better off waiting until 1979, when they could try again to overcome Senate opposition to credits at all levels.

15. INFLATION TARGET. Spurred by growing congressional concern over inflation, the House March 9 came within a few votes of adding a specific anti-inflation target to the Humphrey-Hawkins full employment bill (HR 50).

By a 198-223 vote the House rejected an amendment sponsored by James M. Jeffords, R-Vt., to set a new national goal calling for a reduction in the rate of inflation to 3 percent a year by 1983, in addition to the bill's original goal of a reduction in the unemployment rate to 4 percent by 1983.

House Democratic leaders had to offer their own broad anti-inflation language, without the specific 3 percent target, in order to defuse support for the Jeffords amendment, which had picked up substantial Democratic backing during the days preceding the vote.

Republicans supported the Jeffords amendment overwhelmingly, 142-2, while Democrats voted 56-221 (ND 26-168; SD 30-53) against.

Despite its House victory, however, the coalition of labor and civil rights groups supporting HR 50 eventually had to accept the anti-inflation goal in order to forestall a threatened Senate filibuster in the last days of the 95th Congress.

16. HOUSE TAX BILL. Congressional consideration of tax legislation in 1978 marked a sharp departure from that of recent years.

In January, President Carter proposed a fairly traditional tax cut — one which offered the relatively largest benefits to lower income people, while tightening up on tax "loopholes" which benefited the well-to-do.

But Carter and liberal Democrats in Congress were caught off-guard when a coalition of Republicans and conservative Democrats seized the initiative and pushed through the House Ways and Means Committee a bill that took a very different approach. It directed relatively larger benefits to middle and upper income individuals, and — most controversially — it included a substantial reduction in the tax on capital gains.

The liberals, disunited and lacking direction from the president, were slow to respond to the conservative movement on taxes. But at almost the last moment they did come up with an alternative tax proposal. Sponsored by Reps. James C. Corman, D-Calif., and Joseph L. Fisher, D-Va., and written in consultation with the administration, the alternative reduced the proposed tax cuts for people earning more than $50,000 and provided larger tax cuts to people earning less than that amount. It also called for stricter treatment of capital gains than the committee bill did.

The conservative coalition saw the Corman-Fisher proposal as the key test of their tax philosophy. A vote for the alternative, they warned, would amount to upholding the traditional belief that tax bills should "redistribute income," while a vote for the committee bill would support the philosophy that tax cuts should be uniform for all income groups.

Despite the strong support of the House's Democratic leadership, the Corman-Fisher proposal was defeated in a key vote Aug. 10, 193-225: R 8-134; D 185-91 (ND 164-27; SD 21-64).

1978 Key Votes - 9

	1 2 3 4 5 6 7 8 9 10 11 12 13 14 15
KANSAS Dole (R)	Y N Y Y N Y Y N Y Y Y N Y Y N
MASSACHUSETTS Kennedy (D)	Y Y Y N Y N Y Y Y N N Y Y Y Y
TENNESSEE Baker (R)	Y Y N Y ? ? Y N Y Y Y N Y N N

Y - Yea
N - Nay
? - Did not vote or otherwise make a position known.

1. HR 5289. Natural Gas Pricing. Metzenbaum, D-Ohio, motion to recommit the conference report to the conference committee with instructions to delete all pricing provisions except those related to Alaska gas and to grant certain emergency powers to the president and the Federal Energy Regulatory Commission. Rejected 39-59: R 21-15; D 18-44 (ND 13-40; SD 5-14), Sept. 19, 1978. A "nay" was a vote supporting the president's position.

2. Exec N, 95th Congress, First Session, Panama Canal Treaties. Adoption of the resolution of ratification to the neutrality treaty guaranteeing that the Panama Canal will be permanently neutral and remain secure and open to vessels of all nations. Adopted 68-32: R 16-22; D 52-10 (ND 39-4; SD 13-6), March 16, 1978. A "yea" was a vote supporting the president's position.

3. S Con Res 86. Mideast Fighter Plane Sales. Adoption of the resolution to disapprove the sale of $4.5 billion worth of jet fighter planes to Israel, Saudi Arabia and Egypt. Rejected 44-54: R 11-26; D 33-28 (ND 26-17; SD 7-11), May 15, 1978. A "nay" was a vote supporting the president's position.

4. S 3075. Foreign Military Aid. Baker, R-Tenn., motion to table (kill) the Case, R-N.J., amendment providing that U.S. sanctions against Rhodesia could not be lifted until the president determined that the Rhodesian government of Ian Smith had committed itself to a conference of all the groups contending for power in the country and free elections for a new government, supervised by international observers, were held. Tabling motion rejected 39-57: R 27-11; D 12-46 (ND 2-38; SD 10-8), July 26, 1978.

5. S Con Res 80. Fiscal 1979 Budget Targets. Eagleton, D-Mo., amendment to reduce national defense spending by $1.4 billion in budget authority and $900 million in outlays. Rejected 21-70: R 4-31; D 17-39 (ND 17-20; SD 0-19), April 25, 1978.

6. S Con Res 80. Fiscal 1979 Budget Targets. Tower, R-Texas, amendment to increase national defense spending by $1.6 billion in budget authority and $1.2 billion in outlays. Rejected 21-74: R 17-17; D 4-57 (ND 0-42; SD 4-15), April 26, 1978.

7. S 2493. Airline Deregulation. Kennedy, D-Mass., amendment to direct the Civil Aeronautics Board to authorize a proposed air transportation service unless it determined that the service was not consistent with the public convenience and necessity. Adopted 69-23: R 28-6; D 41-17 (ND 30-9; SD 11-8), April 19, 1978. A "yea" was a vote supporting the president's position.

8. HR 8309. Waterway User Fees/Water Projects. Domenici, R-N.M., amendment to phase in over 10 years a tax on inland waterway barge fuel of 12 cents per gallon, beginning with a 4 cent tax per gallon on Oct. 1, 1977; to require the secretary of transportation to recommend to Congress by Jan. 15, 1981, various ways to pay for the nation's future inland waterway needs, and to require that the Army Corps of Engineers recover, through user charges, 10 percent of the capital costs of any newly authorized water project within the first 10 years of the project's operation. Rejected 43-47: R 16-19; D 27-28 (ND 22-15; SD 5-13), May 3, 1978. A "yea" was a vote supporting the president's position.

9. H J Res 554. D.C. Voting Representation. Passage of the joint resolution to propose an amendment to the Constitution to provide for full voting representation in Congress (both in the House and the Senate) for the District of Columbia and to retain the right granted District residents by the 23rd Amendment to vote for the election of the president and vice president (the resolution would repeal the 23rd Amendment). Passed 67-32: R 19-19; D 48-13 (ND 38-5; SD 10-8), Aug. 22, 1978. A two-thirds majority vote (66 in this case) is required for passage of a joint resolution proposing an amendment to the Constitution. A "yea" was a vote supporting the president's position.

10. H J Res 638. ERA Deadline Extension. Garn, R-Utah, amendment to the resolution extending the deadline for ratification of the ERA amendment to allow a state to rescind its ratification of the ERA amendment at any time after the resolution became effective. Rejected 44-54: R 24-13; D 20-41 (ND 5-37; SD 15-4), Oct. 4, 1978. A "nay" was a vote supporting the president's position.

11. HR 5285. Medicare-Medicaid and Hospital Cost Containment. Talmadge, D-Ga., motion to table (kill) the Nelson, D-Wis., substitute amendment to authorize prospective reimbursement of hospitals by Medicare and Medicaid, to endorse a voluntary effort by hospitals to cut costs, and to authorize national hospital revenue limits if goals of the voluntary effort were not met. Motion rejected 42-47: R 25-6; D 17-41 (ND 4-35; SD 13-6), Oct. 12, 1978. A "nay" was a vote supporting the president's position. (The Nelson substitute for the bill was adopted subsequently by voice vote.)

12. S 1753. Elementary and Secondary Education Act Amendments. Pell, D-R.I., motion to table (kill) the Roth, R-Del., amendment to limit court-ordered busing of students only when there was a discriminatory purpose for segregated education; to require courts to determine whether a greater degree of racial segregation resulted because of the segregation policy; and to delay federal busing orders to provide time for appeals, unless the Supreme Court or a three-member appellate court denied such a delay. Motion agreed to 49-47: R 12-26; D 37-21 (ND 34-8; SD 3-13), Aug. 23, 1978.

13. HR 6782. Emergency Farm Bill. Passage of the bill to provide, for 1978 only, for a paid land diversion program for farmers, an increase in target price and loan levels for wheat, corn and cotton programs, and a flexible parity program of graduated target prices for wheat, corn and cotton. Passed 67-26: R 26-11; D 41-15 (ND 23-14; SD 18-1), March 21, 1978.

14. HR 13511. Revenue Act of 1978. Bumpers, D-Ark., amendment to cut individual income taxes in 1979 $4.5 billion more than the $16 billion recommended by the Finance Committee, with the extra relief going to persons with incomes below $50,000 and especially to those in the $10,000-$30,000 range. Adopted 52-43: R 13-23: D 39-20 (ND 32-9; SD 7-11), Oct. 6, 1978.

15. HR 8410. Labor Law Revision. Byrd, D-W.Va., motion to invoke cloture (cut off debate) on the Byrd, D-W.Va., substitute to the bill to amend the National Labor Relations Act. Motion rejected 58-41: R 14-24; D 44-17 (ND 41-2; SD 3-15), June 14, 1978. A three-fifths majority vote (60) of the total Senate membership is required to invoke cloture.

1978 Key Votes - 10

```
                              1 2 3 4 5 6 7 8 9 10 11 12 13 14 15 16
ILLINOIS
12  Crane (R)                 ? X ? ? N Y Y N Y N N Y Y ✔ Y N
16  Anderson (R)              N N N N Y N N N N N Y Y N N ? N
```

Y - Yea
N - Nay
X - Paired Against
✔ - Paired for
? - Did not vote or otherwise make a position known

1. HR 12928. Public Works — Energy Appropriations, Fiscal 1979. Passage, over the president's Oct. 5 veto, of the bill to appropriate $10,160,483,000 for energy and water development programs of the Corps of Engineers and the Interior and Energy Departments. Rejected 223-190: R 73-62; D 150-128 (ND 92-99; SD 58-29), Oct. 5, 1978. A two-thirds majority vote (276 in this case) is required to override a veto. The president had requested $11,039,449,000. A "nay" was a vote supporting the president's position.

2. H Res 1434. National Energy Act. Bolling, D-Mo., motion to order the previous question [thus ending debate on adoption of the resolution to waive all points of order so that the House could consider en bloc the conference reports on the five pieces of the National Energy Act — (HR 5263, HR 5037, HR 5289, HR 5146, HR 4018)]. (The vote prevented a separate vote on the natural gas pricing section of the bill, which had been sought by its opponents.) Motion agreed to 207-206: R 8-127; D 199-79 (ND 136-55; SD 63-24), Oct. 13, 1978. A "yea" was a vote supporting the president's position.

3. HR 6782. Emergency Farm Bill. Adoption of the conference report on the bill to provide a one-year flexible parity program with graduated land diversion and target price levels for wheat, corn and cotton, and to raise loan rates for these commodities beginning Oct. 1, 1979 (with retroactive payments for 1978 crops). Rejected 150-268: R 70-75; D 80-193 (ND 26-160; SD 54-33), April 12, 1978. A "nay" was a vote supporting the president's position.

4. HR 11983. Federal Election Commission-Public Financing. Sisk, D-Calif., motion to order the previous question (thus ending debate) on the adoption of the rule (H Res 1172) providing for House floor consideration of the fiscal 1979 authorization bill for the Federal Election Commission. (Opponents of the rule sought to defeat the previous question in order to permit drafting an alternative rule that would allow a House vote on public financing of House general elections.) Motion agreed to 213-196: R 106-30; D 107-166 (ND 45-144; SD 62-22), July 19, 1978. The rule subsequently was adopted by voice vote.

5. HR 12514. Foreign Military Aid. Wright, D-Texas, amendment, to the Fascell, D-Fla., amendment, to lift the U.S. arms embargo against Turkey when the president certified to Congress that the action was in the national interest of the United States and NATO and that Turkey was acting in good faith to achieve a settlement of the Cyprus problem. Adopted 208-205: R 78-64; D 130-141 (ND 64-123; SD 66-18), Aug. 1, 1978. A "yea" was a vote supporting the president's position. (The Fascell amendment, as amended, was adopted subsequently by voice vote.)

6. HR 12931. Foreign Aid Appropriations, Fiscal 1979. Miller, R-Ohio, amendment, to the Young, R-Fla., amendment to reduce all appropriations in the bill by 8 percent except funds for Israel and Egypt. Rejected 184-199: R 88-43; D 96-156 (ND 42-133; SD 54-23), Aug. 14, 1978. A "nay" was a vote supporting the president's position.

7. HR 12931. Foreign Aid Appropriations, Fiscal 1979. Young, R-Fla., amendment to prohibit indirect U.S. aid to Uganda, Cambodia, Laos and Vietnam. Rejected 198-203: R 101-35; D 97-168 (ND 52-134; SD 45-34), Aug. 3, 1978. A "nay" was a vote supporting the president's position.

8. HR 9375. Fiscal 1978 Supplemental Appropriations. Mahon, D-Texas, motion that the House recede and concur in the Senate amendment, to the bill, rescinding $462 million appropriated in fiscal 1977 for the Defense Department for production of three B-1 bombers. Motion agreed to 234-182: R 30-106; D 204-76 (ND 155-38; SD 49-38), Feb. 22, 1978. A "yea" was a vote supporting the president's position.

9. HR 10929. Defense Procurement Authorization. Passage, over the president's Aug. 17 veto, of the bill to authorize $36,956,969,000 for Defense Department weapons procurement and military research programs in fiscal 1979. Rejected 191-206: R 107-23; D 84-183 (ND 34-150; SD 50-33), Sept. 7, 1978. A two-thirds majority vote (265 in this case) is required for passage over a veto. A "nay" was a vote supporting the president's position.

10. HR 6805. Consumer Protection Agency. Passage of the bill to establish an independent Office of Consumer Representation within the Executive Branch to represent the interests of consumers before federal agencies and courts. Rejected 189-227: R 17-126; D 172-101 (ND 147-40; SD 25-61), Feb. 8, 1978. A "yea" was a vote supporting the president's position.

11. HR 8494. Lobbying Disclosure. Passage of the bill to require annual registration and quarterly reporting by major lobbying organizations as well as disclosure of grass-roots (indirect) lobbying activities by reporting organizations and the names and addresses of major groups contributing to reporting organizations. Passed 259-140: R 75-67; D 184-73 (ND 143-39; SD 41-34), April 26, 1978. A "yea" was a vote supporting the president's position.

12. H Con Res 559. Fiscal 1979 Budget Targets. Holt, R-Md., amendment to set aggregate budget targets as follows: revenues of $440.1 billion, budget authority of $546.8 billion, outlays of $488.3 billion and a deficit of $48.2 billion. Rejected 197-203: R 139-1; D 58-202 (ND 24-155; SD 34-47), May 3, 1978.

13. HR 12929. Labor-HEW Appropriations, Fiscal 1979. Miller, R-Ohio, amendment to reduce controllable spending in the bill by 2 percent. Adopted 220-181: R 122-18; D 98-163 (ND 47-133; SD 51-30), June 13, 1978.

14. HR 12050. Tuition Tax Credits. Gradison, R-Ohio, motion to recommit the conference report on the bill to provide income tax credits for college and vocational school tuitions to the conference committee, with instructions that House conferees insist on a provision making tuitions paid to private elementary and secondary schools eligible for a credit. Motion agreed to 207-185: R 100-33; D 107-152 (ND 91-86; SD 16-66), Oct. 12, 1978. 1978. A "nay" was a vote supporting the president's position.

15. HR 50. Full Employment Act. Jeffords, R-Vt., substitute amendment, to the Sarasin, R-Conn., amendments, to require the president, beginning with the third year after passage of the bill, to include in his annual economic report goals for reasonable price stability, and to formulate policies for the reduction of inflation; and to define reasonable price stability as reduction of inflation to 3 percent within five years of enactment. Rejected 198-223: R 142-2; D 56-221 (ND 26-168; SD 30-53), March 9, 1978. (The Sarasin amendments, as amended by the Wright amendments, were adopted subsequently by voice vote.)

16. HR 13511. Revenue Act of 1978. Corman, D-Calif., amendment to provide an $18.1 billion tax cut including more benefits to taxpayers earning less than $50,000, and less to those earning more. Rejected 193-225: R 8-134; D 185-91 (ND 164-27; SD 21-64), Aug. 10, 1978. A "yea" was a vote supporting the president's position.

CQ 1979 Key Votes

Energy, Foreign Policy Issues Dominate Key Votes for 1979

Energy and foreign policy issues dominated key House and Senate votes during 1979.

The key votes selected by Congressional Quarterly are a reflection of the session's preoccupation with these issues, particularly energy.

A quarter of the 1979 key votes came on energy legislation. The central matter was a windfall tax to channel to the government some of the new profits that oil companies would make as price controls on oil were phased out and eventually lifted completely. Members also considered creation of a special board to cut red tape for priority energy projects, a multibillion-dollar investment in synthetic fuels and a moratorium on nuclear plant construction.

Congress also showed considerable interest in international affairs and higher defense spending.

During the first six months of the session, much of the time was spent on foreign policy issues. One of the most hotly debated was President Carter's effort to redirect American relations away from Taiwan and toward Communist China. Members of both chambers opposed to this switch fought a losing battle, but produced some anxious moments for the administration when the roll was called.

House Key Votes

1. WINDFALL PROFITS TAX. When President Carter announced in April his plan to end gradually oil price controls, he asked Congress to tax the additional profits the government's move would bring to oil companies.

The president argued that decontrol would give the oil industry an undeserved windfall. Oil selling for $6 a barrel would suddenly triple in price, and other prices would also rise to match the world price. Carter wanted the tax revenues to be used for development of synthetic fuels, fuel assistance for the poor and aid to mass transit.

After some tinkering, the House Ways and Means Committee basically endorsed Carter's proposal. Included in its bill (HR 3919) was the tax considered most onerous by the oil industry: a permanent tax on new oil discoveries.

Getting rid of that permanent tax was the principal goal of two oil-state members of the Ways and Means Committee — James R. Jones, D-Okla., and W. Henson Moore, R-La. They drafted a proposal that would end the tax on newly discovered and hard-to-get oil in 1990 and lower the tax rate on other types of oil from the committee-approved rate of 70 percent to 60 percent. Carter had proposed a 50 percent rate.

The Jones-Moore proposal was designed to appeal to House moderates who wanted a tax similar to the administration's, but also wanted to encourage additional oil production. It also drew support from Republicans and Democrats from oil-producing states, who saw the substitute as their best chance to weaken the committee proposal. On June 28, the House adopted their substitute, 236-183: R 146-10; D 90-173 (ND 28-152; SD 62-21).

2. OIL PRICE CONTROLS. Congress had last squarely faced the question of domestic price controls on oil in 1975. At that time Democrats resisted a move by President Ford to end the controls. But the debate generated a compromise that set a future schedule for gradually lifting the controls, with complete decontrol scheduled for October 1981.

After that timetable was set, liberal Democrats in Congress had scrambled to block moves by Republicans and others to move up the decontrol date. It was clear the decontrol advocates were getting stronger every year.

In April 1979, President Carter announced that he would start ending price controls gradually, in anticipation of the 1981 decontrol date. He argued that controls were only encouraging energy consumption by keeping the price low and were thwarting efforts to push conservation.

But Carter's action led to an outburst from liberal Democrats, who said decontrol would feed the already fat oil industry at the expense of poor and middle income Americans.

Although they realized they were short of votes, supporters of oil price controls wanted House members on the record on the question. During Oct. 11 action on the Energy Department authorization bill (HR 3000), Toby Moffett, D-Conn., proposed an amendment to keep the agency from lifting controls. But he lost, 135-257: R 7-137; D 128-120 (ND 119-53; SD 9-67).

3. ENERGY MOBILIZATION BOARD. The House generally agreed with President Carter's proposal to create a special board to cut red tape for priority energy projects, such as pipelines, refineries and synthetic fuels plants. But it faced a debate over just how much power that board should have.

The Commerce Committee had sparked opposition when it wrote a bill giving the board the authority to recommend to the president a waiver of substantive laws, such as

---

How Votes Were Selected

Congressional Quarterly each year selects a series of key votes on major issues.

Selection of Issues. An issue is judged by the extent it represents one or more of the following:
- A matter of major controversy.
- A test of presidential or political power.
- A decision of potentially great impact on the nation and lives of Americans.

Selection of Votes. For each group of related votes on an issue, only one key vote is usually chosen. This is the vote, in the opinion of Congressional Quarterly editors, that was important in determining the outcome.

In the description of the key votes, the designation ND denotes Northern Democrats and SD denotes Southern Democrats.

clean air rules. A board with more modest powers had been recommended by the Interior Committee.

When the bill (HR 4985) reached the floor, the Interior proposal for a board with more limited powers failed by a narrow margin, 192-215. Then Bob Eckhardt, D-Texas, offered an amendment to strike the provision in the Commerce bill giving the board authority over substantive federal law.

Noting that the president also opposed the substantive waiver provision, Eckhardt argued that it would threaten laws worked out by Congress over many years. Joining him in opposition was conservative Robert E. Bauman, R-Md. In response to arguments that a strong board could improve energy security, Bauman replied: "Some of us feel that if we destroy the Constitution, we have lost the greatest assurance of security we have."

Majority Leader Jim Wright, D-Texas, spoke for the opposition, saying the Eckhardt amendment would "make a shambles of any opportunity Congress might have to expedite an energy project under this legislation." The author of the waiver provision, John D. Dingell, D-Mich., also attacked the amendment.

On Nov. 1, the House opted for a more powerful board and rejected the Eckhardt proposal, 153-250: R 27-121; D 126-129 (ND 112-63; SD 14-66).

4. NUCLEAR PLANT MORATORIUM. The March accident at the Three Mile Island reactor in Pennsylvania prompted nuclear critics in Congress to seek a six-month halt in construction of new reactors.

Rep. Edward J. Markey, D-Mass., and others argued that a six-month pause would allow the Nuclear Regulatory Commission to incorporate into its safety rules any lessons learned from the accident. Because the proposed reactors would not be operating for several years, they said, the moratorium would not reduce energy supplies. Markey had support from the House Interior Committee, but not from the other panel with jurisdiction, the Commerce Committee.

Opponents of a moratorium contended it was intended only as a symbolic attack against the nuclear industry. They noted the moratorium would have little practical effect since the NRC itself had said no new construction permits would be issued for several months, until after reforms prompted by Three Mile Island had been carried out. And they pointed to the situation in Iran, where Americans were being held hostage in the U.S. Embassy, as a reminder of unstable oil supplies, which they said nuclear power could replace.

On Nov. 29, when Markey offered the moratorium plan as an amendment to the Nuclear Regulatory Commission authorization bill (HR 2608), the House overwhelmingly rejected the proposal, 135-254: R 23-121; D 112-133 (ND 105-60; SD 7-73).

5. HOSPITAL COST CONTAINMENT. President Carter suffered a critical loss in his three-year campaign to clamp down on rising hospital costs when the House Nov. 15 emphatically rejected a compromise version of his hospital cost containment legislation (HR 2626).

The vote came on an amendment by a respected younger Democrat, Richard A. Gephardt, Mo., to drop mandatory hospital revenue controls from the bill and authorize only a new national commission to study the problem of hospital costs. The House subsequently passed the commission proposal, which White House press secretary Jody Powell termed "a joke."

Gephardt's substitute was adopted 234-166, with 99 Democrats joining an almost solid bloc of Republicans to defeat the president's proposal: R 135-8; D 99-158 (ND 43-137; SD 56-21).

Conservative members of both parties voted against the president, and so did a significant number of younger Democrats like Gephardt with reputations for loyalty to the president. Gephardt's proposal had originally been proposed by Republicans in House committees.

The American Medical Association, hospital organizations and big business had run a sophisticated, sustained lobbying campaign against the president's bill, overwhelming supporters from groups representing the elderly and organized labor.

Carter tried hard to paint his proposal as a key anti-inflation measure. Administration officials had also substantially compromised their original 1977 bill, bidding for support by providing for exemptions or special treatment for more than half the nation's hospitals.

But opponents argued that the bill would add another costly burden of regulation for hospitals, and that curbing hospital revenues would freeze medical technology and foreclose future life-saving discoveries.

6. RELATIONS WITH TAIWAN. The same day (March 8) that the Senate defeated an attempt to virtually retain the mutual defense treaty with Taiwan, the House turned down a conservative move to restore relations between the United States and the Republic of China on Taiwan. The tandem votes assured congressional acceptance of President Carter's plan to conduct relations with Taiwan on an "unofficial" basis, a key part of the administration's new China policy.

The downgrading of U.S. ties with Taiwan, including the termination of a mutual defense treaty with that nation, had cleared the way for Carter to establish relations with the People's Republic of China on the mainland. Both houses of Congress accepted Carter's new policy toward China in spite of widespread friendship on Capitol Hill for the Taiwan government. Congress did, however, insist on a resolution of support for Taiwan's independence.

The key vote on the House side came on an amendment by Dan Quayle, R-Ind., to the Taiwan relations act (HR 2479) establishing a quasi-government corporation to handle future relations with the Taiwan people on an unofficial basis. Quayle's amendment would have raised the level of the U.S. presence in Taiwan to a "government liaison office," similar to the office the United States had maintained in Peking from 1974 until March 1979. Administration officials said such an office would re-establish formal ties with Taiwan, in violation of Carter's agreement with Peking.

The Quayle amendment was narrowly defeated 172-181: R 113-13; D 59-168 (ND 27-131; SD 32-37). The vote showed that conservatives did not have sufficient support to overturn Carter's China policy.

7. RELATIONS WITH PANAMA. After watching the Senate struggle with the controversial Panama Canal treaties in 1978, the House got its chance in 1979 to take a stand on turning the canal over to Panama. President Carter sent Congress legislation that was needed to carry out the treaties.

Although an overwhelming majority of House members clearly opposed the treaties, the House rejected most attempts by conservatives to tack restrictions on the implementing legislation. Carter said some of the conservative's proposed restrictions violated the treaties, thus legally giving Panama the right to take over the canal immediately if they were enacted. The treaties require the United States and Panama to run the canal jointly until the year 2000, when Panama would assume full control of the waterway.

The major attempt by conservatives to overturn the treaties was on an amendment by George Hansen, R-Idaho, to the implementing bill (HR 111). Hansen's amendment would have required Panama to reimburse the United States for most of its costs in implementing the treaties. The administration said that violated the treaties, which obligated the United States to pay such expenses.

Hansen charged that Carter deliberately lied to the American people in 1978 when he said the treaties would not cost the taxpayers anything. Hansen estimated that moving military bases and other expenses would total $2 billion to $4 billion. The Carter administration initially put the treaty cost at $385 million, but eventually admitted the cost could run as high as $1 billion.

When Hansen offered his amendment on the House floor, John M. Murphy, D-N.Y., introduced a substitute that required some of the U.S. treaty costs to be paid by the users of the canal rather than by the United States or Panama. The administration supported Murphy's substitute as the best alternative to Hansen's amendment.

The House accepted the Murphy substitute by a vote of 220-200: R 25-132; D 196-68 (ND 155-26; SD 40-42). The vote indicated that the administration barely had enough support in the House to defeat conservative attempts to derail the treaties.

Although the House later adopted other provisions that Carter claimed violated the treaties, the Senate approved a bill much closer to the administration position. A compromise finally adopted in September generally resembled the House version, but did not include the Hansen-type provisions that Carter most feared.

8. DRAFT REGISTRATION. In what was widely interpreted as a vote against resuming the military draft, the House Sept. 12 rejected, 259-155, a proposal to initiate registration of 18-year-old males for a future draft should an international emergency occur. The vote came on an amendment by Patricia Schroeder, D-Colo., to delete the proposal from the fiscal 1980 defense procurement authorization bill (HR 4040). The registration provision, which was opposed by President Carter, had been added to the bill by the House Armed Services Committee.

House members still disillusioned by the Vietnam experience were joined in opposition to registration by some conservatives who traditionally take a hard line on defense issues, but also oppose governmental intrusions into Americans' private lives. Majorities of both parties backed the Schroeder amendment: R 83-69; D 176-87 (ND 154-30; SD 22-57).

There was no connection theoretically between the registration proposal and the future of the all volunteer army. Registration supporters argued that the decision to move from conscription to an all-volunteer force in the early 1970s was based, in part, on the assumption that registration would continue so that in the event of a war the draft could be resumed quickly. Under the current skeleton Selective Service structure, it would take months to gear up the system and process the first recruits for the armed services.

Opponents of the committee's provision charged it would be a foot in the door for eventual resumption of peacetime conscription, and that if the Pentagon had easy access to a large manpower pool, presidents would be more likely to consider military interventions around the globe.

Some registration supporters also used the proposal to debate the all-volunteer army. Since early 1977 defense hard-liners had been citing a wide range of Army manpower problems as evidence that U.S. defense needs could not be met by the all-volunteer system. They cited the Army's recurrent shortage of recruits, especially those scoring high on aptitude tests.

But supporters of the all-volunteer system maintained that the shortages could be corrected by offering special bonuses and fringe benefits to attract the kind of recruits wanted by the Army.

9. BUDGET DISCIPLINE. Senate Budget Committee Chairman Edmund S. Muskie, D-Maine, lost his fight to test Congress' fiscal discipline when the House Nov. 8 approved a second fiscal 1980 budget resolution (S Con Res 36) that excluded Senate-passed provisions requiring certain committees to make $3.6 billion in spending cuts. The vote was 205-190: R 0-145; D 205-45 (ND 146-26; SD 59-19).

The House vote doomed the use of "reconciliation" instructions to ensure that committees met the spending limits set in the budget resolution.

The Senate had approved the budget-cutting technique under prodding by Muskie. But House Budget Chairman Robert N. Giaimo, D-Conn., maintained the House would not accept a budget containing such orders.

After the House rejected the enforcement provision, Muskie and his panel worked to create a substitute that would encourage committees to spend within their limits.

Their alternative — language banning a third budget resolution to bail out committees that had overspent — was ultimately approved by both chambers. But many lawmakers questioned whether the "sense of Congress commitment" would prevent Capitol Hill from hiking the fiscal 1980 budget if the economy turned sharply down, as most experts predicted.

10. FEDERAL TRADE COMMISSION POWERS. The controversy over whether Congress should be allowed to veto the Federal Trade Commission's actions continued in 1979. The dispute had forced the agency to receive funds outside the normal authorization-appropriation process since fiscal 1977, with the House demanding a congressional veto while the Senate opposed it.

The House again approved an authorization bill (HR 2313) with provisions to rein in the agency by subjecting all regulatory actions to a congressional veto and banning some activities outright. The veto seemed to have its best chance of passage in 1979 because of the anti-regulatory climate.

FTC rules carry the weight of law for businesses, and critics said the agency was exceeding its mandate to protect consumers and business against fraud and deception. Government should be controlled by elected officials, they said.

Business lobbied heavily for the veto provision. Consumer groups supported the FTC as a protector of their interests in the marketplace.

Opponents, including President Carter, argued that the one-chamber veto was unconstitutional because it encroached on the authority of the executive branch.

The bill allowed congressional veto of any FTC rule and permitted one chamber to veto if the other did not adopt a resolution of disapproval within 30 days. The bill also barred the FTC from regulating the funeral home industry and investigating or prosecuting antitrust cases against agricultural cooperatives. The vote Nov. 27 to pass the bill was 321-63: R 138-2; D 183-61 (ND 110-56; SD 73-5).

11. WELFARE REFORM. House approval of President Carter's scaled-down welfare reform bill (HR 4904) on Nov. 7 showed that a step-by-step approach to changing the welfare system had a much better chance of succeeding in Congress than an effort to make a wholesale restructuring of the system all at once.

The 222-184 victory for the president's plan was in marked contrast to the failure of the administration's comprehensive reform proposal to even reach the House floor in the 95th Congress.

However, the regional and party breakdown of the vote, which showed Northern Democrats sharply split from the conservative coalition of Republicans and Southern Democrats — R 29-118; D 193-66 (ND 165-15; SD 28-51) — illustrated the continuing deep division over what reform of the welfare system — a goal sought by all — really meant.

To supporters of the bill, the provisions establishing a national minimum benefit for welfare recipients and allowing unemployed two-parent families in all states to get benefits were modest but essential steps toward helping the very poorest of the poor.

But to opponents, the provisions were another step on the road to a national guaranteed income and total federal control of welfare. They argued that control should be returned to the states and that welfare recipients should be placed under tougher work requirements.

12. DEPARTMENT OF EDUCATION. Heavy lobbying by educators, led by the powerful National Education Association (NEA), overcame widespread concerns about creation of a new federal bureaucracy when the House July 11 passed a bill establishing a separate Department of Education.

The narrow 210-206 vote for passage of the bill (HR 2444) was a critical victory in the NEA's longtime fight for the department. President Carter, who won the organization's first presidential endorsement in 1976, worked personally for the bill, and was endorsed for re-election the day after it cleared Congress.

The breakdown of the vote, R 35-117; D 175-89 (ND 108-70; SD 67-19), reflected the contrasting criticisms of the new department that came from the coalition of conservatives and liberals who opposed the bill.

Conservative Republicans said establishment of a separate department would lead to more federal control over education and threaten the traditional independence of local schools. Many liberal Northern Democrats, on the other hand, voted against the bill because of their opposition to a series of conservatively oriented amendments, added by the House, on controversial social topics such as abortion, busing and school prayer. They also feared that education programs would suffer if they were split off from health and welfare programs traditionally supported together by education, labor and social welfare interests.

13. ALASKA LANDS. Throughout 1978 and 1979, Congress had been trying to agree on legislation (HR 39) that would establish millions of acres of new national parks, wildlife refuges, forests and wild and scenic rivers in Alaska. The administration, seeking to preserve the land for future generations, had dubbed the bill its top environmental priority.

But the legislation represented a classic conflict between conservationists and developers. The developers argued that by creating national park land in some areas, Congress would preclude mining, logging and oil and gas drilling and cut off access to much-needed natural resources. Alaska's congressional delegation came down on the side of the developers.

Environmentalists had won in the House in 1978. But in 1979 both the Merchant Marine and Interior committees had reported bills considered pro-development, despite the opposition of Interior Chairman Morris K. Udall, D-Ariz.

Udall and John B. Anderson, R-Ill., with the backing of a coalition of conservation groups, then drafted a more pro-conservation bill, which they took to the full House. The measure set aside 125.4 million acres, 67 million of those as wilderness, the most restrictive classification.

When the measure finally came to a vote May 15, environmentalists thought they had the edge, but the outcome was not clear until the final vote. Udall made a motion to substitute the Udall-Anderson version of the bill. It passed 268-157: R 66-90; D-202-67 (ND 154-32; SD 48-35).

But the Senate did not pick up the ball. A version of the bill reported Oct. 30 by the Senate Energy Committee never reached the floor.

14. DIGGS CENSURE. The House voted overwhelmingly in 1979 to censure Rep. Charles C. Diggs Jr., D-Mich., for misuse of his clerk-hire funds.

The July 31 vote to censure Diggs was 414-0. Four members, including Diggs himself, voted present.

Following the reading of the censure resolution by House Speaker Thomas P. O'Neill Jr., D-Mass., Diggs told reporters he intended to serve out the remainder of his term and seek re-election in 1980.

Diggs became only the second member of the House to be censured in this century, and the first to be censured since 1921, when Thomas L. Blanton, D-Texas (1917-37) was disciplined for having objectionable language printed in the *Congressional Record*.

Diggs was censured after he admitted in a letter to the House Committee on Standards of Official Conduct that he had padded his office payroll and accepted kickbacks from five of his congressional office employees. In the letter, he apologized to his colleagues for any "discredit" his actions might have brought to the House and promised to repay the U.S. Treasury $40,031.66 plus interest, which he said represented his personal gain from the kickbacks. In return for agreeing to be censured, he asked that the committee end its investigation into his financial affairs.

Diggs had been charged by the Standards Committee with 18 violations of House rules. The charges were filed after Diggs was convicted in October 1978 on 29 felony counts similar to the House charges against him. Diggs appealed the conviction, which at year's end was pending before the U.S. Court of Appeals for the District of Columbia.

The day before the House was to vote on the censure resolution, a group of Republicans attempted to force a vote on a resolution to expel Diggs from the House. Their attempt failed when the House voted 205-197 to table — and thus kill — the expulsion resolution. Twelve Republicans joined 193 Democrats in voting to table; 134 Republicans and 63 Democrats voted against tabling.

Under the Constitution, a two-thirds majority of the House is required to expel a member. O'Neill later issued a statement critical of the Republicans for injecting partisan politics into what he said had been formerly a non-partisan deliberation.

15. ANTI-BUSING AMENDMENT. The House July 24 decisively turned back a proposed constitutional amendment to ban busing for purposes of school desegregation. The proposal not only fell short of the two-thirds vote needed for passage, but failed to get even a simple majority. It was rejected by a vote of 209-216: R 114-40; D 95-176 (ND 48-138; SD 47-38).

The overwhelming defeat was attributed to an intensive lobbying campaign against the proposal by House liberals and their civil rights allies, and to widespread reluctance, even among many busing foes, to alter the Constitution to accommodate a relatively narrow political issue.

The amendment (H J Res 74) would have barred school systems or the courts from compelling any student to attend a public school other than the one nearest his or her home to achieve racial desegregation. It also would have given Congress the power to pass legislation to enforce the amendment.

The amendment was brought to the floor under the rarely used discharge petition procedure. On June 27, busing foe Ronald M. Mottl, D-Ohio, had lined up a majority of House members (218) to sign a petition discharging the Judiciary Committee from consideration of the amendment and bringing it directly to the floor. The committee had never reported any of the numerous anti-busing amendments referred to it in recent years.

Before the key vote on passage, the House voted 227-183 to formally take the amendment away from the committee.

16. CHRYSLER AID. The House's resounding 271-136 vote Dec. 18 to provide $3.4 billion in aid to the Chrysler Corp., was won with the help of a varied contingent of lobbyists with a stake in the auto firm, lawmakers said.

The administration wanted help for the company to preserve hundreds of thousands of jobs that might be lost if it folded — a goal shared by the United Auto Workers union.

Thousands of dealers and suppliers also pleaded for aid to Chrysler so they could stay in business.

And representatives of the nation's major mayor-governor groups fought for assistance because a Chrysler collapse would double unemployment in Detroit and many other cities.

"It was a crazy combination of votes," commented one Michigan lawmaker after the bill (HR 5860) was approved.

The House-passed version of the legislation authorized $1.5 billion in loan guarantees to Chrysler if the company could raise another $1.9 billion in concessions from parties that would be hardest hit if it failed.

Senate Key Votes

1. FILIBUSTER LIMITATION. The Senate tightened its rules at the beginning of the 96th Congress in an effort to control the use of the post-cloture filibuster tactic by a minority of the Senate's members.

Senate rule 22 already had limited senators to one hour of debate apiece on a bill after the Senate voted to invoke cloture on that bill and thus cut off debate. But Sen. James B. Allen, D-Ala. (1969-78), began in 1976 to use repeated quorum calls, roll-call votes and other parliamentary techniques to delay Senate action even after the Senate had voted to invoke cloture, in order to kill a bill or to demand concessions from the bill's supporters. Allen's techniques soon were picked up by other senators.

Senate Majority Leader Robert C. Byrd, D-W. Va., proposed a package of proposals at the beginning of 1979 to restrict both pre- and post-cloture filibuster delaying tactics. When strong Republican opposition developed to some of Byrd's proposals, however, he decided to go ahead with only one of them.

The proposal that was adopted required the Senate to hold a final vote on a bill within 100 hours of debate after the Senate had voted to invoke cloture. All time spent on quorum calls, roll-call votes and other parliamentary procedures were to be counted in computing the 100-hour debate ceiling. The proposal was approved by the Senate 78-16.

2. OUTSIDE INCOME LIMIT. Acting with little notice and after only a few minutes of debate, the Senate voted in early 1979 to delay for four years one of the most controversial provisions of its two-year-old ethics code. There were only about six senators on the floor at the time. Because none of them requested a recorded vote, none was taken.

The effect of the vote was to put off until 1983 a strict limitation on the amount of money senators could earn in addition to their congressional salaries. The ceiling on earned income was 15 percent of a senator's pay, or $8,625 a year at the annual salary level of $57,500 then in effect.

Government reform groups branded the vote a setback in their battle to maintain rigid standards of conduct for members of Congress and strongly criticized the senators' unwillingness to be recorded on the issue.

A few weeks later, senators agreed to a request by Sen. Gary Hart, D-Colo., to reconsider their earlier voice vote to delay the earned income limit. Senators then voted 44-54 not to reimpose the limitation. Although the second vote did not alter the end result, it quieted criticisms of the Senate's earlier action.

3. TALMADGE DISCIPLINARY ACTION. Sen. Herman E. Talmadge, D-Ga., was "denounced" by the Senate for financial misconduct in 1979 after a lengthy Select Ethics Committee investigation and hearings.

The proceeding against Talmadge was the first to come to a vote on the Senate floor since 1967, when Thomas J. Dodd, D-Conn. (House 1953-57; Senate 1959-71), was censured for financial misconduct.

The Senate Ethics panel began a formal investigation of Talmadge's financial affairs in December 1978 following press reports of irregularities in the senator's campaign finances and office expense account. The committee held hearings in the spring and summer of 1979 on five charges of misconduct against Talmadge.

Throughout the investigation and hearings, Talmadge denied he knowingly violated Senate rules and blamed the irregularities in his finances on accounting errors committed by his staff.

Although the Ethics Committee did not recommend Talmadge's "censure," it concluded he "knew or should have known" of the improper acts he was accused of committing, and should be "denounced." The committee said his conduct was "reprehensible" and constituted "gross neglect of duty" which "tends to bring the Senate into dishonor and disrepute."

The vote to denounce Talmadge was 81-15. Talmadge maintained the Senate action was a "personal victory" because there had been no finding that he intentionally violated Senate rules.

4. NEW CHINA POLICY. The Senate turned back an effort in March by congressional supporters of Taiwan that virtually would have restored the 1955 mutual defense treaty between the United States and the Republic of China on Taiwan.

The downgrading of U.S. ties with Taiwan — including the termination of the mutual defense treaty — had cleared the way for President Carter to establish relations with the People's Republic of China. Both houses of Congress went along with Carter's new policy toward Peking, in spite of widespread friendship on Capitol Hill toward the Taiwan government. Congress did, however, insist on a resolution of support for Taiwan's independence from the mainland.

The key Senate vote on the issue came on an amendment by Charles H. Percy, R-Ill, to the bill (S 245) providing for informal relations between the United States and Taiwan once the U.S. Embassy in Taipei was closed.

As reported by the Foreign Relations Committee, the bill pledged the United States to continue supplying Taiwan with defensive arms, and said any hostile action against Taiwan would be viewed with "grave concern" by the United States.

Percy proposed, instead, a declaration that any attack on Taiwan would be a threat to the "security interests" of the United States. Percy said such a statement would warn mainland China to keep its hands off Taiwan. But administration supporters said that amendment would have had the effect of restoring the defense treaty and cause a break in U.S. relations with Peking.

The Senate rejected Percy's amendment by a surprisingly close vote of 42-50: R 35-5; D 7-45 (ND 3-33; SD 4-12).

5. INTERNATIONAL DEVELOPMENT BANKS. Every year since 1977 the House has voted to prohibit the World Bank and other international development banks from using U.S. contributions to aid Vietnam, Cuba and other communist countries. And each year the Senate eliminated those prohibitions.

The same thing happened in 1979, but the Senate came closer than ever before to adopting the House-passed restrictions. A motion to delete a ban on all aid to Vietnam, Cuba, Angola, the Central African Empire, Cambodia and Laos passed by only three votes, 49-46: R 19-21; D 30-25 (ND 25-12; SD 5-13).

The closeness of the vote seemed to indicate that a growing number of senators were becoming less willing to undo House-passed restrictions on the World Bank.

Conservatives in both chambers argued that American taxpayers did not want their money going to Vietnam and other communist countries. The only way to stop such aid, they said, was to prohibit the international development banks from using U.S. money for those loans.

But the Nixon, Ford and Carter administrations all agreed that the United States could not and should not place restrictions on the "indirect" money it contributes to those banks. No other nation places restrictions on its contributions, administration officials maintained. By restricting its contributions, the United States would be setting a precedent that could eventually kill the banks, they argued.

6. SANCTIONS AGAINST RHODESIA. Ever since Rhodesia illegally declared independence from Great Britain in 1965, Congress has debated whether to use economic sanctions as a lever to force Rhodesia's white minority government to hand power over to the black majority. From 1965 to 1971 the United States complied with sanctions imposed by the United Nations. Congress lifted a ban on importation of Rhodesian chrome in 1971, but reimposed economic sanctions in 1977 at the request of President Carter.

Congressional conservatives, who have always opposed the sanctions, renewed pressure to lift them in 1978 when Rhodesian Prime Minister Ian Smith agreed to give limited power to Rhodesian blacks. In April 1979 Bishop Abel T. Muzorewa was elected Rhodesia's first black prime minister.

Immediately after the election, conservatives renewed their call to lift sanctions. President Carter said the sanctions should remain in effect because the white minority continued to control the key government departments of defense, justice and internal security.

But the Senate on May 15, two weeks after the new government was installed, overwhelmingly passed a resolution urging Carter to lift sanctions. Sponsored by Richard S. Schweiker, R-Pa., the resolution was incorporated in the 1980 State Department authorization bill (HR 3363) by a vote of 75-19: R 38-2; D 37-17 (ND 20-17; SD 17-0).

Although the Senate action could not have forced Carter to lift sanctions, the overwhelming vote showed that most senators felt Rhodesia had done enough to satisfy international demands for black rule. The vote also showed a considerable switch in congressional sentiment: 20 senators who voted in 1978 to retain sanctions supported the Schweiker resolution.

The Senate vote also forced Carter to accept a later compromise that required him to lift sanctions by Nov. 15. Carter finally lifted sanctions Dec. 16, after a British governor assumed temporary authority in Rhodesia in preparation for new national elections.

7. DEFENSE SPENDING. Consideration of the SALT II arms control treaty with the Soviet Union focused the Senate's attention on national defense. A number of senators, both Republicans and Democrats, began insisting on substantial increases in military spending before they could even consider supporting the treaty.

During debate on the second fiscal 1980 budget resolution (S Con Res 36) Sept. 18, the pro-defense senators easily defeated the Senate Budget Committee and pushed an amendment to increase defense spending 3 percent above inflation in fiscal 1980. Then, in a significant — though largely symbolic — vote, they successfully pushed an amendment setting a goal of 5 percent annual real growth in the military budgets for fiscal 1981 and 1982. The vote was 55-42: R 31-7; D 24-35 (ND 9-31; SD 15-4).

8. M-X MISSILE. By an 11-77 vote: R 2-36; D 9-41 (ND 9-26; SD 0-15), the Senate Nov. 9 rejected an amendment by Mark O. Hatfield, R-Ore., that would have eliminated $670 million sought by the administration to begin building prototypes of a mobile, intercontinental missile, called the M-X, to replace the increasingly vulnerable Minuteman missile. The amendment was offered to the fiscal 1980 defense appropriations bill (HR 5359).

The vote reflected a widespread consensus within the Senate that the United States should develop a land-based intercontinental missile powerful enough to destroy Soviet missiles in their underground launchers. Defense experts predicted that by 1982 Soviet missiles would be sufficiently accurate to pose a severe threat to the Minuteman.

For years liberals opposed any improvements in U.S. nuclear weaponry that could pose a direct threat to Soviet weapons. If the Soviet Union thought its missile capability was endangered, it would be more likely to use its nuclear arsenal to avert its possible destruction by the West, these members argued.

Several liberals, who in the past supported this argument, voted against the Hatfield amendment, apparently in hopes of winning conservative support for the SALT II strategic arms control treaty. But several sources doubted that there were enough such votes to kill M-X even if the SALT treaty were rejected.

Nevertheless, uncertainty remained over how to base and protect the M-X. There was strong skepticism in the Senate toward the so-called "racetrack" launching plan for M-X favored by President Carter. This was due primarily to the estimated $30 billion price tag, the complexity of the design and the tremendous human and physical impact the racetrack system would have in Nevada and Utah where it was proposed to be built. Immediately after rejecting the Hatfield amendment, the Senate adopted, 89-0, an amendment by Ted Stevens, R-Alaska, stipulating that none of the funds spent on M-X could be used to commit the missile system to any one launching system.

9. FUEL AID TO THE POOR. An example of the regional differences that frequently divide members of Congress came Nov. 14 when the Senate voted on a formula for distributing federal aid to help poor people heat their homes. Senators from Northern states were almost unanimously opposed to those from Southern states over whether the fuel aid should be "tilted" toward the cold or warm regions.

The vote came on a bill (S 1724) establishing a two-year program, for fiscal years 1981 and 1982, that was designed to respond to the rapidly rising prices of home heating fuels. The bill later was made part of the windfall profits tax measure (HR 3919).

The original version of S 1724, as reported by the Finance and Labor and Human Resources committees, used a formula that was relatively generous to Southern states. This angered Rudy Boschwitz, R-Minn., and Edmund S. Muskie, D-Maine, who responded with an amendment that would have steered much of the fuel aid back to the Northern states.

The regional differences were clearly shown when Muskie moved to table a Robert Dole, R-Kan., amendment that was a modified version of the committees' distribution formula. Muskie's motion to table was rejected 41-50: R 20-19; D 21-31 (ND 21-15; SD 0-16).

The issue was resolved, at least temporarily, when the opposing factions came up with a compromise that was more favorable to the North than the committee bill, but less so than the Boschwitz-Muskie amendment. However, senators from both the North and South made clear that they thought the arrangement was unfairly favorable to the other region.

The House displayed a similar regional split when it voted on the formula for heating aid distribution for the winter of 1979-80.

10. ELECTORAL COLLEGE. A diverse Senate coalition that crossed party and ideological lines combined July 10 to defeat the proposed constitutional amendment to abolish the Electoral College and to elect the president by direct popular vote.

Some Northern liberals aligned with a majority of Republicans and Southern Democrats to thwart passage of the direct election amendment (S J Res 28). With no action on the amendment in the House, the Senate vote terminated consideration of the proposal during the 96th Congress.

For more than a decade, the amendment's major sponsor, Democratic Sen. Birch Bayh of Indiana, chairman of the Judiciary Subcommittee on the Constitution, had promoted the direct vote measure. When it was last brought to the Senate floor in 1970, the amendment fell victim to a late session filibuster.

Bayh and his allies argued that the Electoral College system may have been adequate for electing a president in the nation's early years but was an anachronism in the 20th century. Proponents contended that it constantly ran the risk of a misfire, sending a popular vote loser to the White House because he had obtained an electoral vote majority. Such an event, they warned, could bring a constitutional crisis.

Opponents countered that the system had not misfired since 1888 and that a constitutional change in the method of electing the president could unhinge the whole federal system with its checks and balances, concurrent majorities and separation of powers.

The amendment ran ahead by a vote of 51-48: R 12-28; D 39-20 (ND 31-9; SD 8-11) but fell 15 votes short of the required two-thirds majority of those present and voting needed to approve a constitutional amendment.

11. TELLICO DAM/ENDANGERED SPECIES. The floodgates of Tennessee's Tellico Dam were closed Nov. 30 and 16,000 acres of adjacent land were slowly innundated as environmentalists lost their fight to kill the controversial $130 million project.

In 1978, the Supreme Court had halted construction of the dam, agreeing with the argument of conservationists that it would destroy the habitat of a tiny endangered fish, the snail darter. The federal Endangered Species Act barred federal public works projects that threatened an endangered species or its habitat.

But proponents of the dam and others successfully amended the law later in the year by creating a commission that would have the power to grant projects an exemption from the act. The panel took up the Tellico question in January, but it refused to allow construction to proceed.

So dam proponents went back to Congress. In June, Sen. Howard H. Baker Jr., R-Tenn., tried to get the Senate to exempt Tellico, but members refused to go along, 43-52.

Dam proponents were more successful in the House, however, and slipped a Tellico exemption into the energy and water development appropriations bill (HR 4388). Nevertheless, when that bill got to the Senate, members again refused to give Tellico the go-ahead.

But on Sept. 10, with it became clear that the House intended to stand by its position, the Senate gave up the struggle and agreed to let the project proceed. The vote was 48-44: R 28-10; D 20-34 (ND 7-29; SD 13-5).

12. SYNTHETIC FUELS. Two Senate committees considered President Carter's proposal for a multibillion-dollar national investment in synthetic fuels, which are liquids and gases made from coal, shale and other unconventional energy sources. The program was designed to reduce U.S. dependence on imported oil.

The Energy Committee, enthusiastic about the program, agreed to spend $20 billion on synfuels development and to establish a government corporation that could, if necessary, actually own a synthetic fuels plant.

But the Banking Committee was skeptical. The panel approved only a $3 billion proposal and emphasized aid that would boost private industry development. They opposed any government ownership of plants and refused to set up the special corporation. Their proposal was supported by an odd coalition that included the Sierra Club, which worried about environmental damage from synfuels, and the U.S. Chamber of Commerce, which opposed heavy government involvement.

When the question was put to a floor vote, senators endorsed the more ambitous Energy Committee version (S 932), which was the measure on the floor. A move to substitute the Banking version failed, 37-57: R 24-15; D 13-42 (ND 11-25; SD 2-17).

13. ENERGY MOBILIZATION BOARD. Congress was already interested in putting priority energy projects on a "fast track" through the bureaucracy when President Carter asked in July for an energy mobilization board to cut through red tape.

The Senate Energy Committee approved a board (S 1308) that could streamline procedures, such as hearings, and could even waive a procedural requirement in federal, state or local law.

But some senators argued that the board, with the president's consent, should be able to waive substantive laws, such as clean air rules, if they stood in the way of construction of an oil pipeline or other important national energy project.

Sen. Walter (Dee) Huddleston, D-Ky., offered an amendment to give the board that substantive waiver authority. It was opposed by senators who said such broad powers could be used to unravel environmental and other laws written by Congress over the past decade.

On Oct. 3, the Senate rejected the amendment, 37-56: R 16-21; D 21-35 (ND 8-29; SD 13-6).

14. NUCLEAR PLANT MORATORIUM. The March accident at the Three Mile Island reactor in Pennsylvania prompted nuclear critics in Congress to seek a six-month halt in construction of new reactors.

Sen. Gary Hart, D-Colo., and others argued that a six-month pause would allow the Nuclear Regulatory Commission to incorporate into its safety rules any lessons learned from the accident. Because the proposed reactors would not be operating for several years, they said the moratorium would not reduce energy supplies.

But opponents of a moratorium contended it was intended only as a symbolic attack against the nuclear industry. They were willing to force improvements in safety, such as requiring that states have evacuation plans in case of emergencies. But they didn't want to add to the nuclear industry's already shaky standing in the financial community or the public opinion polls. They also wanted to wait until after a presidential commission had made its report on the accident.

On July 17, Hart attempted to attach the moratorium proposal as an amendment to the Nuclear Regulatory Commission authorization bill (S 562). The move failed, 35-57: R 8-31; D 27-26 (ND 25-12; SD 2-14).

15. WINDFALL PROFITS TAX. Although the House had approved an oil windfall profits tax that would bring in $277 billion in revenues by 1990, the Senate Finance Committee had drafted a bill with a tax bite less than half that size — $138 billion.

When the bill (HR 3919) got to the Senate floor, many senators wanted to stiffen the tax. They argued that the Carter administration's decision to lift controls on oil prices combined with rising world prices generally would give the oil industry more income than it needed for additional production and exploration. Some of the extra money, they said, should go to alternative energy development, to help low-income families pay their heating bills and to improve mass transit. President Carter had urged similar uses for the funds when he first proposed the tax.

But Republicans and oil-state Democrats argued that if the tax were too stiff the oil industry would cut back on exploration and development. Congress should encourage new production, not discourage it with a heavy tax, they said. They particularly opposed any tax on new discoveries and on oil that was expensive to recover, two categories that had been exempted from the tax by the Finance Committee.

But Abraham Ribicoff, D-Conn., Bill Bradley, D-N.J., Majority Leader Robert C. Byrd, D-W.Va., and others wanted to add a tax on new discoveries. And they proposed a "minimum tax" of 20 percent, which would increase revenues by about $23 billion by 1990.

On Dec. 12, Finance Chairman Russell B. Long, D-La., tried to kill the Ribicoff amendment by tabling it. But, with Treasury Secretary G. William Miller and Energy Secretary Charles W. Duncan watching from the gallery, the Senate refused, 44-53: R 34-6; D 10-47 (ND 4-36; SD 6-11).

The action prompted a filibuster by amendment opponents, led by Robert Dole, R-Kan. Later, a compromise was reached that reduced the rate on newly discovered oil to 10 percent. On Dec. 14, the compromise was adopted, 78-13.

The vote on Long's tabling motion was a turning point in Senate action on the tax because it clearly showed that those wanting a tougher tax were in the majority in the Senate.

16. CHRYSLER AID. Senate passage by a 53-44 vote Dec. 19 of legislation (HR 5860) to provide $3.6 billion in aid to the ailing Chrysler Corp. ended five months of lobbying by the giant corporation for federal backing.

The company made its initial plea for help in August, arguing that record losses would push it over the brink by early 1980 unless the government helped it out with loan guarantees.

President Carter refused Chrysler's initial advances, however. He demanded more information about the company's finances, and said he would need assurances that parties with a stake in its survival — workers, dealers, creditors — also would be willing to help out.

The company, the nation's third largest auto maker, finally clocked in late in October with its financial plan, and the White House sent a $3 billion aid bill to Capitol Hill Nov. 1.

Administration officials argued that bankruptcy by the huge company would throw hundreds of thousands of workers off the job and hurt the economy.

They designed a plan that required the company to raise $1.5 billion on its own in exchange for $1.5 billion in federal loan guarantees.

The administration's decision triggered a series of frantic hearings and markups, which concluded when the Banking Committee approved a $4 billion assistance plan requiring workers to take a three-year wage freeze.

That was modified on the floor to require $525 million in concessions from union workers and $150 million from non-union workers — for a total of $3.6 billion. Congress ultimately approved a $3.5 billion compromise plan.

1979 Key Votes - 9

	1 2 3 4 5 6 7 8 9 10 11 12 13 14 15 16
KANSAS Dole (R)	N N Y Y N Y + N N Y Y Y N N Y Y
MASSACHUSETTS Kennedy (D)	? Y Y N Y N N ? ? Y N ? N Y N Y
TENNESSEE Baker (R)	Y N Y ? Y Y Y ? N Y Y ? N ? Y ?

Y - Voted for (yea).

N - Voted against (nay).

+ - Announced for.

? - Did not vote or otherwise make a position known.

1. S Res 61. Senate Filibuster Rule. Adoption of the resolution to amend Senate Rule 22 to require the Senate to take a final vote on a measure on which cloture has been invoked once 100 hours of post-cloture debate have been consumed and to provide that senators who have not used time during the 100 hours of debate may speak on the measure for 10 minutes, notwithstanding the 100-hour limit. Adopted 78-16: R 23-15; D 55-1 (ND 39-0; SD 16-1), Feb. 22, 1979.

2. S Res 115. Senate Income Limitation. Adoption of the resolution to reinstate a Senate ethics code provision prohibiting a senator, beginning Jan. 1, 1979, from earning outside income of more than 15 percent of his or her Senate salary, or $8,625 at the 1979 salary level then in effect. Rejected 44-54: R 12-28; D 32-26 (ND 22-18; SD 10-8), March 28, 1979.

3. S Res 249. Sen. Herman E. Talmadge Investigation. Adoption of the resolution to "denounce" Sen. Herman E. Talmadge, D-Ga., for "reprehensible" conduct and "gross neglect of his duty" to supervise his office and employees. Adopted 81-15: R 34-7; D 47-8 (ND 35-4; SD 12-4), Oct. 11, 1979.

4. S 245. Taiwan Relations. Percy, R-Ill., amendment to declare that hostile action against Taiwan would be a threat to the "security interests of the United States." Rejected 42-50: R 35-5; D 7-45 (ND 3-33; SD 4-12), March 8, 1979. A "nay" was a vote supporting the president's position.

5. HR 4473. Foreign Aid Appropriations, Fiscal 1980. Adoption of the committee amendment to delete a House-passed prohibition on direct (bilateral) and indirect (multilateral) U.S. aid to Vietnam. Adopted 49-46: R 19-21; D 30-25 (ND 25-12; SD 5-13), Oct. 9, 1979. A "yea" was a vote supporting the president's position.

6. S 586. State Department Authorization. Schweiker, R-Pa., amendment to express the sense of Congress that Rhodesia had met the U.S. conditions for lifting the economic sanctions and to urge the president to lift sanctions 10 days after a black majority government was installed. Adopted 75-19: R 38-2; D 37-17 (ND 20-17; SD 17-0), May 15, 1979. A "nay" was a vote supporting the president's opinion.

7. S Con Res 36. Fiscal 1980 Binding Budget Levels. Part two of the Hollings, D-S.C., amendment to increase the 1981 defense spending target to $159.8 billion in budget authority and $145.6 billion in outlays (an increase of $12.5 billion and $7.3 billion respectively over the Budget Committee recommendation) and to increase the 1982 defense spending target to $180.4 billion in budget authority and $163.3 billion in outlays ($21.4 billion and $15.4 billion over the Budget Committee recommendation). Adopted 55-42: R 31-7; D 24-35 (ND 9-31; SD 15-4), Sept. 18, 1979.

8. HR 5359. Defense Appropriations, Fiscal 1980. Hatfield, R-Ore., amendment to eliminate $670 million for development of the M-X mobile missile and include instead $20 million for conversion of existing Minuteman missiles to be carried by submarines. Rejected 11-77: R 2-36; D 9-41 (ND 9-26; SD 0-15), Nov. 9, 1979. A "nay" was a vote supporting the president's position.

9. S 1724. Home Energy Assistance. Muskie, D-Maine, motion to table (kill) the Dole, R-Kan., amendment, to the Boschwitz, R-Minn., amendment, to allocate heating assistance to the states according to a formula based half on heating degree days and half on residential energy expenditures, and establishing a minimum level for state allocations. Motion rejected 41-50: R 20-19; D 21-31 (ND 21-15; SD 0-16), Nov. 14, 1979.

10. S J Res 28. Direct Popular Elections. Adoption of the joint resolution to propose a constitutional amendment to abolish the electoral college and provide for direct popular election of the president and vice president. Rejected 51-48: R 12-28; D 39-20 (ND 31-9; SD 8-11), July 10, 1979. A two-thirds majority vote (66 in this case) is required for passage of a joint resolution proposing an amendment to the Constitution. A "yea" was a vote supporting the president's position.

11. HR 4388. Energy and Water Appropriations, Fiscal 1980. Johnston, D-La., motion to recede from the Senate amendment to the conference report that would have removed from the bill a House-passed provision to allow completion of the Tellico Dam in Tennessee by exempting the project from the Endangered Species Act and other federal laws and instead to agree to the House position. Motion agreed to (thus clearing the bill for the president) 48-44: R 28-10; D 20-34 (ND 7-29; SD 13-5), Sept. 10, 1979. A "nay" was a vote supporting the president's position.

12. S 932. Defense Production Act/Synthetic Fuels. Proxmire, D-Wis., amendment to substitute the Banking Committee version of Title I to provide $3 billion for synthetic fuels production, but which did not establish a special corporation to administer the funds and barred government-owned plants for the Energy Committee version of Title I of the bill. Rejected 37-57: R 24-15; D 13-42 (ND 11-25; SD 2-17), Nov. 7, 1979. A "nay" was a vote supporting the president's position.

13. S 1308. Energy Mobilization Board. Huddleston, D-Ky., amendment to authorize the president, on the board's recommendation, to waive any substantive federal law that impeded construction of a priority energy project. Rejected 37-56: R 16-21; D 21-35 (ND 8-29; SD 13-6), Oct. 3, 1979. A "nay" was a vote supporting the president's position.

14. S 562. Nuclear Regulatory Commission. Hart, D-Colo., amendment to defer issuance of any new construction permits for nuclear power plants in the first six months of fiscal 1980. Rejected 35-57: R 8-31; D 27-26 (ND 25-12; SD 2-14), July 17, 1979.

15. HR 3919. Windfall Profits Tax. Long, D.-La., motion to table (kill) the Ribicoff, D-Conn., amendment, to set a 20 percent tax on three types of oil: 1) newly discovered, 2) tertiary and 3) heavy oil. Motion rejected 44-53: R 34-6; D 10-47 (ND 4-36; SD 6-11), Dec. 12, 1979.

16. HR 5860. Chrysler Loan Guarantees. Passage of the bill to authorize $1.5 billion in federal loan guarantees, to be matched by $2.1 billion from other sources, and to establish a $175 million employee stock ownership plan. Passed 53-44: R 12-27; D 41-17 (ND 30-10; SD 11-7), Dec. 19, 1979. A "yea" was a vote supporting the president's position.

1979 Key Votes - 10

```
                                    1 2 3 4 5 6 7 8 9 10 11 12 13 14 15 16
ILLINOIS
12  Crane (R)            Y ? ? ? ? # N Y ? ? X N N Y Y X
16  Anderson (R)         ? ? # ? ? ? ? ? ? ? Y ? Y ? N N

Y - Voted for (yea).

N - Voted against (nay).

# - Paired for.

? - Did not vote or otherwise make a position known.
```

1. HR 3919. Windfall Profits Tax. Jones, D-Okla., substitute providing for a tax rate of 60 percent, discontinuation of the windfall tax at the end of 1990 and other changes. Adopted 236-183: R 146-10; D 90-173 (ND 28-152; SD 62-21), June 28, 1979.

2. HR 3000. Energy Department Authorization — Civilian Programs. Moffett, D-Conn., amendment to prohibit use of funds appropriated by the bill for expenditures related to lifting price controls on certain types of domestic crude oil. Rejected 135-257: R 7-137; D 128-120 (ND 119-53; SD 9-67), Oct. 11, 1979. A "nay" was a vote supporting the president's position.

3. HR 4985. Energy Mobilization Board. Eckhardt, D-Texas, amendment to eliminate the authority of the Energy Mobilization Board to waive substantive laws. Rejected 153-250: R 27-121; D 126-129 (ND 112-63; SD 14-66), Nov., 1, 1979. A "yea" was a vote supporting the president's position.

4. HR 2608. Nuclear Regulatory Commission. Markey, D-Mass., amendment to put a moratorium on NRC issuance of new nuclear plant construction permits through April 1, 1980 (the first six months of fiscal 1980). Rejected 135-254: R 23-121; D 112-133 (ND 105-60; SD 7-73), Nov. 29, 1979.

5. HR 2626. Hospital Cost Control. Gephardt, D-Mo., substitute amendment, to the Commerce Committee substitute, to establish for three years a National Study Commission on Hospital Costs, and to authorize $10 million in fiscal 1980 and sums as needed for fiscal 1981-82 to state hospital cost control programs. Adopted 234-166: R 135-8; D 99-158 (ND 43-137; SD 56-21), Nov. 15, 1979. A "nay" was a vote supporting the president's position. (The Commerce Committee substitute, as amended by Gephardt, was adopted subsequently by voice vote.)

6. HR 2479. Taiwan Relations. Quayle, R-Ind., amendment to conduct relations with Taiwan through a government "liaison office," rather than through the unofficial American Institute in Taiwan proposed by the Carter administration. Rejected 172-181: R 113-13; D 59-168 (ND 27-131; SD 32-37), March 8, 1979. A "nay" was a vote supporting the president's position.

7. HR 111. Panama Canal Treaties Implementation. Murphy, D-N.Y., amendment, to the Hansen, R-Idaho, amendment, to restore the original language in the bill dealing with annual payments to Panama from canal revenues, property transfers to Panama and U.S. costs in implementing the 1978 canal treaties. Adopted 220-200: R 25-132; D 195-68 (ND 155-26; SD 40-42), June 20, 1979. A "yea" was a vote supporting the president's position.

8. HR 4040. Defense Procurement. Schroeder, D-Colo., amendment to delete the provision in the bill as reported by the Armed Services Committee requiring mandatory draft registration and providing for a presidential study of the issue. Adopted 259-155: R 83-68; D 176-87 (ND 154-30; SD 22-57), Sept. 12, 1979. A "yea" was a vote supporting the president's position.

9. S Con Res 36. Fiscal 1980 Binding Budget Levels. Giaimo, D-Conn., motion to approve binding fiscal 1980 budget levels recommended by Senate-House conferees, but excluding Senate reconciliation instructions that directed various committees to achieve $3.6 billion in spending cuts (the conference version of the resolution set the following budget levels: budget authority, $638 billion; outlays, $547.6 billion; revenues, $517.8 billion; and deficit, $29.8 billion). Motion agreed to 205-190: R 0-145; D 205-45 (ND 146-26; SD 59-19), Nov. 8, 1979.

10. HR 2313. Federal Trade Commission Authorization. Passage of the bill to authorize $75 million for Federal Trade Commission operations in fiscal 1980; $80 million in 1981 and $85 million in 1982; and to allow for a one-house veto of the commission's regulatory actions (provided the other house did not overturn the action within 30 days). Passed 321-63: R 138-2; D 183-61 (ND 110-56; SD 73-5), Nov. 27, 1979. A "nay" was a vote supporting the president's position.

11. HR 4904. Welfare Reform. Passage of the bill to establish a national minimum welfare benefit, require states to provide coverage to unemployed two-parent families with children, reduce state costs, and make administrative changes designed to reduce benefits to some recipients. Passed 222-184: R 29-118; D 193-66 (ND 165-15; SD 28-51), Nov. 7, 1979. A "yea" was a vote supporting the president's position.

12. HR 2444. Education Department. Passage of the bill to establish a separate Department of Education. Passed 210-206: R 35-117; D 175-89 (ND 108-70; SD 67-19), July 11, 1979. A "yea" was a vote supporting the president's position.

13. HR 39. Alaska Lands. Udall, D-Ariz., substitute amendment (HR 3561) to create 125.4 million acres of national parks, wildlife refuges and forests in Alaska. Adopted 268-157: R 66-90; D 202-67 (ND 154-32, SD 48-35), May 26, 1979. A "yea" was a vote supporting the president's position.

14. H Res 378. Diggs Censure. Adoption of the resolution to censure Rep. Charles C. Diggs Jr., D-Mich., to order Diggs to repay the Treasury $40,031.60 and to require Diggs' employees to certify to the House Committee on Standards of Official Conduct for the remainder of the 96th Congress that they are being paid by Diggs in full compliance with House rules. Adopted 414-0: R 153-0; D 261-0 (ND 178-0; SD 83-0), July 31, 1979.

15. H J Res 74. School Busing Amendment. Passage of the joint resolution to propose an amendment to the Constitution to prohibit compelling students to attend a school other than the one nearest their home to achieve racial desegregation. Rejected 209-216: R 114-40; D 95-176 (ND 48-138; SD 47-38), July 24, 1979. A two-thirds majority vote (262 in this case) is required for passage of a joint resolution proposing an amendment to the Constitution. A "nay" was a vote supporting the president's position.

16. HR 5860. Chrysler Loan Guarantees. Passage of the bill, as amended to authorize $1.5 billion in federal loan guarantees, for the Chrysler Corp. to be matched by $1.93 billion from other sources, including $400 million in wage concessions by the company's unionized workers and $100 million by other employees. Passed 271-136: D 62-88; R 209-48 (ND 154-21; SD 55-27), Dec. 18, 1979. A "yea" was a vote supporting the president's position.

Selected Bibliography

Anderson, John B. *Vision and Betrayal in America.* Chicago: World Books Encyclopedia, 1975.

Anderson, John B. et al. *Congress and Conscience.* Philadelphia: J. B. Lippincott, 1970.

Ashman, Charles. *Connally: The Adventures of Big Bad John.* New York: William Morrow, 1974.

Baker, James T. *A Southern Baptist in the White House.* Philadelphia, Pa.: Westminster Press, 1977.

Barone, Michael et al. *The Almanac of American Politics: The Senators, the Representatives, the Governors, Their Records, States and Districts.* New York: E. P. Dutton, 1979.

Bourne, Peter. *Jimmy Carter.* Boston, Mass.: Little, Brown, 1977.

Boyarsky, Bill. *The Rise of Ronald Reagan.* New York: Random House, 1968.

Brereton, Charles. *First Step to the White House: The New Hampshire Primary 1952-1980.* Hampton, New Hampshire: The Wheelabrator Foundation Inc., 1979.

Brown, Edmund G. Sr. *Reagan and Reality: The Two Californias.* New York: Praeger, 1970.

Brown, Edmund G., Jr. *Thoughts.* San Francisco, Calif.: City Lights Books, 1976.

Burns, James M. *Edward Kennedy and the Camelot Legacy.* New York: W. W. Norton & Co., 1976.

Cannon, Lou. *Ronnie and Jesse: A Political Odyssey.* Garden City, N.Y.: Doubleday, 1969.

Carter, Jimmy. *A Government As Good As Its People.* New York: Simon & Schuster, 1978.

Carter, Jimmy. *Why Not the Best?* Nashville, Tenn.: Broadman Press, 1977.

Crane, Philip M. *Democrat's Dilemma: How the Liberal Left Captured the Democratic Party.* Whittier, Calif.: Constructive Action, 1964.

Crane, Philip M. *The Sum of Good Government.* Ottawa, Ill.: Green Hill, 1976.

Crane, Philip M. *Surrender in Panama: The Case Against the Treaty.* Ottawa, Ill.: Green Hill, 1978.

Crawford, Ann F. *John B. Connally: Portrait in Power.* Austin, Texas: Jenkins Publishing Co., 1973.

David, Lester. *Ted Kennedy, Triumphs and Tragedies.* New York: Grosset & Dunlap, 1972.

Davis, James W. *Springboard to the White House: Presidential Primaries: How They Are Fought and Won.* New York: Thomas Y. Crowell, 1967.

Drew, Elizabeth. *American Journal: The Events of 1976.* New York: Random House, 1977.

Edwards, Lee. *Reagan: A Political Biography.* San Diego, Calif.: Viewpoint Books, 1967.

Glad, Betty. *Jimmy Carter: From Plains to the White House.* New York: W. W. Norton & Co., 1978.

Hadley, Arthur T. *The Invisible Primary.* Englewood Cliffs, N.J.: Prentice-Hall, 1976.

Hersh, Burton. *The Education of Edward Kennedy: A Family Biography.* New York: William Morrow, 1972.

Hobbs, Charles D. *Ronald Reagan's Call to Action: Realistic Democracy.* New York: Thomas Nelson, 1976.

Honan, William H. *Ted Kennedy, a Profile of a Survivor; Edward Kennedy After Bobby, After Chappaquiddick, and After Three Years of Nixon.* New York: Quadrangle, 1972.

Keech, William R. and Matthews, Donald R. *The Party's Choice: With An Epilogue on the 1976 Nominations.* Washington, D.C.: Brookings Institution, 1976.

Kennedy, Edward M. *Decisions for a Decade: Policies and Programs for the 1970s.* Garden City, N.Y.: Doubleday 1968.

Kennedy, Edward M. *In Critical Condition: The Crisis in America's Health Care.* New York: Simon & Schuster, 1972.

Kennedy, Edward M. *Our Day and Generation.* New York: Simon & Schuster, 1979.

Kucharsky, David. *The Man from Plains.* New York: Harper & Row, 1976.

Lippman, Theo, Jr. *Senator Ted Kennedy: The Career Behind the Image.* New York: W. W. Norton & Co., 1976.

Lurie, Leonard. *The King Makers.* New York: Coward, McCann & Geoghegan, 1971.

Matthews, Donald R., ed. *Perspectives on Presidential Selection.* Washington, D.C.: Brookings Institution, 1973.

Miller, William L. *Yankee From Georgia.* New York: Times Books, 1978.

Meyer, Peter. *James Earl Carter: The Man and the Myth.* Mission, Kan.: Sheed Andrews & McMeel, 1978.

Overacker, Louise. *The Presidential Primary.* New York: Arno Press, 1974.

Pack, Robert. *Jerry Brown: The Philosopher-Prince.* New York: Stein & Day, 1978.

Pippert, Wesley G. *The Spiritual Journey of Jimmy Carter: In His Own Words.* New York: Macmillan, 1978.

Reagan, Ronald. *The Creative Society: Some Comments on Problems Facing America.* New York: Devin-Adair, 1968.

Reagan, Ronald and Hobbs, Charles. *Ronald Reagan's Call to Action.* New York: Warner Books, 1976.

Schram, Martin. *Running for President 1976: The Carter Campaign.* New York: Stein & Day, 1977.

Shogan, Robert. *Promises to Keep: Carter's First 100 Days.* New York: Thomas Y. Crowell, 1977.

Stroud, Kandy. *How Jimmy Won: The Victory Campaign from Plains to the White House.* New York: William Morrow, 1977.

Tedrow, Richard L. and Tedrow, Thomas L. *Death at Chappaquiddick.* Ottawa, Ill.: Green Hill, 1976.

Turner, Robert W. *I'll Never Lie to You: Jimmy Carter in His Own Words.* New York: Ballantine Books, 1976.

Von Damm, Helene. *Sincerely, Ronald Reagan.* Ottawa, Ill.: Green Hill, 1976.

Witcover, Jules. *Marathon: The Pursuit of the Presidency 1972-1976.* New York: Viking Press, 1977.

Wooten, James. *Dasher: The Roots and the Rising of Jimmy Carter.* New York: Summit Books, 1978.

INDEX

Abortion. See Health and Welfare
AFL-CIO Committee on Political Education (COPE). See Interest Group Ratings
Agriculture
  Campaign issues - 53
  Emergency farm aid - 92, 93
  Farm labor legislation - 12
  Wheat price supports - 81
American Conservative Union (ACU)
  Crane's presidential campaign - 49
Americans for Constitutional Action (ACA). See Interest Group Ratings
Anderson, John B. (R Ill.)
  Background - 26
  Campaign staff - 26
  Early primary strategy - 27
  Election results (1960-78) - 71
  Interest group ratings - 27
  Key votes - 88, 98, 108
  Political odyssey - 23
  Presidential ambition - 26
  Public career - 25, 26
  Vote study scores - 24

Baker, Howard H. Jr. (R Tenn.)
  Background - 30
  Campaign staff - 32
  Election results (1964-78) - 71
  Interest group ratings - 31
  Issue positions - 29, 30
  Key votes - 87, 97, 107
  Political flexibility - 28, 29
  Senate career - 31
  Strategy - 32
  Vote study scores - 29
  Watergate - 31
Baker, James A.
  Bush campaign - 38
Bayh, Birch (D Ind.) - 20, 105
Boschwitz, Rudy (R Minn.) - 33
Bradford, William G.
  Anderson campaign - 23, 26, 27
Brock, Bill - 26
Brown, Edmund G. Jr. See also Election 1976
  Background - 11, 12
  Balanced budget amendment - 10
  Campaign staff - 10
  Coalition building - 11
  Criminal issues - 10
  Governorship - 12
  Gubernatorial races - 71
  Political synthesis - 9
  Presidential primaries (1976) - 12
  Proposition 13 - 12
  Strategy - 13
Buckley, William F. Jr. - 34

Bush, George
  Background - 35
  Campaign staff - 38
  Centrist politics - 34
  Early career - 37
  Early primary strategy - 28, 33
  Election results (1964-70) - 71
  Executive career - 38
  Fund for a Limited Government - 39
  Interest group ratings - 37
  Issue stands - 36, 37
  Strategy - 38
  Vote study scores - 36

Campaign Finance
  Federal Election Commission (FEC)
    Anderson statement - 25
    Brown statement - 11
    Bush statement - 35, 39
    Connally's rejection of public funds - 45
    Reagan statement - 63
  Political Reform Proposition 9 - 12
  Public financing law contribution limits - 27, 45
  Public financing of House campaigns - 24
Carter, President Jimmy. See also Election 1976
  Background - 6
  Campaign staff - 7
  Election 1976 - 6, 7, 71, 73-77
  Foreign affairs - 89
  Governorship - 6
  Issue positions - 5
  Political obstacles - 1
  Strategy - 8
Chafee, John H. (R R.I.) - 33
Church, Frank (D Idaho) - 7, 38, 73-77
Civil Rights
  Candidate Positions
    Anderson - 23, 24
    Baker - 29
    Bush - 35
    Carter - 6
    Dole - 51
    Reagan - 61
Cohen, William S. (R Maine) - 33, 39
Committee for the Survival of a Free Congress - 28, 49
Committee on Political Education (COPE). See Interest group ratings
Congress and Government. See also Ethics
  Congressional feistiness - 2
  Government reform - 6
  Key Votes
    Consumer protection agency - 95

  D.C. voting rights - 91
  Federal Trade Commission powers - 101
  Filibuster limitation - 103
  How votes were selected - 79
  Public financing of congressional races - 82, 94
  Senate committee chairmanships - 80
  Leadership
    Campaign issues - 1, 17
    Power of incumbency - 4
Connally, John B.
  Background - 41, 42
  Campaign funds - 45
  Campaign staff - 43
  Election results (1962-63) - 71
  Governorship - 43
  Middle East plan - 41, 42
  Military position - 41
  Milk funds acquittal - 44
  Party switch - 44
  Political outlook - 40
  Strategy - 44
Constitution, U.S.
  Anti-abortion amendment - 24, 29
  Anti-busing amendment - 24, 103
  Balanced budget amendment - 10, 36, 52
  D.C. voting rights - 31, 91
  Electoral College reform - 35, 52, 105
  18-year-old vote - 20, 35, 36
  Equal rights amendment (ERA) - 24, 29, 36, 91
  First Amendment, freedom of the press - 47
Crane, Daniel B. (R Ill.) - 48
Crane, Philip M. (R Ill.)
  Background - 47, 49
  Campaign staff - 49
  Election results (1969-78) - 71
  Interest group ratings - 48
  Key votes - 88, 98, 108
  Philosophical roots - 46
  Presidential campaign - 48, 49
  Vote study scores - 47
Crime
  Brown position - 10
  Kennedy views - 21
  Reagan position - 61
Curb, Mike - 13

Danforth, John C. (R Mo.) - 33
Defense policy. See National Defense
Dole, Robert (R Kan.)
  Background - 53, 54
  Campaign staff - 54
  Cuba policy - 81
  Election results (1968-74) - 72

  Financial worth - 55
  Interest group ratings - 55
  Issue positions - 52, 53
  Key votes - 87, 97, 107
  Personal style - 55
  Political philosophy - 51
  Strategy - 56
  Vice presidential candidate - 55
  Vote study scores - 52

Economy and Labor
  Candidate Views
    Anderson - 24
    Baker - 30
    Brown - 10
    Bush - 36
    Carter - 4, 5
    Connally - 41, 42
    Crane - 46, 47
    Dole - 52
    Reagan - 58, 60
  Chrysler bail-out - 37, 103, 106
  Farm labor legislation - 12
  Key Votes
    Budget discipline - 101
    Carter's tax rebate proposal - 79, 83
    Common-site picketing - 84
    1978 Fiscal policy issues - 89, 95, 96
    Labor law reform - 93
    Minimum wage, youth differential - 86
  Lockheed bail-out - 44
  Revenue Sharing
    Anderson views - 25
    Reagan views - 58
  Tax Relief
    Bush proposal - 36
    Key votes - 81, 83, 92, 96
    Proposition 13 - 12, 60
    Roth-Kemp proposal - 60
Education
  Connally's Texas record - 43
  Court-ordered busing - 92
  Education Department - 46, 102
  Reagan's California record - 60
  Tuition tax credits - 96
Edwards, Mickey (R Okla.) - 47
Eizenstat, Stuart E.
  Carter record - 4
Election 1976
  Carter campaign - 6, 7
  Presidential race results - 71
  Primary results - 73-78
Electoral College reform. See Constitution, U.S.
Energy and Environment
  Candidate Views
    Anderson - 24

111

Index - 2

Baker - 29, 30
Brown - 11, 12
Bush - 35, 36
Carter - 5, 6
Kennedy - 17
Reagan - 60
Key Votes
Alaska lands - 102
Auto emissions - 84
Carter's energy program - 79, 93, 99
Clinch River breeder reactor - 82
Crude oil tax - 85
Energy Mobilization Board - 99, 106
Natural gas pricing - 83, 85, 90
Nuclear plant moratorium - 100, 106
Oil price controls - 99
Synthetic fuels - 105
Tellico Dam/Endangered species - 105
Water projects - 85, 93
Windfall profits tax - 99, 106
Ethics
Key Votes
Diggs censure - 102
Financial disclosure/Watergate - 82
House Obey reforms - 86
House office allowance ban - 83
How votes were selected - 79
Senate franking privilege - 80
Senate income limit - 80, 103
Talmadge disciplinary action - 103

Federal Election Commission (FEC). See Campaign Finance
Fernandez, Benjamin - 23, 65
Fonda, Jane - 11, 41
Ford, Gerald R. See also Election 1976
Role in Bush career - 38
Role in Dole career - 55
Foreign Policy
Candidate Views
Baker views - 29, 30
Bush issue stands - 37
Carter philosophy - 5
Connally's Middle East plan - 41, 42
Dole position - 52, 53
Kennedy-Carter differences - 16
Reagan position - 60, 61
Key Votes
China policy - 104
Cuba policy - 81

Foreign aid cuts - 94
Human rights - 86
International development banks - 94, 104
Korea policy - 81
Mideast jet sales - 90
Panama Canal treaties - 90, 100
Rhodesian policy - 90, 104
Taiwan relations - 100
Turkish arms embargo - 94

Government Operations. See Congress and Government
Gregory, Dick - 24

Hayakawa, S.I. (Sam) (R Calif.) - 60
Hayden, Tom - 11
Health and Welfare
Abortion - 80, 83, 85
Carter views - 5
Dole health insurance plan - 53
Fuel aid to the poor - 105
Hospital cost control - 92, 100
Kennedy health insurance plan - 17
Social Security financing - 83
Welfare reform - 102

Interest Group Ratings
Anderson - 27
Baker - 31
Bush - 37
Crane - 48
Dole - 55
Kennedy - 19

Johnson, Lyndon B.
Role in Connally's career - 40, 42

Kemp, Jack F. (R N.Y.)
Anderson House race - 26
Reagan campaign - 60, 61
Kennedy, Edward M. (D Mass.)
Background - 18
Campaign staff - 21
Differences with Carter - 16
Election results (1962-76) - 72
Interest group ratings - 19
Judiciary Committee career - 20
Key votes - 87, 97, 107
Legislative style - 20
Liberal image - 15
Strategy - 21
Vote study scores - 16
Key Votes
1977 votes - 79-88
1978 votes - 89-99
1979 votes - 100-108
Kissinger, Henry A.
Anderson House race - 26
Baker foreign policy views - 30

Labor. See Economy and Labor
Laxalt, Paul (R Nev.)
Baker campaign strategy - 33
Reagan campaign - 61-63
Lobby disclosure - 95
Loeb, William - 49
Lugar, Richard G. (R Ind.)
Baker campaign - 32, 33

McGovern, George (D S.D.) - 51, 52, 54, 81
Milliken, William G. - 58
Mondale, Walter F. - 1, 7, 8
Muskie, Edmund S. (D Maine) - 80, 81, 92, 101, 105

National Defense
Candidate Views
Anderson position - 24
Baker stands on issue - 29, 30
Bush position - 36, 37
Carter position - 5
Connally position - 41
Dole position on SALT II - 52
Reagan - 60, 61
Key Votes
Aircraft carrier veto - 95
B-l bomber controversy - 79, 86, 95
Defense spending - 84, 89-91, 104
Draft registration - 101
M-X missile - 104
Neutron bomb production - 82
Warnke nomination - 80
National Farmers Union (NFU). See Interest Group Ratings
Nixon, Richard M.
Role in Bush career - 38
Role in Connally career - 44
Role in Dole career - 54
Watergate - 25, 31
Nofziger, Lyn - 62, 63

Ogilvie, Richard B. - 26

Primaries (1980)
Anderson's early strategy - 27
Baker's late start - 28, 33
Bush strategy - 38, 39
Carter strategy - 8
Connally's image problem - 44, 45
Crane's campaign crises - 49
Dates of state primaries - vi
Dole's organizational problems - 56
Public financing law. See Campaign Finance

Reagan, Ronald. See also Election 1976
Actor and politician - 57
Background - 61

Campaign staff - 61
Citizens for the Republic (CFTR) - 63
Governorship - 59
Gubernatorial races - 72
Issue positions - 60, 61
'North American accord' - 58
Party switch - 62
Strategy - 62
Republican Party
Anderson orthodoxy - 24
Connally party switch - 44
Gallup and the GOP presidential candidates - 59
11th Commandment
Baker conviviality - 32
National Hispanic Society - 62
Reagan party switch - 62
Republican National Committee (RNC)
Bush chairmanship - 34, 38
Dole chairmanship - 54
Roth, William V. Jr. (R Del.) - 60

Schweiker, Richard S. (R Pa.) - 62, 104
Sears, John P.
Reagan campaign - 58, 61, 62
Stassen, Harold - 65
'States Rights'
Crane views - 46
Reagan views - 58

Transportation/Commerce
Airline deregulation - 6, 20, 91
Oil cargo preference - 86
Trucking deregulation - 20
Waterway user fees - 81, 91

Udall, Morris K. (D Ariz.) - 73-77, 102

Viguerie, Richard - 26, 49
Vote studies. See also Individual candidates
Explanation - 67
Key Votes
How votes were selected (box) - 79
1977 in review - 79-88
1978 in review - 89-98
1979 in review - 99-108

Welfare Reform
Carter's social policy - 5
Reagan's actions as governor - 60
Weyrich, Paul - 28, 49